STUDY SKILLS

third edition

STUDY SKILLS
Do I Really Need This Stuff?

STEVE PISCITELLI

PEARSON

Boston • Columbus • Indianapolis • New York • San Francisco • Upper Saddle River
Amsterdam • Cape Town • Dubai • London • Madrid • Milan • Munich • Paris • Montreal • Toronto
Delhi • Mexico City • Sao Paulo • Sydney • Hong Kong • Seoul • Singapore • Taipei • Tokyo

Editor-in-Chief: Jodi McPherson
Acquisitions Editor: Katie Mahan
Managing Editor: Shannon Steed
Editorial Assistant: Clara Ciminelli
Executive Marketing Manager: Amy Judd
Senior Production Editor: Gregory Erb
Editorial Production Service: Electronic Publishing Services Inc.
Manufacturing Buyer: Megan Cochran
Electronic Composition: Jouve
Interior Design: Electronic Publishing Services Inc.
Photo Researcher: Annie Fuller
Cover Designer: Studio Montage
Cover Administrator: Diane Lorenzo

Many of the designations by manufacturers and sellers to distinguish their products are claimed as trademarks. Where those designations appear in this book, and the publisher was aware of a trademark claim, the designations have been printed in initial caps or all caps.

Library of Congress Cataloging-in-Publication Data

Piscitelli, Stephen.
  Study skills : do I really need this stuff? / Steve Piscitelli. — 3rd ed.
    p.   cm.
  1. Study skills. 2. College student orientation. I. Title.
LB2395.P59 2013
371.3028'1--dc23

                                        2011043788

ISBN 10: 0-13-278951-5
ISBN 13: 978-0-13-278951-6

Dedication

To Laurie

for her constant inspiration,
friendship, and love

ABOUT THE AUTHOR

Steve Piscitelli has dedicated himself to the processes of teaching and learning for more than three decades. An award-winning teacher, he has taught students of varying abilities and levels, from middle school through the university level. Currently, Steve is a tenured professor at Florida State College at Jacksonville. Steve earned degrees from Jacksonville University, the University of North Florida, and the University of Florida.

In addition to this Third Edition of *Study Skills: Do I Really Need This Stuff?*, Pearson Education has published *Choices for College Success* (Second Edition, 2011). Steve has also written, recorded, and produced two music CDs. His nationally known workshops combine interaction, practicality, music, and humor to connect participants with practical strategies. More information is available at www.stevepiscitelli.com.

Steve lives with his wife, Laurie, and canine companion, Buddy, in Atlantic Beach, Florida.

BRIEF CONTENTS

CONTENTS

Chapter 2
CRITICAL THINKING   15

Chapter 3
PRIORITY MANAGEMENT   37

Chapter 4
INFORMATION LITERACY   65

Chapter 7
CLASS-TIME LISTENING AND NOTE TAKING   145

Chapter 10
MEMORY 211

Chapter 11
TEST PREPARATION AND TEST PERFORMANCE 233

Chapter 12
CIVILITY 259

Chapter 13
THE CHOICES YOU MAKE 279

When my editor and I first spoke about doing a revised edition of *Study Skills: Do I Really Need This Stuff?* I was excited—but also a little concerned. A little voice inside me (call him "Critical Steve") kept saying things like "What else can you possibly say about study skills? How many different ways can you write about success strategies?" Probably the most biting question from "Critical Steve" was "What in the world do you have to say that has not already been said?"

No pressure, right?

Those questions inspired me to contribute the new perspective you will find here. Thanks to "Critical Steve" whispering (yelling?) in my ear, this third edition incorporates some simple yet very powerful changes. The biggest change is the use of the R.E.D. Model for critical thinking. It serves as the backbone for this text, providing a solid base not only for effective study skills but also for effective life skills.

Studies conducted by business organizations and universities consistently list critical thinking as a key—yet often missing—skill for workplace readiness.* While knowledge of academic content is obviously important, so are the skills of communication, analysis, evaluation, and creation. This book provides practice for each of those skills.

This new edition still retains its student-friendly tone and reliance on reflective activities to help students understand what they do well—and what they can do better. The bullet points that follow highlight the major changes, additions, and features of *Study Skills: Do I Really Need This Stuff?* Third Edition.

NEW TO THE THIRD EDITION

■ **The R.E.D. Model† is introduced in Chapter 2 and used throughout the book.** It is the basis for chapter-opening and -ending activities, and it is also used consistently in internal chapter activities as needed to support the chapter topic.

■ **Each chapter begins with a student scenario.** These stories incorporate typical and specific challenges that students encounter. For instance, in the chapter about information literacy (Chapter 4),

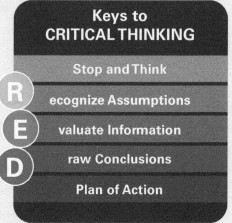

Keys to
CRITICAL THINKING

Stop and Think

R ecognize Assumptions

E valuate Information

D raw Conclusions

Plan of Action

*For example, see The Conference Board, Inc., Corporate Voices for Working Families, the Partnership for 21st Century Skills, and the Society for Human Resource Management, "Are they really ready to work? Employers' perspectives on the basic knowledge and applied skills of new entrants to the 21st century U.S. workforce" (2006), available online at http://p21.org/documents/FINAL_REPORT_PDF09-29-06.pdf (accessed June 9, 2011). Also see "The skills and abilities for the 21st Century: A workforce readiness initiative," The Career Center and the Community/Mental Health Counseling Program, The University of South Florida, available online at http://www.coedu.usf.edu/zalaquett/workforce/sa.htm (accessed June 9, 2011).

†Watson-Glaser Critical Thinking Appraisal, Forms A/B (WGCTA). Copyright © 2007 NCS Pearson, Inc. Reproduced with permission. All rights reserved. "Watson-Glaser Critical Thinking Appraisal" is a trademark, in the US and/or other countries, of Pearson Education, Inc., or its affiliates(s).

the student situation looks at the issues of personal privacy and integrity in the world of social media. Each scenario ends with a challenge for the reader to solve.

■ **Each chapter ends with a section titled Critically Thinking: What Have You Learned in This Chapter?** Here, the reader must apply the chapter learning outcomes, key terms, strategies, and the R.E.D. Model to offer a plan of action for the student in the scenario.

■ **The chapters have been reordered.** While changing the organization of the content is always a debatable subject, in this case, it reflects the immediate needs of most students:

- Given the importance and prevalence of social media, online personal profiles, and personal reputation issues, information literacy was moved from Chapter 11 in the second edition to Chapter 4 in this third edition.

- Priority management has been moved from Chapter 4 to Chapter 3. This is a critical success tool students need to master early in the term.

- All other chapters (until Chapter 12) appear one chapter later than in the second edition.

■ **Chapter 3 (Priority Management) has a new perspective.** Whereas the second edition emphasized *time management*, this edition builds on the premise that time management is impossible. We cannot manage time. What we have to do is manage priorities. In doing so, we are taking the action and using the resources that move us closer to our goal. More information and strategies are also provided on the topic of procrastination.

■ **Chapter 4 (Information Literacy) has been totally revamped.**

- The first half of this chapter addresses traditional information literacy, defined as finding, evaluating, and using information. The second part of the chapter takes an in-depth focus on social media and communication in the Internet age.

- The topic of communication has been rewritten to include tips for creating and posting appropriate social media updates, as well as establishing (or not) an online profile. Privacy issues are explained, and the concept of a "digital tattoo" is emphasized.

- Information on repetitive strain injuries has been moved to Chapter 3 (Priority Management).

- A postwriting checklist has been added.

■ **A section on multiple intelligences has been added to the chapter on learning styles (Chapter 6).** A practical activity has been included to connect the concept to personal success.

■ **The brief overview of left-brain, right-brain, and whole-brain processing provided in the second edition has been removed and replaced.** In this edition, see Chapter 7, which provides an introduction to the topic of attention.

■ **The new version of the VARK Questionnaire (7.1) is included** in this third edition.

■ **Information on strategic highlighting has been added to the reading chapter (Chapter 9).**

■ **The "forgetting curve" is introduced, explained, and connected to memory strategies (Chapter 10).**

■ **The chapter on testing (Chapter 11) has been reorganized** to more accurately reflect the clear distinction between two separate processes: test preparation and test performance. The second edition used the terms *preparation* and *performance* interchangeably. Separating the two concepts in this new edition drives home the point that testing is multifaceted—and not just a night-before-the-test event.

■ **The activities in Chapter 1 and Chapter 13 have been thoroughly revised.** This edition has fewer but more focused activities.

■ **A new Glindex replaces the subject and problem-solving indexes.** This new feature provides a glossary that defines every key term in every chapter. This section provides a concise and easy reference for students and faculty.

■ **The book has been redesigned with the full use of color to highlight the features** and make for a more interesting, interactive, and engaging reading experience.

FEATURES OF THE THIRD EDITION

In addition to what was listed in the previous section, students and instructors will find the following features in this edition:

■ Chapters start with the same learning components:

- A student scenario and a challenge to the reader to "think critically" about the student situation
- Chapter Learning Outcomes
- Key Terms
- Chapter Introduction
- An assessment activity for students to reflect on their level of skill with the chapter topic

■ The R.E.D. Model icon will appear throughout the chapters to signal when critical-thinking skills need to be applied.

■ Each chapter has activities to reinforce the study skills introduced.

■ At least one of the chapter activities (before the end of the chapter) relates directly to the student scenario at the beginning of the chapter.

■ Chapters end with a section called Critically Thinking: What Have You Learned in This Chapter? It provides a review of the chapter learning outcomes and offers a final chance to critically think through the student situation presented in the chapter-opening scenario.

■ The test-preparation and test-performance chapter (Chapter 11) now includes specific item examples for each type of test described.

■ Over the course of the book, students have the opportunity to complete a number of reflective activities. They can compile these activities into a portfolio of strategies. Doing so will help them be able to answer the question "What am I doing to get what I want?"

■ Source citations are provided within each chapter (and a list of sources is included at the end of the book) for instructors and students who want to conduct further research.

OVERVIEW OF THE CHAPTERS

Introduction Today Is the Tomorrow You Created Yesterday

The introduction reinforces the idea that the choices students make today will create their tomorrow. In short, if they want their dreams to become realities, they have to act—they have to apply their knowledge and skills.

Chapter 1   Do I *Really* Need This Stuff?

The core principles of the book are introduced (critical thinking, the power of practice, and locus of control). Students learn that there are no "quick fixes" and that they will need to take action and make appropriate choices to achieve the success they would like to see in their lives. The opening of this chapter is a bit different from the openings of Chapters 2 through 12. Rather than start with a scenario about a student dilemma, this chapter places the readers at the center of a situation, thus involving them from the outset. Students complete an assessment of strengths and challenges regarding their own study skills.

Chapter 2   Critical Thinking

The first student scenario is introduced. Each chapter (through Chapter 12) will use a scenario. The R.E.D. Model for critical thinking is introduced and explained. This is the model that students will apply for the remainder of the book. R.E.D. stands for Recognize assumptions, Evaluate information, and Draw conclusions.

Chapter 3   Priority Management

Although college requires considerable work, students will also have more unstructured time than they have probably ever had before. They will need to organize their schedules to include studies, family responsibilities, recreation, and the like. The key is learning to identify and manage priorities. Additionally, students will have to organize a personal study space so it will work efficiently. This chapter also examines the causes of and strategies to deal with procrastination and stress.

Chapter 4   Information Literacy

Students live in an age that allows them to get information from virtually anywhere in the world with a couple of keystrokes and the push of the "Enter" button. But students have to understand that this explosion of data does not necessarily equate to an explosion of credible knowledge. Consequently, once students have found information, they need to know how to evaluate it before they decide to use it. This chapter contains significant coverage of social media. Not only is an overview of social media provided, but strategies for appropriate communication in the Internet age are introduced, as well.

Chapter 5   Motivation and Goal Setting

This chapter goes beyond how to write a goal. It examines the connection between locus of control and being able to achieve a goal. This new edition provides additional tips on developing and carrying out specific action steps associated with goal attainment. Students are encouraged to remove three words from their vocabulary: *try, but, can't.*

Chapter 6   Learning Styles

This edition presents the VARK 7.1 Questionnaire (updated from 7.0). Also, a new section briefly explains multiple intelligences and applies it to organizing how one studies.

Chapter 7   Class-Time Listening and Note Taking

This chapter describes strategies that will help students become more actively engaged and intentional learners inside the classroom. Success skills introduced in this chapter include understanding instructor expectations, developing a respectful student/instructor relationship, and practicing various note-taking strategies.

Chapter 8   Reviewing and Using Your Notes Outside the Classroom

This chapter demonstrates how to remain academically engaged outside the classroom. Specifically, students examine ways to review classroom notes outside class to help them understand the "big picture."

Chapter 9   Reading

The level and quantity of college reading assignments comes as a shock to many students. This chapter examines how to approach a reading assignment in an organized and effective manner. Students practice the SQ4R reading strategy. Information also is provided on the proper use of highlighting as a strategic reading practice.

Chapter 10   Memory

The Ebbinghaus "forgetting curve" sets the stage for the importance of not only doing something with the material students are learning but also doing it in a timely and effective manner. The three basic components of memory are introduced and reinforced with chapter activities.

Chapter 11   Test Preparation and Test Performance

A clear distinction between the two separate processes of test preparation and test performance distinguishes this edition from the last. Separating the two drives home the point that testing is multifaceted. Before students can perform, they must prepare. Specific item examples for different types of tests are included.

Chapter 12   Civility

This chapter examines basic tenets of respectful and honest relationships. College work requires more than passively listening to lectures and taking notes. Group work, study teams, debates, lab experiments, oral presentations, and conferences with professors all demand behaving with civility and responsibility. Students will study strategies to develop fulfilling collaborative relationships. Whether the association is a short-term group project or a conference about grades, demonstrating respect for all involved will help build meaningful relationships. A new section on setting boundaries and establishing limits helps students understand they must let people know just how far they will go—and how far they will allow others go with them.

Chapter 13   The Choices You Make

As students complete the final activities of the book, they are asked two questions: (1) Are you satisfied with the choices you have made this term? and (2) Did your results match your expectations? While this chapter is short in terms of length, it requires students to look back at previous chapters and activities to integrate the important themes and concepts of the book. The same assessment of strengths and challenges from Chapter 1 is offered again to gauge progress.

There is no chapter scenario. As in the first chapter, the focus here is clearly on the reader, providing a nice symmetry.

One last note about this third edition: Since the time that I wrote the second edition of *Study Skills: Do I Really Need This Stuff?* I have had the good fortune to write and publish *Choices for College Success*, Second Edition (Boston: Pearson Education, 2011). Some material from that book has been used in the chapters that follow.

ACKNOWLEDGMENTS

At every step of the writing process, I have been blessed with nurturing friendships, honest critiques, and professional guidance. Thanking everyone would be impossible, but I would like to mention a few of the people who have added immeasurably to the book you hold in your hands.

As the author, I put words to paper, but the final product is the work of a larger team. This book benefited from the scrutiny and suggestions from my peers in the field—professionals who helped me shape rough, and at times confused, ideas into reader-friendly chapters.

■ **Pearson Education.** I am fortunate to continue my relationship with Pearson Education. My Editor-in-Chief, Jodi McPherson, saw the wisdom in this revision and provided the resources for it to come to fruition. Shannon Steed, Managing Editor, kept me focused and balanced throughout the process. She encouraged me and challenged me. As cliché as it sounds, her questions and suggestions invariably moved the revision to a better level. Thanks to Claire Hunter, Development Editor, for her guidance down the homestretch of the manuscript development. Clara Ciminelli, Editorial Assistant, patiently took time to answer innumerable e-mails and phone calls about the "nuts and bolts" of the process.

Content is one piece of the process. Production is another. A huge thank you to Greg Erb, Senior Production Editor, who has worked his magic once again. This is the second project I have completed with Greg and his very creative team. I hope we get to collaborate on more projects in the future.

Thanks to Amy Judd, Executive Marketing Manager, and her entire team for their continuous support. And I have nothing but respect and gratitude for the Pearson representatives who match instructors with the appropriate books and resources for their students. Thanks as well to the reviewers for this edition: Elizabeth Huggins, Augusta State University; Dr. Cari Kenner, St. Cloud State University; Chad Luke, Tennessee Tech University, Cookeville, TN; Brenda Marks, Ed. D. Clackamas Community College.

■ **Students.** There is more than a kernel of truth in the adage that "Teachers learn as much from their students as they teach their students." I am a better teacher and writer for having worked with my students.

■ **"Road warriors."** I am lucky to count Amy Baldwin and Robb Sherfield among my friends and colleagues. Both are successful authors, speakers, and teachers. We have traveled together, presented collaboratively, shared publishing ideas, and enjoyed many light-hearted moments. I continue to learn from them.

■ **My best friend.** Once again, my wife, Laurie, has been there every step of the way. She unselfishly sacrificed weekends and evenings as I wrote. Without her love, support, and friendship, this book would not have been completed.

■ **Buddy.** And finally, Buddy, my canine companion. Whether lying beside my desk as I typed or leading me down the beach at sunrise, he reminds me to find the joy in the simple things in life.

I continue to be a fortunate man!

Steve Piscitelli
Atlantic Beach, Florida

Supplemental Resources

INSTRUCTOR SUPPORT – Resources to simplify your life and support your students.

Book Specific

Online Instructor's Manual – This manual is intended to give professors a framework or blueprint of ideas and suggestions that may assist them in providing their students with activities, journal writing, thought-provoking situations, and group activities. The test bank, organized by chapter includes: multiple choice, true/false and short-answer questions that support the key features in the book. This supplement is available for download from the Instructor's Resource Center at www.pearsonhighered.com/irc

Online PowerPoint Presentation – A comprehensive set of PowerPoint slides that can be used by instructors for class presentations or by students for lecture preview or review. The PowerPoint Presentation includes bullet point slides for each chapter, as well as all of the graphs and tables found in the textbook. These slides highlight the important points of each chapter to help students understand the concepts within each chapter. Instructors may download these PowerPoint presentations from the Instructor's Resource Center at www.pearsonhighered.com/irc

MyStudentSuccessLab – Are you teaching online, in a hybrid setting, or looking to infuse technology into your classroom for the first time? MyStudentSuccessLab is an online solution designed to help students build the skills they need to succeed for ongoing personal and professional development. For more information and to access activites, videos, and test items for your course visit www.mystudentsuccesslab.com

Other Resources

"Easy access to online, book-specific teaching support is now just a click away!"
Instructor Resource Center – Register. Redeem. Login. Three easy steps that open the door to a variety of print and media resources in downloadable, digital format, available to instructors exclusively through the Pearson 'IRC'. www.pearsonhighered.com/irc

"Provide information highlights on the most critical topics for student success!"
Success Tips is a 6-panel laminate with topics that include MyStudentSuccessLab, Time Management, Resources All Around You, Now You're Thinking, Maintaining Your Financial Sanity, and Building Your Professional Image. Other choices are available upon request. This essential supplement can be packaged with any student success text to add value with 'just in time' information for students.

Supplemental Resources

Other Resources

"Infuse student success into any program with our "IDentity" Series booklets!" - Written by national subject matter experts, the material contains strategies and activities for immediate application. Choices include:
- Financial Literacy (Farnoosh Torabi)
- Financial Responsibility (Clearpoint Financial)
- Now You're Thinking about Student Success (Judy Chartrand et.al.)
- Now You're Thinking about Career Success (Judy Chartrand et.al.)
- Ownership (Megan Stone)
- Identity (Stedman Graham).

"Through partnership opportunities, we offer a variety of assessment options!"
LASSI– The LASSI is a 10-scale, 80-item assessment of students' awareness about and use of learning and study strategies. Addressing skill, will and self-regulation, the focus is on both covert and overt thoughts, behaviors, attitudes and beliefs that relate to successful learning and that can be altered through educational interventions. Available in two formats: Paper ISBN: 0131723154 or Online ISBN: 0131723162 (access card).

Robbins Self Assessment Library – This compilation teaches students to create a portfolio of skills. S.A.L. is a self-contained, interactive, library of 49 behavioral questionnaires that help students discover new ideas about themselves, their attitudes, and their personal strengths and weaknesses. Available in Paper, CD-Rom, and Online (Access Card) formats.

"For a truly tailored solution that fosters campus connections and increases retention, talk with us about custom publishing."
Pearson Custom Publishing – We are the largest custom provider for print and media shaped to your course's needs. Please visit us at www.pearsoncustom.com to learn more.

STUDENT SUPPORT – Tools to help make the grade now, and excel in school later.

"Now there's a Smart way for students to save money."
CourseSmart is an exciting new choice for students looking to save money. As an alternative to purchasing the printed textbook, students can purchase an electronic version of the same content. With a CourseSmart eTextbook, students can search the text, make notes online, print out reading assignments that incorporate lecture notes, and bookmark important passages for later review. For more information, or to purchase access to the CourseSmart eTextbook, visit www.coursesmart.com

"Today's students are more inclined than ever to use technology to enhance their learning."
MyStudentSuccessLab will engage students through relevant YouTube videos with 'how to' videos selected 'by students, for students' and help build the skills they need to succeed for ongoing personal and professional development. www.mystudentsuccesslab.com

"Time management is the #1 challenge students face."
Premier Annual Planner - This specially designed, annual 4-color collegiate planner includes an academic planning/resources section, monthly planning section (2 pages/month), weekly planning section (48 weeks; July start date), which facilitate short-term as well as long term planning. Spiral bound, 6x9.

"Journaling activities promote self-discovery and self-awareness."
Student Reflection Journal - Through this vehicle, students are encouraged to track their progress and share their insights, thoughts, and concerns. 8½ × 11. 90 pages.

MyStudentSuccessLab

Start Strong. Finish Stronger.
www.MyStudentSuccessLab.com

MyStudentSuccessLab is an online solution designed to help students acquire the skills they need to succeed for ongoing personal and professional development. They will have access to peer-led video interviews and develop core skills through interactive practice exercises and activities that provide academic, life, and professionalism skills that will transfer to ANY course.

It can accompany any Student Success text or used as a stand-alone course offering.

How will MyStudentSuccessLab make a difference?

Is motivation a challenge, and if so, how do you deal with it?

Video Interviews – Experience peer led video 'by students, for students' of all ages and stages.

How would better class preparation improve the learning experience?

Practice Exercises – Practice skills for each topic - leveled by Bloom's taxonomy.

What could you gain by building critical thinking and problem-solving skills?

Activities – Apply what is being learned to create 'personally relevant' resources through enhanced communication and self-reflection.

MyStudentSuccessLab

Start Strong. Finish Stronger.
www.MyStudentSuccessLab.com

As an instructor, how much easier would it be to assign and assess on MyStudentSuccessLab if you had a Learning Path Diagnostic that reported to the grade book?

Learning Path Diagnostic

- For the **course**, 65 Pre-Course questions (Levels I & II Bloom's) and 65 Post-Course questions (Levels III & IV Bloom's) that link to key learning objectives in each topic.

- For each **topic**, 20 Pre-Test questions (Levels I & II Bloom's) and 20 Post-Test questions (Levels III & IV Bloom's) that link to all learning objectives in the topic.

As a student, how much more engaged would you be if you had access to relevant YouTube videos within MyStudentSuccessLab?

Student Resources

A wealth of resources like our FinishStrong247 YouTube channel with 'just in time' videos selected 'by students, for students'.

MyStudentSuccessLab Topic List -

1. A First Step: Goal Setting
2. Communication
3. Critical Thinking
4. Financial Literacy
5. Information Literacy
6. Learning Preferences
7. Listening and Taking Notes in Class
8. Majors and Careers
9. Memory and Studying
10. Problem Solving
11. Professionalism
12. Reading and Annotating
13. Stress Management
14. Test Taking Skills
15. Time Management

MyStudentSuccessLab Feature set

Learning Path Diagnostic: 65 Pre-Course (Levels I & II Bloom's) and 65 Post-Course (Levels III & IV Bloom's) / Pre-Test (Levels I & II Bloom's) and Post-Test (Levels III & IV Bloom's).

Topic Overview: Module objectives.

Video Interviews: Real video interviews 'by students, for students' on key issues.

Practice Exercises: Skill-building exercises per topic provide interactive experience and practice.

Activities: Apply what is being learned to create 'personally relevant' resources through enhanced communication and self-reflection.

Student Resources: Pearson Students Facebook page, FinishStrong247 YouTube channel, MySearchLab, Online Dictionary, Plagiarism Guide, Student Planner, and Student Reflection Journal.

Implementation Guide: Grading rubric to support instruction with Overview, Time on Task, Suggested grading, etc.

PEARSON

Pearson Success Tips, 1/e

ISBN-10: 0132788071 • ISBN-13: 9780132788076

Success Tips is a 6-panel laminate that provides students with information highlights on the most critical topics for student success. These topics include MyStudentSuccessLab, Time Management, Resources All Around You, Now You're Thinking, Maintaining Your Financial Sanity, and Building Your Professional Image. Other choices are available upon request via our www.pearsoncustomlibrary.com program, as well as traditional custom publishing. This essential supplement can packaged with any student success text to add value with 'just in time' information for students.

Features

- **MyStudentSuccessLab** — Helps students 'Start strong, Finish stronger' by getting the most out of this technology with their book.
- **Time Management** — Everyone begins with the same 24 hours in the day, but how well students use their time varies.
- **Resources All Around You** — Builds awareness for the types of resources available on campus for students to take advantage of.
- **Now You're Thinking** — Learning to think critically is imperative to student success.
- **Maintaining Your Financial Sanity** — Paying attention to savings, spending, and borrowing choices is more important than ever.
- **Building Your Professional Image** — Students are motivated by preparing for their future careers through online and in person professionalism tips, self-branding, and image tips.
- **Additional Topics** — Topics above are 'default.' These topics include MyStudentSuccessLab, Time Management, Resources All Around You, Now You're Thinking, Maintaining Your Financial Sanity, and Building Your Professional Image. Other choices are available upon request via our www.pearsoncustomlibrary.com program, as well as traditional custom publishing. This essential supplement can be packaged with any student success text to add value with 'just in time' information for students.

Topic List

- MyStudentSuccessLab*
- Time Management*
- Resources All Around You*
- Now You're Thinking*
- Maintaining Your Financial Sanity*
- Building Your Professional Image*
- Get Ready for Workplace Success
- Civility Paves the Way Toward Success

- Succeeding in Your Diverse World
- Information Literacy is Essential to Success
- Protect Your Personal Data
- Create Your Personal Brand
- Service Learning
- Stay Well and Manage Stress
- Get Things Done with Virtual Teams
- Welcome to Blackboard!

- Welcome to Moodle!
- Welcome to eCollege!
- Set and Achieve Your Goals
- Prepare for Test Success
- Good Notes Are Your Best Study Tool
- Veterans/Military Returning Students

NOTE: those with asterisks are 'default' options; topic selection can be made through Pearson Custom Library at www.pearsoncustomlibrary.com, as well as traditional custom publishing.

ALWAYS LEARNING

PEARSON

PERSONALIZE THE EXPERIENCE WITH

PEARSON LEARNING SOLUTIONS

FOR STUDENT SUCCESS AND CAREER DEVELOPMENT

The Pearson Custom Library Catalog

With Pearson Custom Library, you can create a custom book by selecting content from our course-specific collections. The collections consist of chapters from Pearson titles like this one, and carefully selected, copyright cleared, third-party content, and pedagogy. The finished product is a print-on-demand custom book that students can purchase in the same way they purchase other course materials.

Custom Media

Pearson Learning Solutions works with you to create a customized technology solution specific to your course requirements and needs. We specialize in a number of best practices including custom websites and portals, animation and simulations, and content conversions and customizations.

Custom Publications

We can develop your original material and create a textbook that meets your course goals. Pearson Learning Solutions works with you on your original manuscript to help refine and strengthen it, ensuring that it meets and exceeds market standards. Pearson Learning Solutions will work with you to select already published content and sequence it to follow your course goals.

Online Education

Pearson Learning Solutions offers customizable online course content for your distance learning classes, hybrid courses, or to enhance the learning experience of your traditional in-classroom students. Courses include a fully developed syllabus, media-rich lecture presentations, audio lectures, a wide variety of assessments, discussion board questions, and a strong instructor resource package.

In the end, the finished product reflects your insight into what your students need to succeed, and puts it into practice.
Visit us on the web to learn more at www.pearsoncustom.com/studentsuccess or call 800-777-6872

ALWAYS LEARNING

PEARSON

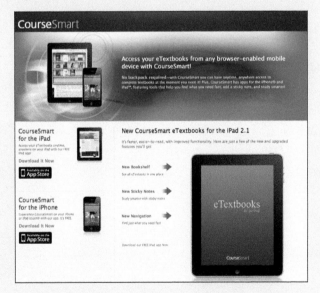

Today Is the Tomorrow You Created Yesterday

> *When you have to make a choice and don't make it, that is in itself a choice.*
> —William James, psychologist and philosopher

After having their planes shot out from under them in 1965, Fred Cherry and Porter Halyburton found themselves in a Vietnamese prisoner of war camp. During their seven years of captivity, they suffered some of the most horrific and brutal conditions any human being could be expected to endure. But endure they did—with courage, dignity, and a strong sense of purpose (Hirsch, 2004).

Without trivializing their experiences or those of their fellow captives, the philosophy that enabled these men to survive can be summed up in three words: *dreams, action, and reality.* "Your dreams are followed by action, which creates reality" (Hirsch, 2004, p. 195).

THE CHOICES YOU MAKE CREATE YOUR REALITY

Those words—*dreams, action, reality*—had a profound impact on me as I read these men's stories. Isn't this what success in school and life is really about? Our dreams will never make it to reality if we do not make the choices needed to put them into action. And those choices have to be made daily. What you do today will have an impact on what happens to you tomorrow. And when you have reached tomorrow, today will be yesterday.

Got that? Today is the tomorrow you created yesterday!

Perhaps you have heard someone (or even yourself) say, "If only I had done that (or not done that) yesterday, things would be different today." While you cannot predict the future, you certainly can have an impact on what the future looks like. Are you someone who believes the future "happens to you"? Or do you believe "you create" the future.

Para-Olympian gold medalist Dame Tanni Grey-Thompson has put it simply: "You can change your life. You don't wait for someone else to do it for you" (Hughes, 2011, p. 35). That change begins today with the choices you make to create a bright future.

This book will help you examine your choices and how they have made—or will make—your academic dreams a reality. As you journey toward your dreams, be sure to pay attention to your physical and emotional needs, as well as your academic demands. In this way, you will have a better chance to achieve your dreams and maintain a high level of energy for continued success. In short, take care of yourself!

As you work through the activities in the following chapters, you will find that there is nothing particularly magical about study skills. You have used these skills, in one form or another, in your past academic experiences. Still, you may feel a bit intimidated when confronted with new challenges. "Will I be able to do this? I've never done anything like this before. Maybe college wasn't such a great idea for me. I really don't think I can handle failing."

When confronted with such thoughts, review the choices you have before you and take the steps needed for academic success. Chapter strategies will help you accomplish this.

USE THIS BOOK— *REALLY* USE THIS BOOK

You will find activities, models, figures, tables, photos, graphics, and lots of strategies throughout this book. Use them! Obviously, they will do you little good if you do not read, relate, review, and realize how to apply them to your studies. Even if your instructor does not assign all of the activities—give yourself the luxury of completing them anyway. Each provides an opportunity for you to reflect on what you have read—and then immediately apply the knowledge.

In education and life, it is not so much about what you know. It's much more about what you do with what you know!

CRITICAL THINKING

Critical thinking is the central theme in this book. It permeates all chapters and all activities. You will be asked to analyze your current level of skills, connect those skills with skills you will learn, and then evaluate your level of competence. In other words, by engaging you in critical-thinking activities, the study skills strategies will come alive with practical applications that will help you achieve your academic goals. Resist taking short cuts. Give your full attention to each strategy and activity.

Starting with the chapter-opening scenario and continuing all the way to the chapter-ending activity (which builds on the opening scenario), you will have opportunities to apply your skills in real time. When you see the R.E.D. Model icon, be prepared to apply the knowledge you have just learned. These critical-thinking checks will allow you to reflect on your current level of skills while responsibly adding to your repertoire of study skill strategies.

Whatever your level of academic skill, this book will allow you to "raise your game" to a new level. Just as athletes strive to improve from game to game and from season to season, successful students continually look for ways to add to their academic accomplishments.

The strategies in the following chapters will help you put your dreams into action so they will become reality. The choices will be yours.

Dreams, action, reality. What you do today will create your tomorrow.

STUDY SKILLS

Do I *Really* Need THIS STUFF?

Simply put, discipline is doing what you really don't want to do so you can do what you really want to do.

—John C. Maxwell, leadership expert and author

CHAPTER LEARNING OUTCOMES

By the time you finish reading this chapter and completing its activities, you will be able to do the following:

- Identify at least two study skill challenges that you have.

- Identify at least two study skill strengths that you have.

- Explain how you can use your study skill strengths to minimize one of your study skill challenges.

- List at least five study skill topics covered in this book that you can use immediately.

The First Day of CLASS

It is the first day of the college term. Your instructor asks you to take out a piece of paper and respond to the following statements:

1. You have been placed in a study skills course this term. Explain why you do NOT really need this stuff! There must be some mistake. After all, you have spent many years in

© Shutterstock

Key Terms

Challenge
Critical thinking
Discipline
Locus of control
Strength
Study skills

INTRODUCTION
Chapter

What do you think of when you hear the term study skills? Most students approach a study skills course (or book) with little or no enthusiasm. It's not one of the most popular topics in the course catalog.

For many students, college is a means to an end: a career and the ability to earn money. They want to get in, get out, and get on with their lives.

Others come to campus excited about the activities, clubs, and social experiences that await them. They want to encounter more than just the classroom.

classrooms. You know what to do and how to do it.

2. You have been placed in a study skills course this term. Explain why you *DO really need this stuff!* Even though you have spent many years in classrooms, you need to improve in some areas as you begin the term.

CRITICALLY THINKING
about *Your* situation

Take a quiet moment to reflect on the statements just presented:

1. What reasons come to mind that explain why you feel you do *not* need to be in a study skills course?

2. What reasons explain why a study skills course is the *correct* placement for you this term?

And most students come to postsecondary education believing they have the tools needed to succeed in college. They finished high school without much difficulty and with fairly good grades—and so they don't see any problems with jumping right into their college classes. Other nontraditional students may have postponed college for a number of years. They are here now after years of real-life experiences. Whether they spent time working, raising a family, or serving in the military, they stand ready for this next adventure in their lives. While some might be a bit apprehensive about handling the course work, they are excited to be back in school.

MyStudentSuccessLab

MyStudentSuccessLab (www .mystudentsuccesslab.com) is an online solution designed to help you 'Start strong, Finish stronger' by building skills for ongoing personal and professional development.

With all of these life experiences and college expectations, it is not unusual for students to be a bit put off when an adviser tells them they have to enroll in a study skills course. You might even hear students say things like the following:

- "Why do I need that? That's a course for students with problems—not me!"
- "I am too smart for this course!"
- "Why do I need this course? I do my homework every night. Isn't that studying?"
- "My adviser made me take this course. What a waste of time!"
- "Sounds like an easy A!"

Perhaps you had a similar reaction. Or at least, maybe you thought taking this course was just another "hoop" you had to jump through. You did not like it, but you rolled your eyes, gritted your teeth, and enrolled. "I do not really need this stuff, but I don't have much choice. Anyway, how difficult can this be? I'm sure I don't have to be Bill Gates to figure this stuff out."

So, for whatever reason you ended up in this course, recognize that it is not designed for problem students, slow learners, or struggling students. It remains a course for students who wish to discover the best ways to learn and excel on campus—and beyond.

As you work through the activities in this book, identify obstacles to your learning as well as the strengths that help you learn. What stands in your way of being as successful as you would like to be? Are these obstacles related to attitude or ability? In the past, what strengths have helped you to achieve in the classroom? How can you build on those strengths to help minimize your challenges?

Activity 1.1, Assessment of Strengths and Challenges, will help you focus on some of your academic challenges—as well as your strengths. All students—including you—bring academic experiences, skills, and strategies that will help them be successful in the college classroom.

Activity 1.1

Assessment of Strengths and Challenges

Before you can work on your **challenges**, you need to know what they are. That may seem obvious, but sometimes we miss the obvious. This activity will help you focus on your challenges while reminding you of your **strengths**— those things you do well. You may be able to use your strengths to minimize or eliminate your challenges. For instance, your ability to think critically may help you determine the best way to address a test-taking challenge.

The challenges you want to be concerned with at this point are process challenges, not content challenges. For this activity focus on what you do, rather than what you learn. Concentrate, for instance, on what you can do (steps you can take) to become a more capable student in math (or English, or history, or science, or Spanish, or some other class).

First, check your strengths when it comes to academic success. What do you do well? Check as many or as few of the following qualities as apply. Take your time, and think about each choice carefully.

___ Setting goals   ___ Completing goals

___ Supporting an opinion with facts   ___ Organizing an essay

___ Establishing priorities

___ Writing and completing a strong essay

___ Completing work on time

___ Establishing relationships and connections with class notes

___ Eliminating distractions

___ Taking notes from class lectures

___ Remembering important information for exams

___ Controlling test anxiety

___ Taking notes from the textbook

___ Allowing plenty of time to prepare for exams

___ Taking organized notes

___ Completing exams in the time allotted

___ Getting to class on time

___ Learning from previous exam mistakes

___ Participating in class

___ Taking study breaks

___ Keeping an organized notebook

___ Studying alone

___ Regularly reviewing and organizing class notes

___ Studying with friends

___ Coming to class prepared

___ Locating information for research projects

___ Understanding and using my learning style

___ Evaluating information for research projects

___ Using critical-thinking skills to solve problems

___ Using social media for academic and career purposes

___ Getting the main point from a reading assignment

___ Developing respectful relationships with faculty and classmates

___ Other: _____

___ Other: _____

Now, check your challenges when it comes to academic success. In what areas do you need to improve? Check as many or as few as apply. Take your time, and think about each choice carefully.

___ Setting goals

___ Supporting an opinion with facts

___ Completing goals

___ Organizing an essay

___ Establishing priorities

___ Writing and completing a strong essay

___ Completing work on time

___ Establishing relationships and connections with class notes

___ Eliminating distractions

___ Taking notes from class lectures

___ Remembering important information for exams

___ Controlling test anxiety

___ Taking notes from the textbook

___ Allowing plenty of time to prepare for exams

___ Taking organized notes

___ Completing exams in the time allotted

___ Getting to class on time

___ Learning from previous exam mistakes

___ Participating in class

___ Taking study breaks

___ Keeping an organized notebook

___ Studying alone

___ Regularly reviewing and organizing class notes

___ Studying with friends

___ Coming to class prepared

___ Locating information for research projects

___ Understanding and using my learning style

___ Evaluating information for research projects

___ Using critical-thinking skills to solve problems

___ Using social media for academic and career purposes

___ Getting the main point from a reading assignment

___ Developing respectful relationships with faculty and classmates

___ Other: _____

___ Other: _____

Review the items you checked in each previous section. List below the five strengths you consider your biggest assets, ranking them from 1 to 5 (high to low). Do the same for your challenges.

Strengths

1. ....

2. ....

3. ....

4. ....

5. ....

Challenges

1. ....

2. ....

3. ....

4. ....

5. ....

Look at the strengths you listed. In what ways might you be able to use them to help you minimize or eliminate your challenges? For instance, if one of your challenges is "Getting the main point from a reading assignment" and one of your strengths is "Taking organized notes," how can you use that strength to help with the challenge? That is, how can one of your strengths be used to minimize one of your challenges?

Write your response here:

....

....

....

HOW CAN STUDY SKILLS HELP YOU GET WHAT YOU WANT?

Action expresses priorities.
—Mohandas Gandhi, Indian independence leader

Obvious similarities exist between college and high school experiences. For instance, your instructors organize class activities and assign textbook readings. There are tests and projects to complete. You will have classmates you like and some that may irritate you. You will have a deep passion for some classes but find others difficult and tiring. Overall, the outward structure of college will appear very similar to what you have experienced in your past schooling.

You will quickly discover, however, that there is also a great deal of difference between college and high school. For example, you will be given a syllabus on the first day of class. More than likely, all of your assignments for the entire term will be on that handout. You will not be reminded daily about your assignments and due dates. You will have to keep track of them on your own. It is possible that you will not even get a hard copy (that is, a printed version) of the syllabus. Your instructor may post it online and expect you to find and use it from there.

In college, you may find yourself in very large lecture halls with more students than you ever had in a class before. Your instructors may not even know your name—and you may only see them when they walk into your classes. If you want to talk with them about your grades, you may have to search and find their campus offices.

In high school, your teachers may have given you many opportunities to earn grades. But in college, you may find that in some of your classes, you will receive only two, three, or four grades for the entire term. A lot rides on your performance on each exam or assignment.

You will also learn that if you miss your 8:00 a.m. history class, there is a better than average chance that no one will come looking for you. College life offers a great deal of freedom of choice and unstructured time. You will need to master how to use your unstructured time for positive results. Assignments, exams, group projects, social engagements, and personal responsibilities will all compete for your time (Piscitelli, 2011, p. 8). Having good study skills will help you complete assignments and still have time for a full social life, as well.

In short, you will need to develop **discipline** to effectively structure and carry out your day. When you act with discipline, you develop habits that move you closer to your goals. You focus on what needs to be done, and you do it when it needs to be done.

That is what having effective study skills will help you do: Develop discipline. Primarily, the focus will be on academic success, but you will see—as you read through these chapters—that the skills you develop in this course will carry over to your life outside class. These are life skills that are transferable to your career and your relationships.

Having disciplined study skills is necessary for students to master their academic work. Applying these skills helps develop strategies and techniques to focus energies on efficient and effective studying. And having sound study skills contributes to developing positive self-esteem. A student who can achieve in the classroom will feel better about his or her capabilities. Competence will foster confidence. In short, study skills are important for all students.

UNDERSTANDING THE CONCEPT

Break the concept of study skills into its two parts:

- **Study:** This is your personal effort to learn something. It could be academic (learning how to speak a foreign language), athletic (learning how to play tennis), occupational (learning how to do a particular job), or emotional (learning how to control anxiety or anger). You have "studied" your entire life—even before you ever set foot in a school. That is, you have learned how to do certain things. This book will concentrate on learning within the school setting. Synonyms include *think deeply, inspect, reflect, contemplate, review, analyze,* and *concentrate.*

- **Skill:** When someone has a skill, he or she can do something with a degree of expertise. A skill is sharpened through practice and experience. Even someone with a natural talent—say, in music—practices to become expert or skilled in his or her area. When you have a skill, you are able to do something well. Typically, when someone develops a skill it involves a certain amount of studying. Synonyms include *ability, mastery, competence, command, aptitude,* and *expertise.*

For our purposes, the term **study skills** will refer to your abilities to learn how to do academic things well and in a disciplined manner. Look at the table of contents of this book, and you will find typical study skill topics listed. Some, you will have no problem with, but others may cause you some concern.

Activity 1.2

Let's Get Personal (Part I)

It's time to make this very personal. Flip to the table of contents. Read the chapter titles and section headings listed there. Pick the one chapter that you believe will have the biggest impact on your academic success when you read it.

Look at the boldface headings, tables, and figures of that chapter. Choose three items (information, tips, strategies) you can use right now.

List and then briefly explain your interest in each item.

1. ....

....

....

2. ....

....

....

3. ....

....

Each new term in college presents its own set of challenges. New courses, new instructors, and new demands all require students to reevaluate their study and relationship skills in and out of the classroom. Having study skills can help you successfully navigate various courses and instructor personalities.

Reading this chapter will also give you the opportunity to identify what will help you get what you want from your school term.

A QUICK PREVIEW OF COMING ATTRACTIONS

> *Continuous effort— not strength or intelligence—is the key to unlocking our potential.*
> —Winston Churchill, prime minister of the United Kingdom

Movie "trailers"—those quick advertisements that appear on TV—give previews of coming attractions. After watching a couple of clips from a movie, viewers have an idea of what a movie has to offer. Effective trailers draw people to movies.

Consider, if you would, this book to be the "movie" and the following chapters to be the "scenes." Together, they all make up the "main feature." This section of the chapter will help you preview some of the "coming attractions"—the coming topics—and how they relate to you. It will warm you up and prepare you for what is to come. It will also help you locate information that is of immediate interest.

Activity 1.2, which you just completed, allowed you the opportunity to review the chapter you believe could have the biggest impact on your academic success. In Activities 1.3, 1.4, and 1.5, you will be able to dig a little deeper into this book. You will not only see what this book has to offer, but you will also be able to locate the topics that will be most helpful to you at this point in your college term.

Following one simple guideline will help you make the most of your time with this activity—and not see it as overwhelming: Spend no more than 10 minutes on each activity. If you desire, you can spend more time, but remember that you will have plenty of time to spend on each chapter later in the term. For the time being, invest no more than one-half hour on the following three activities combined. That's it—just 30 minutes!

You have only two purposes:

1. Familiarize yourself with the content of this textbook.
2. Concentrate on which study skills can help you right now.

By the time you are done with the activities, you will have identified topics of immediate interest to you. And you will have done this in less time than it would take you to watch a television news program or have a cup of coffee with friends at a café. What a valuable investment in a short period of time! Wouldn't you say you and your academic success are worth 30 minutes? (And you will have practiced a reading strategy known as SQ4R: survey, question, read, recite, record, and review.)

Activity 1.3

Let's Get Personal (Part 2)

This activity builds on Activity 1.2. Once again, flip to the table of contents. Read the chapter titles and section headings. Pick another chapter that you believe will have an impact on your academic success when you read it.

Look at the boldface headings, tables, and figures of that chapter. Choose three items (information, tips, strategies) you can use right now.

List and then briefly explain your interest in each item.

1. ....

....

2. ....

....

3. ....

....

Activity 1.4

Let's Get Personal (Part 3)

This activity builds on Activities 1.2 and 1.3. Turn to the table of contents. Read the chapter titles and section headings. Pick another chapter that you believe will have an impact on your academic success.

Look at the boldface headings, tables, and figures of that chapter. Choose three items (information, tips, strategies) you can use right now.

List and then briefly explain your interest in each item.

1. ....

....

2. ....

....

3. ....

....

Activity 1.5

Let's Get Personal (Part 4)

This activity builds on Activities 1.2, 1.3, and 1.4. Flip to the table of contents. Read the chapter titles and section headings. Pick one more chapter that you believe will have an impact on your academic success.

Look at the boldface headings, tables, and figures of that chapter. Choose three items (information, tips, strategies) you can use right now.

List and then briefly explain your interest in each item.

1. ....

....

2. ....

....

3. ....

....

CORE PRINCIPLES

" All the so-called 'secrets of success' will not work unless you do. "

—Unknown

You will find three core life-skill principles running throughout this book: critical thinking, the power of practice, and locus of control.

CRITICAL THINKING

Critical thinking requires gathering information, weighing it for accuracy and appropriateness, and then making a rational decision based on it. Critical thinkers are active learners who seem to never stop asking questions about whatever is before them.

As you read each chapter, apply your critical-thinking skills to determine how you can best use the strategies to help you become more successful as a student. To make both the book and your course more meaningful, try constantly to make connections that go beyond the classroom. That is, critically examine each skill for its connection to your life in general. For instance, studying how to most effectively use your time will develop a life skill that will help you in your personal relationships and career development.

THE POWER OF PRACTICE

The study skill strategies covered in the following chapters will be virtually useless unless you take the time to study them, practice them, and apply them. It won't help simply to think about using them or to think about the success you will have with them. You need to actually use the strategies again and again. Practice until you make using the strategies a habit—a good habit.

When you find a reflective self-assessment activity in a chapter, set aside some quiet time and complete it carefully. After all, the time you invest is time you are investing in yourself. What a wonderful investment!

LOCUS OF CONTROL

Generally speaking, **locus of control** describes how people explain events in their lives. Do you accept responsibility for your life and make things happen, or do you look for reasons (excuses) that things happen to you?

An individual with an internal locus of control may explain poor test grades by looking into the mirror, pointing at himself, and saying, "I should have studied more." This student accepts the responsibility for what happens to him. On the other hand, a student who is more apt to blame the teacher exhibits an external locus of control. A comment such as "That teacher is not fair and does not know how to write a test" reflects a student looking to assign responsibility elsewhere.

Refer to Figure 1.1. As with all continuums, few people are found at the extremes. Most of us fall somewhere in between. But upon reflection, we notice that we tend to lean to one end or the other.

As you progress through the semester, think of this continuum. Listen to your words. Pay attention to your actions. Are you a person who generally takes responsibility for your actions (leaning toward the "internal" end)? Or are you someone who tends to blame others (leaning toward the "external" end)? Use this information to heighten your awareness.

Figure 1.1

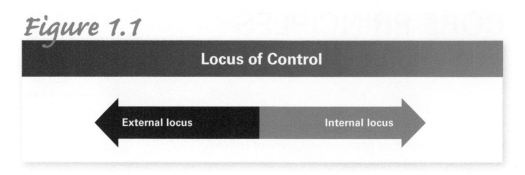

Locus of Control

External locus   Internal locus

IT'S CALLED *WORK*

THERE IS NO "QUICK FIX"

This book does not offer a way to "beat the system" to earn the highest possible grades. It provides no gimmicks, no tricks. To offer a "quick fix" would be like going on a trendy diet to lose weight but never changing the behaviors that resulted in the extra pounds. Unfortunately, becoming a better student is not as easy as reading a book or watching an Internet video. So, if you want a quick-fix approach, reading the following chapters will not help much.

The material in this book will help you identify and change those behaviors that are keeping you from being the best student you can be. It will also help you strengthen and maintain the habits that have worked for you in the past.

The following chapters concentrate on practical skills to build academic success and a positive self-image. Having these skills will help you make the transition from being a student who simply gets by to being a successful student who is aware, insightful, and confident.

NO "QUICK FIX" DOES NOT MEAN TEDIOUS WORK

Interestingly enough, academic success does not have to be accompanied by tedious hours of tortuous work. Yes, there will be hours of work, but the work will be productive. Consider the following example.

© Shutterstock

Have you ever studied a long time for an exam only to be baffled by receiving a lower-than-expected grade? How frustrating. Many students complain, "I sat at that desk for hours last night—and I still bombed!"

In situations like this, the problem may be your study strategy, not the number of hours you have studied. There is a way to be more effective and reduce the number of hours you spend reviewing your material. The key is to know when to study so that you will maximize what you remember.

Memory—a study skill topic—will improve if you organize your study time into a number of sessions, rather than one big "cram" session. Research suggests this is one way to retain and recall more of what you study. It is not so much how long you study as it is how often you study (Medina, 2008, p. 133).

Study skill strategies will provide you with tools to do this.

A COVENANT WITH MYSELF

Because this academic journey is about you—your desires, your needs, and your successes—take a moment and complete the covenant in Figure 1.2. Consider two things about this document:

- This is a covenant, not a contract. The term contract too often has connotations of distrust: "I'm not sure you will do what you say. Therefore, I want you to sign this contract." For our purposes, let's use a much more positive approach. A covenant implies respect and trust. It is a public proclamation of that respect.
- This covenant is strictly personal. It is an agreement you make with yourself. If you don't follow through on it, you don't follow through with yourself. Your signature indicates your desire to improve, your respect for yourself and those around you, and the trust you place in your intention to do the best you can.

Figure 1.2

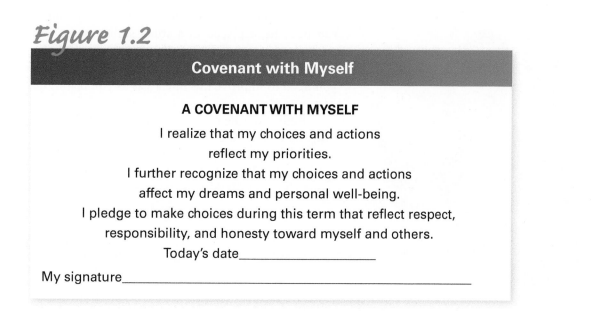

Covenant with Myself

A COVENANT WITH MYSELF

I realize that my choices and actions
reflect my priorities.
I further recognize that my choices and actions
affect my dreams and personal well-being.
I pledge to make choices during this term that reflect respect,
responsibility, and honesty toward myself and others.

Today's date_____

My signature_____

Chapter

SUMMARY

Before leaving this chapter, keep the following points in mind:

- Developing effective study skills will help you discover the best ways to learn and excel in college.
- You have strengths. Use them. You have challenges. Recognize them and work to minimize them.

- Use your critical-thinking skills to examine your strengths and challenges. Practice strategies that will help you.

- Develop disciplined habits that will take you to the highest levels you can reach as a student.

CRITICALLY THINKING

What Have You Learned in This Chapter?

© Shutterstock

Return to the situation that was described (and that you wrote about) at the beginning of the chapter. Specifically, look at the second part of that scenario, which stated the following:

You have been placed in a study skills course this term. Explain why you DO really need this stuff! Even though you have spent many years in classrooms, you need to improve in some areas as you begin the term.

Reflect on the answer you wrote in response to this statement. After you complete that, review your notes from this chapter, the key terms, the boldface chapter headings, and the figures. Also reacquaint yourself with the Chapter Learning Outcomes:

- Identify at least two study skill challenges that you have.

- Identify at least two study skill strengths that you have.

- Explain how you can use your study skill strengths to minimize one of your study skill challenges.

- List at least five study skill topics covered in this book that you can use immediately.

Based on what you have read in this chapter, write a revised response to the statement from the beginning. Also explain what has caused you to adjust (or maintain) your evaluation. How do you see study skills differently now than when you started the chapter? How will you use your strengths to minimize your challenges?

Critical THINKING

2

What we think, we become.

—*Buddha*

CHAPTER LEARNING OUTCOMES

By the time you finish reading this chapter and completing its activities, you will be able to do the following:

- Define critical thinking.

- Use the R.E.D. Model to establish a clear and precise plan to minimize (or eliminate) a study skill problem you have.

- Understand the language of critical thinking.

- Create solutions for a study skill problem you have.

- Explain how critical-thinking skills can help you maintain balance and wellness in your life.

The Case of RICKY

Ricky is a first-semester student. His initial excitement about attending college has turned to panic. His first shock hit when he went to the bookstore to get his books. Besides the "sticker shock" of how much the books cost, he was overwhelmed by the sheer number of books he had to buy for each class. Initially, he thought, "There is no way the professors will expect us to read all of these books. I'll wait until the first day of class to see if there has been some sort of mistake."

© Shutterstock

Key Terms

Accuracy
Analyzing
Assumption
Benjamin Bloom
Clarity
Confirmation bias
Creative thinking
Critical thinking
Evaluate
Higher-order thinking skills
Logic
Lower-order thinking skills
Problem solving
Problem-solving trap
R.E.D. Model
Relevance

Chapter
INTRODUCTION

"But it's my opinion! How can it be wrong?" You may have heard someone blurt out some such statement. Perhaps the person wanted to support an argument with a degree of certainty that would make the point sound reasonable and logical. Unfortunately, such a statement will not meet the test of **critical thinking**—a skill that your professors will expect you to demonstrate on assignments, on tests, and in class discussions. While "But it's my opinion!" might work with a friend or as a sound bite on television, it will not carry much weight in an intellectual discussion.

The first day came—and sure enough, there was no mistake. Each instructor plopped a large syllabus and reading assignments page at his seat. He then learned that each instructor required the students to critically read each assignment. Ricky's idea of reading has been to skim the chapter for words that might be on a quiz, memorize them, and spit them back when asked. Now, he will have to write or orally explain his readings. He has very little experience doing this.

Ricky is considering quitting school.

CRITICALLY THINKING
about *Ricky's* situation

You are Ricky's best friend.
What advice would you
give your friend?

This chapter provides strategies to use in all of the succeeding chapters of this book. You will learn to use the R.E.D. Model, which will help you logically think through both academic and personal issues.

As you move through each study skill topic in this book, you will critically assess your skill level as it exists at the beginning of each chapter. From there, you will have the opportunity to build a selection of strategies that will improve your chances for achieving academic success. Activity 2.1 is the first of these assessments.

MyStudentSuccessLab

MyStudentSuccessLab (www .mystudentsuccesslab.com) is an online solution designed to help you 'Start strong, Finish stronger' by building skills for ongoing personal and professional development.

Activity 2.1

Reflecting on Your Current Level of Critical Thinking Skills

Before you answer the items that follow, reflect on your school experiences. Maybe it was last year—or as long as 20 years ago. Can you remember the types of questions your teachers asked you? Not the content of the questions but rather the difficulty level of the questions? Were you asked to memorize lists of terms and "spit them back" (known as a lower-order thinking skill), or did you have to *understand* and *analyze* and *evaluate* terms and concepts (higher-order thinking skills)?

There are no right answers for the questions below. It's okay if you cannot recall exactly which type of questions you most often faced; remember as best you can. As with all of the reflective activities in this book, write from your heart. This exercise is not meant for you to answer just like your classmates—or to match what you may think the instructor wants to see. Take your time to give a respectful and responsible general accounting of your experiences with critical thinking. A truthful self-assessment now will help you build on skills you possess while developing those you lack.

For each of the following items, circle the number that best describes your typical experience with critical thinking. The key for the numbers is as follows:

0 = never, 1 = almost never, 2 = occasionally, 3 = frequently, 4 = almost always, 5 = always

When considering your past schoolwork, how often:

1.	Did you have to *memorize* things such as terms, dates, and formulas?	0	1	2	3	4	5
2.	Were you rewarded (with a good grade) for "*spitting back*" nearly exact wording from textbooks, definitions, or lectures?	0	1	2	3	4	5
3.	Did you have to *summarize* a passage in your own words?	0	1	2	3	4	5
4.	Were you assigned to read a chapter (or book or essay or Internet site) and then asked to *evaluate* (judge) what you read according to specific standards or criteria?	0	1	2	3	4	5
5.	Did your teachers ask you to *develop* (create) your own theory or explanation for an event?	0	1	2	3	4	5
6.	Did your teachers expect you to *apply* (use) the knowledge you learned in class to solve a problem you had never seen before?	0	1	2	3	4	5
7.	Were you encouraged and rewarded for developing *new* and *unusual* solutions to a problem?	0	1	2	3	4	5
8.	Did you have to answer questions simply by searching for the *correct* answers in the textbook or lecture notes?	0	1	2	3	4	5

Lower-order thinking skills experience. Add up your scores for items 1, 2, 3, and 8. Divide by 4. Write your answer here:

Using the key explanations provided for each number (0, 1, 2, 3, 4, 5) for this activity, complete this sentence: When it comes to thinking, I have _____ used lower-order thinking skills.

Higher-order thinking skills experience. Add up your scores for items 4, 5, 6, and 7. Divide by 4. Write your answer here:..

Using the key explanations provided for each number (0, 1, 2, 3, 4, 5) for this activity, complete this sentence: When it comes to thinking, I have _____ used higher-order thinking skills.

Based on your answers, what insights do you have about your experiences with higher-order (critical) thinking skills?

....

....

DEFINING CRITICAL THINKING

> *Learning without thinking is labor lost; thinking without learning is dangerous.*
> —Chinese proverb

When your instructors ask you to think, read, write, or discuss an issue critically, they want you to examine, argue, analyze, evaluate, or create something. Such critical thinking requires gathering information, weighing it for accuracy and appropriateness, and then making a rational decision based on the facts you have gathered.

Critical thinkers demonstrate command of basic information about an issue as they logically, precisely, and systematically examine the issue from many sides—even if that examination may uncover information that differs from a deeply held personal belief. College life exposes students to situations that will challenge what they already "know" to be certain. For instance, your opinion may tell you there is no need to read the textbook assignments or come to class every day. However, as you gain experience—such as failing quizzes or exams—you may revisit and then change that mindset. You may also "know" that you can exist on minimal sleep. But a few weeks into the semester, you may question that "truth."

You have no doubt encountered similar revelations in your life outside college. At the writing of this chapter, loud debates can be heard about the issues of national health care reform and the power of the collective bargaining process. On television, on the floor of the U.S. Congress, and in state legislatures across the country, people are voicing their opinions. Unfortunately, there have been times when critical thinking has given way to shouting, name-calling, and even lying. While it might seem impossible in the midst of the shouting, having critical-thinking skills can help to distinguish between accuracies and inaccuracies regarding these important issues.

Active learning involves many forms of thinking. Some people use the terms *critical thinking, problem solving,* and *creative thinking* interchangeably, freely substituting one term for another.

A more precise view would be to think of each as a distinct thinking process; one leads to the other; one builds on the previous and uses deeper thinking skills. Each will be described and demonstrated in this chapter.

THE R.E.D. MODEL*

> *The harder you fight to hold on to specific assumptions, the more likely there's gold in letting go of them.*
>
> —John Seely Brown, scholar

It is difficult to imagine a decision that you make that doesn't involve critical thinking. Even buying a cup of coffee at the local coffee shop requires a degree of critical thinking. What size will it be? Is it so strong you will need extra sweetener? Is it a better deal to buy the large or small size?

If you drive a car, have you ever had to stop at a four-way stop sign intersection? Determining when to tap the accelerator and move through the intersection required critical thinking.

If you have a Facebook account and have ever received a "friend" request, you were using critical-thinking skills to make your decision to "confirm" or "quietly ignore."

We all have done this. Critical thinking is not new. But still, aren't you amazed by the number of people who seem to stumble through life making one uninformed decision after another? (And it is even more worrisome to think that there are people who vote without using critical-thinking skills!)

Let's examine a model that will help you *make sure* you are thinking critically and not, in fact, using noncritical "stinkin' thinkin'."

Models provide a systematic, step-by-step way to accomplish a task. The **R.E.D. Model** does just that for your critical thinking. The easy-to-remember acronym will help you remember the process steps. (An *acronym* is formed by taking a letter or two from a series of words. It creates another word—one that will help you remember the original series.)

Mark this page with a sticky note or paper clip so that you can easily refer to it. You will draw on the concepts presented throughout the book. Whenever you see the R.E.D. Model icon in the margin, it will be your reminder to apply your critical-thinking skills.

Step #1. STOP AND THINK

This is old yet sage advice. Before you can start the critical-thinking process, you have to stop all of the chatter and distractions in your mind. Prior to diving into an issue, pause, take a breath, and focus your thoughts.

Step #2. RECOGNIZING ASSUMPTIONS: Separating Fact from Fiction

Think about this: One of our First Amendment rights is freedom of speech. Is this an absolute right? Can we say anything we want? Can we utter statements that are deemed as cruel, hurtful, and even hateful to and by others?

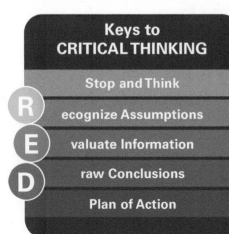

Keys to CRITICAL THINKING

- Stop and Think
- **R** ecognize Assumptions
- **E** valuate Information
- **D** raw Conclusions
- Plan of Action

When we assume (make an **assumption**), we make a decision based on many things—but not necessarily facts. Consider an assumption to be a theory, paradigm, or one's view of the world. When we *assume*, we accept something to be correct. We may or may not have actual proof, but we believe the opinion or position to be accurate. When we question

*Watson-Glaser Critical Thinking Appraisal, Forms A/B (WGCTA). Copyright © 2007 NCS Pearson, Inc. Reproduced with permission. All rights reserved. "Watson-Glaser Critical Thinking Appraisal" is a trademark, in the US and/or other countries, of Pearson Education, Inc. or its affiliates(s).

assumptions, we **evaluate** whether what we assume to be true is actually true. When you read the questions about the First Amendment, do you immediately form an opinion—an assumption—about what freedom of speech really means? What makes you sure that *you* are correct?

We may *assume*, for example, a political candidate is telling the truth because he belongs to the political party we belong to. Or we *assume* posting a comment on a social media site will never be seen by anyone except our "friends." Or maybe a student *assumes* she cannot be an engineer because females just *cannot do* math.

Each of these assumptions is based on an opinion. Sometimes, that opinion comes from past experience; other times, it evolves from personal prejudices and biases. The problem with assumptions is that they can very easily be more fiction than fact.

Critical thinking requires that you understand the issue or situation in front of you. That requires that you question your own positions, theories, and assumptions.

Step #3. EVALUATING INFORMATION: Remaining Objective and Unemotional

Think about this: In the case of *Snyder v. Phelps* (2011), the Chief Justice of the Supreme Court of the United States issued an opinion that said, in part, "As a nation we have chosen . . . to protect even hurtful speech on public issues to ensure that we do not stifle public debate." Another judge stated in a dissenting opinion, "Our profound national commitment to free and open debate is not a license for the vicious verbal assault that occurred in this case." The final 8–1 decision held that the First Amendment does in fact protect hurtful speech in public.

When you read what the two justices said, do you automatically gravitate to one side of the debate? If you are like most people, you probably do. Be careful in this step. Avoid **confirmation bias**. That is, don't let your preconceived ideas get in the way of an unbiased decision.

Can you see beyond the emotion and objectively judge the information that is before you? Did the judges actually say these things? Do you understand the vocabulary? Do you need additional facts? Once you have determined that the information presented is actually factual, you are on your way to understanding whether an argument is credible or not.

Step #4. DRAWING CONCLUSIONS: Making a Decision

The next step of our critical-thinking model logically follows the preceding two. Once you have separated fact from fiction and have objectively analyzed and evaluated the information presented, you are in a good position to make a decision about what you have before you.

Based on the information presented, you are now in a position to arrive at a conclusion.

If you think about it, this is what learning is all about (or, at least, it should be). We have an experience or gain some knowledge and draw a conclusion based on the experience or knowledge. Perhaps what we have learned reinforces our behavior, or maybe we change how we act. In either case, we have made an evaluation that to act or not act a certain way works or does not work for us.

Step #5. PLAN OF ACTION

Once you have a basic understanding of the facts and have formed your educated opinion about the issue at hand, you are ready to plan your next step. This could

Figure 2.1

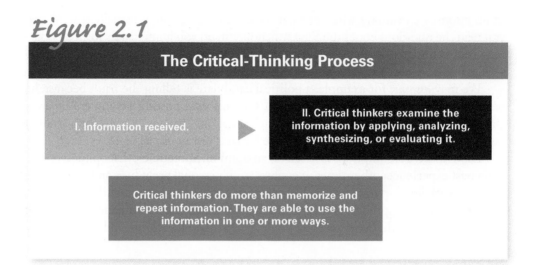

The Critical-Thinking Process

I. Information received.

II. Critical thinkers examine the information by applying, analyzing, synthesizing, or evaluating it.

Critical thinkers do more than memorize and repeat information. They are able to use the information in one or more ways.

range from thinking about the findings to sharing them with someone else to using the information to solve a problem.

The critical-thinking process is illustrated in Figure 2.1.

Activity 2.2

Seeing R.E.D.

CRITICALLY THINKING ABOUT ACADEMIC CHALLENGES

R
E
D

Identify one academic challenge you have had in school. Using the R.E.D. Model for critical thinking, examine the cause of this challenge.

THE LANGUAGE OF CRITICAL THINKING

The important thing in science is not so much to obtain new facts as to discover new ways of thinking about them.

—*Sir William Bragg, physicist*

When it comes to understanding a problem and moving toward a solution, critical thinkers have to set aside emotion. They must examine the issue on a number of intellectual levels. And they can tell when someone else's argument lacks the basic standards of critical thinking

USING C.A.R.L. TO UNDERSTAND CRITICAL THINKING

Certain terms and concepts constantly pop up when talking about critical thinking. Here are four such terms:

Table 2.1 **Applying standards of critical thinking to a current event**

Critical Thinking Standard	Application to Ricky's Situation
Clarity	Can you clearly state Ricky's assumptions and surprises about college?
Accuracy	How do you know this analysis is accurate? What facts can you present to support your interpretation of the arguments?
Relevance	How is Ricky's situation similar or dissimilar to your life, your well-being, and the choices you make—or will make?
Logic	Based on your evidence, in what ways do Ricky's reactions make sense to you? In what ways do you disagree with him?

- **Clarity.** Facts and arguments are presented clearly and unambiguously.
- **Accuracy.** The information presented is factual.
- **Relevance.** The information presented relates to the argument or problems at hand.
- **Logic.** The position makes sense.

Table 2.1 provides a quick example of how to judge the merit of an argument using commonly accepted standards.* For this example, let's return to the case of Ricky you read about at the beginning of the chapter.

In 1956, educational pioneer **Benjamin Bloom** developed a six-tier thinking skills model that has become the backbone of the critical-thinking process. Again, these terms, listed in Table 2.2, are commonly used with critical thinking. Become familiar with them.

LOWER-ORDER THINKING SKILLS

Remembering facts or names is the most basic level of thinking. When you memorize a list of vocabulary words and then repeat those words on a classroom quiz, you have recalled the information from your memory. These **lower-order thinking skills** are basic building blocks in the learning process, as they help lay the foundation for the higher-level thinking skills.

The next thinking step—understanding—indicates that you comprehend the information presented. When you can read or hear something and then put it into your own words, you have an increased chance of remembering it.

HIGHER-ORDER THINKING SKILLS

To make the most appropriate use of the **higher-order thinking skills** (described later in this section), you must master the smaller details noted earlier. The effectiveness of

*The intellectual standards used here—clarity, accuracy, relevance, and logic—are commonly cited in the literature. Three other standards may be used as well: precision, breadth, and depth. See Linda Elder and Richard Paul, "Universal Intellectual Standards," The Critical Thinking Community. Retrieved from www.criticalthinking.org/page.cfm?PageID=527&CategoryID=68.

Table 2.2   **The language of Bloom**

Step in Critical Thinking	At This Step, You Can
Remembering	Define, memorize, and recall facts, names, or dates.
Understanding	Describe, explain, paraphrase, and put things into your own words.
Applying	Demonstrate or use something you have learned in a new situation.
Analyzing	Compare, contrast, examine, and break down information into smaller pieces.
Evaluating	Criticize, defend, or judge the worth of information.
Creating	Design, develop, or put together something new (an idea, product, service).

critical thinking, problem solving, and creative thinking will be significantly reduced if you do not understand the basics.

Let's use your class syllabus as an example.

The first two categories (remembering and understanding) exhibit *noncritical thinking characteristics*, but the last four levels describe forms of *critical* thinking. Table 2.3 outlines Bloom's levels of higher-order thinking and suggests that a critical thinker is actively and deeply involved in processing information by applying, **analyzing**, evaluating, and/or creating information and ideas.

If you can read your syllabus and tell a classmate when the next assignment is due, that is important basic-level knowledge. Knowing the due dates of your course assignments and being able to explain in your own words what each assignment requires are important steps to success. This basic understanding lays the foundation for the higher-level thinking skills—similar to a football receiver, who must remember the pass pattern he needs to run before he can catch a football successfully in a game.

Activity 2.3

Using the R.E.D. Model to Examine Your Study Skills

R
E
D

Consider your study skills, and identify one area of challenge. Using the R.E.D. Model, *clearly and precisely* state what your specific problem or challenge is with the study skill you identified. For example, perhaps you have difficulty taking notes in class or from reading assignments. Or maybe you run out of time and do not complete assignments.

■ **Stop and think.** Identify your study skill challenge, and write it here.

....

....

- **Recognize assumptions.** How do you know this is actually a challenge for you? Has anyone ever pointed this out to you? Or perhaps you might say, "I am no good at math because everyone in my family is bad at math. It is genetic!" Write your response here.

  ....

  ....

- **Evaluate information.** Why do you have this challenge? What evidence exists? Is the problem a study skills problem—or something else? For instance, you may say, "I do poorly on tests because I am a poor test taker." The reality might be that you never get enough sleep before tests and are therefore too tired to perform effectively. Write your response here.

  ....

  ....

- **Draw conclusions.** If you can do this step well, you are able to bring together all pieces of the situation and logically use the evidence to come to a reasonable conclusion. For instance, after you have reviewed the evidence, separated fact from fiction, and put emotion aside, you might find yourself saying something like the following: "I was brought up in a family that feared math. I believe that fear has transferred to me. There is nothing genetic about it! I need to work with a tutor and get a good night's sleep." Write your response here.

  ....

  ....

Table 2.3 Using higher-level thinking skills

Type of Thinking	Example	Why It Is Critical Thinking
Applying	Using your priority management skills, you transfer all of the syllabus assignment and test dates to your calendar. You put yourself on a schedule so that all assignments will be completed on time.	You understand the information and can use it in a new situation.
Analyzing	Once you have all of the due dates on your calendar, you classify your assignments according to which ones will take the most/least time to complete. You ask yourself, "Which items will I need help with?"	You understand the information and demonstrate this understanding by separating or splitting the information into its pieces or parts. By doing this, you can see the essential features of an argument, issue, or process.
Evaluating	After completing the first three weeks of the course, you make a judgment as to how useful your scheduling has been. What worked? What did not work?	You have the ability to judge or critique the value of the information.
Creating	You understand all of the individual requirements of the course, and you start to see the "whole picture" of how much time you will need to devote to this course to earn an A.	You understand the information and then bring the pieces of the information together to form a "big picture" or new idea. You create a new weekly schedule for yourself.

Source: Piscitelli, 2011, p. 81.

PROBLEM SOLVING*

> *We can't solve problems by using the same kind of thinking we used when we created them.*
>
> —Albert Einstein, physicist

Problem solving is a process that requires the use of critical-thinking skills to examine a dilemma, situation, or person that presents us with difficulty—the problem. A proposed solution follows this examination.

For an example, let's look at our friend Ricky from the beginning of the chapter. A critical thinker must first examine Ricky's assumption that "no way" will his professors expect him to read all of these books. How does he "know" this? The same holds true for what Ricky "knows" to be true about reading an assignment. Where did he get this information, and how does it relate to his new college reality?

Once Ricky has identified his assumptions (and separates his facts from fiction), he can begin to gather more information about what his professors expect. He might schedule an appointment with each professor. He might talk with classmates. Perhaps a trip to his campus advisor might help. All of this requires deep thinking, fact finding, and time. However, if our critical thinker gathers the information, analyzes, and submits a report *without a solution*, then the problem has not been solved.

A problem solver looks at the information *and then* proposes alternatives and answers.

THE PROCESS OF PROBLEM SOLVING

Problem solving generally involves a series of steps. When done effectively, each step is well thought out and answers a question. These answers methodically lead to a solution. Problem solving requires five strategic steps:

1. **Reflecting.** This step asks for careful and thoughtful consideration about the problem. Before you can solve your problem, you must clearly define it and why you think it exists. What assumptions exist? Evaluate your answers.
2. **Brainstorming.** When problem solvers brainstorm, they let their ideas tumble from their minds like rain from the sky—the more rain, the better. The purpose of a brainstorming session is to come up with as many ideas as possible—without judgment. What possible actions could solve this problem? No evaluation is needed for this step. Be as creative as you possibly can.
3. **Choosing.** Once you have listed the possible solutions, choose the best and establish a plan to carry it out. Remember that which solution you decide on needs to address your identified problem (see step 1). Evaluate your choice. Why do you consider it to be the best choice? Again, are you making any assumptions?
4. **Implementing.** Now, it is time to move from *thinking* to *doing*. Put your planning into motion. This may lead you directly to the solution of your problem, or you may experience a series of starts and stops. In other words, you may choose a solution and put it into action—only to discover that it does not work like you had thought it would. At that point, based on your evaluation, you may need to return to brainstorming, then choose another alternative, and implement that again. It may be helpful to periodically ask yourself, "Is this solution working?"

*This section based on Piscitelli (2011), pp. 83–86.

5. **Evaluating.** Effective problem solvers do this along the way *and* at the end of the process. As noted in step 4, once you implement your solution, you will need to stop every so often to make sure you are moving in the correct direction. Make adjustments as needed. Once you have completed all the action steps of your plan, make a final judgment as to the effectiveness of your choices and actions. Has the problem been solved—or do you need to do something else? Did your choice work—or do you need to make some new choices?

Using the steps in Figure 2.2, consider the following student dilemma—and solution.

1. Reflecting (on the identified problem)

   "I read my assigned history chapters from the textbook. But when it comes to reading quizzes, I never score above a D. My assumption is that the effort I put into my studies does not match my quiz grades. I want to earn B's and A's on my history reading quizzes."

2. Brainstorming (possible solutions)

   a. I can withdraw from the class.
   b. I can read the entire chapter the night before the quiz. Maybe I will retain more information if I read everything at the last minute.
   c. I can begin reading earlier in the week—and concentrate on fewer pages per night.
   d. I can seek out the services of a tutor and see if there are problems with my reading abilities.

3. Choosing (the most appropriate alternative)

   a. I can withdraw from the class. (NO. Reasons: I will still have to take the course; withdrawing may affect my financial aid; and I still need to deal with my reading comprehension problem. This is based on the assumption that running from the problem will fix it.)
   b. I can read the entire chapter the night before the quiz. Maybe I will retain more information. (NO. Reasons: I have trouble enough understanding the subject; if I had to read 25 pages of this material in one night, I think I would fall asleep!)
   c. I can begin reading earlier in the week—and concentrate on fewer pages per night. (YES! Reason: Breaking the assignment into more bite-sized portions will help me focus on less material at one time—and improve my chances of comprehension and a better grade.)
   d. I can seek out the services of a tutor and see if there are problems with my reading abilities. (YES! Reason: This option actually addresses the assumption that just because I am putting in time reading does not mean I am reading effectively. Perhaps there are some reading strategies I need to learn.)

4. Implementing (the chosen alternative)

   a. My next history quiz is in six days. I will read 5 pages per day of my 25-page chapter. That will give me the last day to review my reading notes and highlighting.
   b. I will set up an appointment with the campus tutoring center (or with a reading instructor on campus) and discuss alternative reading strategies.

5. Evaluating (your plan)

   I got a C on my most recent quiz. The new strategies seem to have worked—but I am not satisfied with a C. I plan on visiting my professor to see if he has any suggestions.

Using this example as a guide, complete Activity 2.4 and Activity 2.5.

Figure 2.2

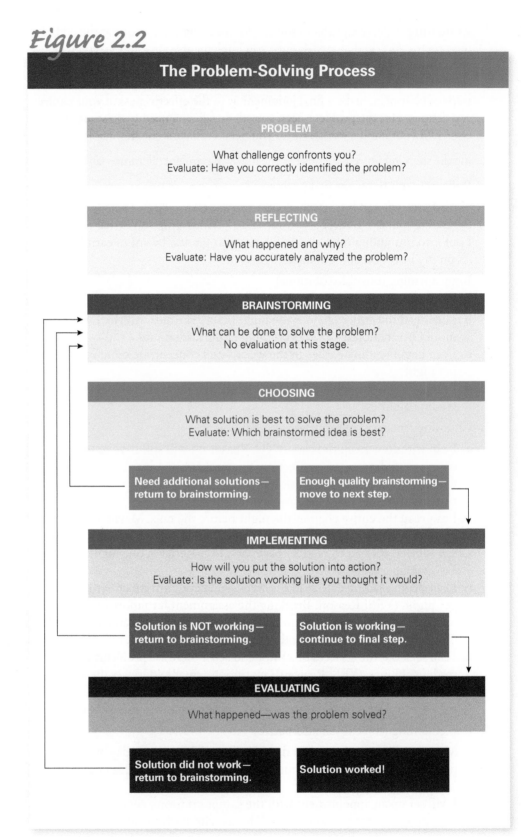

Activity 2.4

Practicing Brainstorming

USING CRITICAL THINKING FOR ACADEMIC SUCCESS

Earlier in this chapter, you identified and examined one academic challenge you have this school term. Now, brainstorm three potential solutions to your academic challenge.

CRITICAL THINKING AND PERSONAL WELL-BEING

When we tend to our social, emotional, physical, and social well-being, we use critical-thinking skills.

There may be a point in the school term when you begin to feel overwhelmed—when the weight of all your responsibilities and obligations seem impossible to handle. Especially during those times, your critical-thinking skills will prove valuable. Let's see what course of action you would suggest to help Tina. As you can see in the following activity, she is about ready to call it quits.

Activity 2.5

Seeing R.E.D.

USING CRITICAL-THINKING SKILLS TO EXAMINE LIFE'S BALANCE

R
E
D

For this activity (based on Piscitelli, 2011, p. 86), read about Tina's situation. Then, work with a classmate to complete the items that follow.

> Twenty-five-year-old Tina is in her first semester of college. In addition to taking two college classes, she works 20 hours a week as a server in a restaurant. Doing her best to make ends meet, she recently took in a roommate to help with rent. Tina has sole custody of her two little girls (2 years old and 7 years old). She also faithfully participates in a 12-step program. She is proud that she has been "clean" of all drugs and alcohol for nearly three years.
>
> Tina is determined that her past will not become her future. Having a strong faith and loving her two children have helped her to keep focused. Lately, though, she has been gripped by panic and anxiety. As a child, she was always told that she was not very smart. The few relatives with whom she still stays in contact believe she is wasting her time with college. Today, Tina told one of her professors she has lost confidence in her ability to do college work—and is considering withdrawing from college.

While Tina's battle with her past "demon" of addiction may not be typical of students you know, her insecurities and doubts reflect the issues that can and do paralyze students. Using the strategies you have learned thus far, help Tina critically examine those dimensions of life that may be out of balance.

1. Reflecting: State Tina's problem or problems as clearly as you can. Identify those that may have an impact on her well-being. Are any assumptions present?

2. Brainstorming:

List potential solution 1. _____

List potential solution 2. _____

List potential solution 3. _____

3. Choosing: Evaluate all information. Are any assumptions present here? Which solution seems most appropriate in this situation?

4. Implementing: How can Tina implement this solution?

5. Evaluating: What can Tina do to judge how effective the solution is?

THE PROBLEM-SOLVING TRAP

Sometimes, we are blinded to new alternatives because we are stuck in a routine or trapped by our assumptions. Perhaps we continue to look at a particular problem from the same point of view. For example, if your quiz grades have been lower than you had hoped for, your response may be, "I will study harder!" After all, that is what you have heard all your life: "If you want to do better, just try harder! Give it more effort. Focus!" Let's examine this assumption—and why it may be a **problem-solving trap** for you.

If you were to base your entire problem-solving strategy on the premise that "studying harder" will bring better grades, you could find yourself going nowhere fast.

While the intent is admirable, "study harder" generally means "I'll continue to use the same study methods that have not worked—but I'll do them longer and with more effort." Think about that. Does that *really* make sense to you? It is limited, because you have not questioned your initial assumption—and thus your alternatives are limited. What you need is some new thinking—some new eyeglasses with which to examine the problem.

CREATIVE THINKING

> *Logic will get you from A to B.*
> *Imagination will take you everywhere.*
> —Albert Einstein, physicist

YOU HAVE TO DO IT DIFFERENTLY IF YOU WANT DIFFERENT RESULTS

Just because you put more effort into preparation for your math exam, for example, does not mean that you will see better results on the next test. **Creative thinking**—thinking that develops (creates) a *new* or *different* product—requires that we look at situations in new ways—from different angles or unique perspectives.

Let's look at the issue of campus security. Solutions to curbing crime on campus might include hiring more security officers for the campus, improving lighting, or installing more emergency phones in high-risk areas on campus. However, a *new* approach might be to explore the possibility of developing a campus "citizens watch" program, in which student organizations work with campus security personnel to increase student confidence about campus safety.

By *creatively* tackling a problem, we become more aware of the greater number of possibilities for solving it. We will become better equipped to broaden our thinking and develop new patterns of problem solving.

LEARNING TO THINK CREATIVELY

While some people seem to be naturally creative, others struggle to come up with an original idea. One strategy is to use what you already know. Let's use the problem-solving process you learned earlier to boost your creativity.

Even when you do not need to solve a dilemma, you can use those same steps. For instance, if you would like to write a short story or compose a song, the process of reflecting, brainstorming, choosing, implementing, and evaluating can be used effectively. Table 2.4 gives some guidance.

Table 2.4 **The creative-thinking process**

Problem-Solving Process Steps	Suggestions to Increase Creativity
Reflecting	• Slow down and think about the problem. Do not "solve" it until you understand it.
	• Be kind to yourself. If you constantly tell yourself, "I would not recognize a creative idea if it hit me in the head," you are establishing a negative attitude. Refer to the chapter-opening quote, "What we think, we become."
	• Associate with people who seem to be able to "think outside the box." Listen to creative people. Read about creative people.
	• Challenge any assumptions that might shut down creativity. Silence internal dialogue such as "Don't be foolish" or "I'm not creative."
Brainstorming	• Brainstorm effectively. List your ideas on a piece of paper, but do not stop to judge whether they are good or bad. Making judgments will slow down your flow of ideas and inhibit your free thinking. There will be time later to judge practicality.
	• Accept the fact that there are different ways to look at your problem or situation. Look at it from different perspectives. How would your instructor view the problem? How about a friend? If you can see the issue from different angles, chances are you can find multiple solutions, as well. Again, challenge assumptions.
	• Avoid the temptation to grab the first solution that comes to your mind. Brainstorm as many solutions as you can think of. Ask a trusted friend to help you. This will give you the opinions of someone who is not personally involved in the problem.
Choosing	• Identify what types of solutions have been used in the past with similar problems. If you can, determine whether the solutions were successful.
Implementing	• Practice. Listen to or read the news. Can you propose a creative solution to a current event? Opportunities are all around. Do this frequently.
Evaluating	• Go beyond thinking about creativity. Feel it, taste it, hear it, and see it. Use every sense you have to understand the world around you.

Activity 2.6

Creative Solutions

CRITICAL THINKING FOR ACADEMIC SUCCESS

One last time, return to the academic challenge you identified and examined earlier in this chapter. Review the three solutions you brainstormed. With the help of a trusted friend or mentor, come up with two more solutions. Make them as creative as you can. Step outside the traditional thinking "box." Review your potential solutions. Come up with at least one creative idea to address the challenge. Go ahead. For the purpose of this activity, be bold. Even if your ideas seem silly or outlandish, write them here or on a separate piece of paper.

....

....

As you learned earlier, once you have solutions, you will need to evaluate (a higher-level thinking skill) the potential consequences of each solution. Do that now for your creative ideas.

....

....

Finally, based on this exercise, which solution do you favor—and why do you think it will successfully address your study skill challenge?

....

....

ADAPTING OLD SKILLS TO NEW SITUATIONS: MAKING CHOICES

It is our choices that show what we truly are, far more than our abilities.

—J. K. Rowling, author

You will continually confront situations in which you must apply the skills you have developed over the years. You learn something in one school year or subject area—for example, how to take notes—and you must apply it in another school year or subject area. Occasionally, a new situation presents itself, in which the old skills do not easily work. You must then make some sort of adjustment. In some cases, this may be minor; in others, quite dramatic. Frustration may very likely occur. In such situations you have four broad choices—and each requires critical thinking:

1. Quit or remove yourself from the situation:
   - The new instructor is requiring things that you have either not done before or have done but not done well. Rather than confront the

situation, you drop the class. Think about the assumptions being made here.

■ A similar scenario may be a catalyst for you to quit a job.

2. Stay in the new situation without adjusting your skills and suffer a miserable existence.

■ This situation is the same as the first, except you cannot or will not drop the class. You dislike the class, but you refuse to modify your skills. Consequently, you are one unhappy student!

■ Do you know someone who cannot adapt to a new boss or manager? Rather than look for ways to improve the situation, the person suffers a miserable existence in the job.

3. Modify your skills to get by in the new situation.

■ You are not particularly happy about the new challenge, but you realize you have to make some adjustments. You might not make a dramatic change, but you do enough to get by.

■ The new position at work requires you to develop some new techniques to be successful. You may not like the adjustment, but you realize it is necessary to stay with a job you otherwise like.

4. Change and adapt your old skills so that they better fit the new demands.

■ You take the challenge head on. You may stumble a couple of times, but you make the needed changes in your skills to serve you better.

■ You want to thrive in the company and move up the promotion ladder. You search for ways to learn and grow each day.

It is possible for a student to go through all of these choices within a given class or situation. It can begin with the fear of a particularly challenging instructor at the beginning of the semester—bringing on the desire to quit. You are not allowed to quit (perhaps your financial aid requirements will not allow you to withdraw), so you stay in the class, dreading each day. Along the way, the teacher catches your attention, or another student helps you, or you have some inner change, and you realize some adjustment must be made. Finally, you know you must completely modify your old skill so it works well with the new situation.

You need to consciously identify and review where you are in your thought process. First ask yourself, "What assumptions am I making?" Then ask yourself, "What can I do?" Sometimes, the first option—quit—is the best. You may be "overplaced" in a class (for example, you did not take a prerequisite course that taught the skills needed). Or the job is just not matched to your skills. But don't jump to this choice because it seems like the easy way out. Many times, quitting only postpones the inevitable. You will eventually need the skill in question. Let's examine Activity 2.6 to assess how you adapt old skills to new situations.

© Shutterstock

Activity 2.6

Making Choices Outside the Classroom

For this activity, think of a situation outside this classroom or course. It could be another class, or it could involve a relationship with a friend, teammate, or co-worker. Using these questions as guides, complete the items that follow. The questions in each item are meant to get you thinking. You do not have to answer each one.

1. When was the last time you either quit a situation (class or job, for instance) or seriously considered quitting a situation? What were the circumstances? Were there alternatives, such as seeking assistance or asking for clarification? With what assumptions were you working?

....

....

2. When was the last time you stayed in a miserable situation? What were the circumstances? Were there other alternatives? How did you feel? What were the results?

....

....

3. When was the last time you made some minor adjustments to old skills to adjust to a new situation? What were the circumstances? What were the results? Would you do it differently now?

....

....

4. When was the last time you made a major change to an old skill to be successful in a new situation? What were the results? Would you be able to apply this process of change to another situation in the future?

....

....

Chapter SUMMARY

CRITICAL THINKING
EXPANDS YOUR CONFIDENCE

In this chapter, you have examined the critical-thinking process. More specifically, you have been introduced to and practiced the R.E.D. Model for critical thinking.

Before moving on to the next chapter, take a moment to reflect on the following points:

- You have been in school before—and you have been successful in school before. Respect the study skills you have, and critically think about how you can apply these skills to your new college environment.

- Critical thinking requires reflection and analysis (as well as application and evaluation) of issues or events.

- Problem solving requires the use of critical-thinking skills to examine a dilemma and then propose a solution.

R **E** **D**
- When solving a problem, use creative-thinking strategies to look at multiple perspectives. This will help you see that problems and issues generally have more than two sides.

Use the R.E.D. Model to recognize assumptions, evaluate information, and draw conclusions.

CRITICALLY THINKING
What Have You Learned in This Chapter?

At the beginning of this chapter, you read about Ricky. You might remember that he had worked himself into such a state that he was considering dropping out of school.

Each chapter of this book will end with a section titled *Critically Thinking: What Have You Learned in This Chapter?* You will then use (apply) what you have learned to the chapter-opening situation. In this chapter, that is the situation concerning Ricky. However, before you dive into Ricky's problem and propose your solution, stop and think about the main points of the chapter.

Review your notes from this chapter, as well as the key terms, chapter outcomes, and bold-faced chapter headings, and the figures and tables. For instance, consider how the chapter outcomes may be used to help Ricky:

© Shutterstock

- Define critical thinking. (Ricky will need to weigh the facts of his situation before he can make a rational decision.)

- Use the R.E.D. Model to establish a plan. (Gathering facts is one of the steps of critical thinking. Ricky will also need to identify any opinions he holds that may lead him to an inappropriate conclusion.)

- Understand the language of critical thinking. (To appropriately use the R.E.D. Model, Ricky will need to understand how to analyze and evaluate information.)

- Provide creative solutions. (Sometimes, we have to look at problems from new and unusual perspectives. Ricky may need your help with this.)

- Explain how critical-thinking skills can help maintain balance and wellness. (Ricky is not in a good place right now. You will be able to offer him ideas on how to solve his problem and maintain his health in the process.)

TEST YOUR LEARNING

Now that you have reviewed the main steps of the critical-thinking and problem-solving processes, reread Ricky's story. Pretend that you are Ricky's best friend. Using the R.E.D. Model for critical thinking, help Ricky critically review his problem before he does something he may regret.

R

Recognize Assumptions:

Facts: What are the facts in Ricky's situation? List them.

Opinions: What opinions do you find in this situation? List them here.

Assumptions: Are Ricky's assumptions accurate?

E

Evaluate Information:

Ricky is considering dropping out of school. Before he makes this decision, help him by compiling a list of questions that will help him make the most appropriate decision.

What emotions seem to be moving Ricky toward his decision?

Is there anything missing from his thought process?

Do you see a confirmation bias?

D

Draw Conclusions:

Based on the facts and the questions you have presented, what conclusions can you draw?

What advice do you have for Ricky? What solutions do you propose?

Based on your suggestions, do you see any assumptions?

Finally, based on what you learned about using critical thinking to problem solve, what plan of action do you suggest for Ricky?

Priority
MANAGEMENT

3

Today is the tomorrow
you created yesterday.
—*Author unknown*

CHAPTER LEARNING OUTCOMES

By the time you finish reading this chapter and completing its activities, you will be able to do the following:

- Develop a written schedule that provides at least two hours of study time for every hour scheduled in the classroom.

- Use and evaluate at least one priority management tool (a calendar or planner).

- Develop a weekly to-do list that ranks your tasks in order of importance.

- Identify at least three types of procrastination and a strategy to deal with each.

- Describe how applying organizational skills can help you balance your life's demands.

The Case of MARIE

Marie is a single mother with one child. She has four on-campus classes and one online class. In addition to her financial aid, she earns income by working 30 hours a week at a store in the mall.

It is now the fourth week of the term, and Marie is feeling overwhelmed by all of the projects, tests, and reading assignments she must complete for her classes. She has not had a good night's sleep in more than two weeks, and the stress of everything is beginning to show.

Marie's class averages are not impressive—one C and three Ds. One week, she spends too much time focusing on math and doesn't have time to study for other classes. The next week, she

© Shutterstock

Key Terms

Activation energy
Calendar
Habit
Personal storage area
Personal study area
Priorities
Procrastination
Repetitive strain injuries
   (RSIs)
Stress
Study time

Chapter

INTRODUCTION

THE MYTH OF TIME MANAGEMENT*

When you hear the word organization, what comes to mind? Perhaps you think about wasting time, spending time, finding time, stealing time, and needing more time. Or maybe you immediately think of calendars, PDAs, procrastination, and time management.

*This section based on Piscitelli (2011), pp. 22–23.

catches up in history but falls behind in everything else. She has been late to most of her classes—not by much, but she is never on time. And her homework is always late. Things constantly "slip her mind."

Marie has thought about dropping one of her classes, but she believes that will affect her eligibility for financial aid. In addition, she looks at dropping a class as being the same as failing it. "I'm not a quitter," she recently told a friend. "All I want to do is hang on for the rest of the semester. I want to earn my degree as soon as possible. Dropping classes will not get me closer to my goal. I'll just have to sleep less and work more."

CRITICALLY THINKING
about *Marie's* situation

You are Marie's mentor. What strategies would you suggest for her to follow?

A recent (April 15, 2011) Bing.com search on the key term "time management" brought up approximately 530,000,000 hits. This concept is the subject of books, videos, seminars, and class discussions. Considering how much attention time management receives, it is difficult to believe that the topic is a myth.

That's right! You read that correctly. Time management is a myth. It cannot be done. Period. You can manage your finances. You can manage the amount of food you eat or the level of exercise you perform. You even can manage relationships. But you cannot manage time.

MyStudentSuccessLab

MyStudentSuccessLab (www .mystudentsuccesslab.com) is an online solution designed to help you 'Start strong, Finish stronger' by building skills for ongoing personal and professional development.

Consider the following:

- Everyone has the same number of hours in a week (168).
- No matter who you are—rich or poor, a college student or a college president, a mailroom worker or a corporate executive—you cannot increase the number of hours in a week. You cannot move some to next week, and you cannot borrow any from last week. You cannot manage to have more hours than the person next to you.
- Each hour is 60 minutes long. You cannot speed it up, and you cannot slow it down. You cannot manage to stretch that hour.
- Regardless of what you do (or anyone does), at the beginning of each day, you have the same 24 hours as everyone else with which to work. You cannot manage to sneak in an additional hour or two.

Rather than focus on something you cannot do—manage time—consider managing your priorities.

Priorities are the things that are important in your life—those things that help you get what you want. So, it makes more sense to practice priority management. When you do this, you are putting the important things first on your daily calendar. You are organizing your day around what moves you closer to your goals.

When you manage your priorities, you will also decrease your stress and improve the balance and health in your life. (For more on this concept, see Winget, 2004, Ch. 22.) Effective priority management will make your life easier. It really is an essential life skill (Urban, 2003, p. 123).

The clock keeps ticking no matter what you do. You cannot control time. You cannot create time. However, you can effectively use time for your benefit.

TIME IS ONLY ONE RESOURCE YOU HAVE TO PRIORITIZE

Priority management challenges even the best students during their first term in college. A typical college student may have only two or three hours of class on a particular day. The increased amount of unstructured time he or she has can be troublesome. For other students, returning to school can create a new set of challenges as they juggle family, work, and school.

But time is only one resource you have to organize. You also need to consider space: Where will you study, how will you file your papers, and where will you keep your supplies? Whether you live on campus, in an off-campus apartment, or at home with your family, you will benefit by designating a place for your out-of-class study time.

Getting organized will not only improve your study habits and grades, but it will also allow you to feel in control of your life. This chapter* will explain how to organize time and space to improve efficiency and effectiveness while minimizing stress.

*This section based on Piscitelli (2008), pp. 70–91.

Activity 3.1

Reflecting on Your Current Level of Organizational Skills

Before you answer the items that follow, reflect on your current level of organizational skills. Think of how well (or poorly) you have organized your priorities and your workspace.

There are no "right" answers for the questions that follow. As you do in completing all of the reflective activities in this book, you should write from your heart. It is not meant for you to answer just like your classmates or to match what you may think your instructor wants to see. Take your time to give a respectful and responsible general accounting of your experiences with organization. Conducting a truthful self-assessment now will help you build on skills you have while developing those you lack.

For each of the following items, circle the number that best describes your typical experience with organizational skills. Here is the key for the numbers:

0 = never, 1 = almost never, 2 = occasionally, 3 = frequently, 4 = almost always, 5 = always

When considering your past successes and challenges with organization, how often:

1.	Were you able to find an item (a paper, a book, your keys) after you put it somewhere?	0	1	2	3	4	5
2.	Did you arrive on time for class or another appointment?	0	1	2	3	4	5
3.	Did you turn in assignments on time?	0	1	2	3	4	5
4.	Did you work in a study space dedicated specifically to you?	0	1	2	3	4	5
5.	Did you not overwhelm and stress yourself by limiting your workload?	0	1	2	3	4	5
6.	Were you able to handle your stress in an effective and healthy manner?	0	1	2	3	4	5
7.	Did you seek advice from a classmate, adviser, or professor about ways to better organize your class work and to reduce stress?	0	1	2	3	4	5
8.	Did you organize your class notes and materials using an effective notebook?	0	1	2	3	4	5

Add up your scores for items 2, 3, and 5. Divide by 3. Write your answer here: _____.

Using the key provided to explain each number (0, 1, 2, 3, 4, 5), complete this sentence: When it comes to organizing priorities, I _____ organize my priorities effectively.

Add up your scores for items 1, 4, and 8. Divide by 3. Write your answer here: _____.

Using the key provided to explain each number (0, 1, 2, 3, 4, 5), complete this sentence: When it comes to organizing space, I _____ organize my space effectively.

Add up your scores for items 5, 6, and 7. Divide by 3. Write your answer here: _____.

Using the key provided to explain each number (0, 1, 2, 3, 4, 5), complete this sentence: When it comes to organization in general, I _____ can organize myself so as to minimize stress.

Based on your answers, what insights have you gained about your experiences with organization?

ORGANIZATION AND TIME

> *This time, like all times, is a very good one, if we but know what to do with it.*
> —Ralph Waldo Emerson, author

No one can give you a foolproof or crisis-proof system for priority management. But successful students can adapt to changes and unforeseen events. No matter what they have planned, they can deal with both expected and unexpected events. Anticipation will help to reduce pressure on you and avoid crisis.

YOU HAVE A LOT TO DO!

With coursework, homework, after-school activities, family responsibilities, and personal activities, you have many demands on your time. A partial list of what you have to do may look like this:

- Find personal free time.
- Find time to do activities with friends.
- Find recreation time.
- Find quality family time.
- Find time to study.
- Juggle work hours, school hours, and study hours.
- Get enough good sleep.
- Juggle family responsibilities with school expectations.

The strategies discussed in this chapter will help you appropriately handle all of the obligations that look you in the face each day.

STUDY TIME: How Much?

This question is nearly impossible to answer. If you are taking a full load of classes, then your homework and class time could very well add up to a 40-hour workweek. That is based on the long-referenced formula of spending two or three hours a week out of class for every hour you spend in class. According to that formula, if you spend 12 hours in class each week, you should devote another 24 to 36 hours to study time: reading, writing, researching, meeting with study groups, completing assignments, and preparing for tests outside class. Doing these tasks is what is meant by **study time**.

Keep in mind that the type of work you do will also dictate how much time is necessary. For instance, if you are reviewing elementary concepts in an introductory math course, your amount of study time may be less than that of someone tackling higher-level calculus for the first time. Likewise, writing English papers may take much more time than studying for a math test (regardless of the level).

HOW DO YOU ESTABLISH A STUDY SCHEDULE?

Let's ask the "How much study time?" question in a different way. How much time do you have available for homework and study purposes?

Complete Activity 3.2, and then examine Table 3.1.

Activity 3.2

Where Does Your Week Go?

Again, there are 168 hours in every week. Whether you are a first-year student or a graduating senior, the number of hours remains constant. You cannot create or eliminate any of them.

In the first column of the table that follows, list all of the things you do in a week. You will find some common categories already entered for you. Add as many as apply to your week's schedule. Once you have completed that, go back and estimate the number of hours per week you devote to each category. Enter those numbers in the next column. (It is difficult to be exact with this type of exercise, but estimate as best you can.) The third column asks you to rate how necessary the activity is to you. That is, was this something you had to do? (For more on this concept, see Hallowell [2007], pp. 148–161.)

What I Do Each Week	Number of Hours I Spend Doing It	How Necessary Is This to My Life? 1 = not very necessary 5 = extremely necessary
Sleep		
Eat meals		
Hygiene (showers, haircuts, general grooming)		
Time in class		
Time at employment		
Practice (sports, music, theater)		
Travel (time I spend on the road each week)		
Child care		
Religious or spiritual activities		
Recreation		
Chores and errands		
Other family obligations		
Club activities		
Other		
Total time spent on all activities		

Recognize assumptions: Look at your responses for column 3. Do you have many 5s? If you find yourself with more things to do than hours to do them, perhaps it has something to do with how you look at these things. If everything is "extremely necessary," then the reality is that nothing is extremely necessary. How do you know the 5s are in fact "extremely necessary"? Separate fact from fiction here.

Table 3.1 **Determining study time**

Number of Each Course You Are Taking This Semester	Course Name	Number of Credits/Hours in the Classroom for This Course	Study Time (based on 2 hours for each 1 hour in class)	Total Hours per Week for the Course (in class and out of class)	Cumulative Hours for All Courses You Are Taking This Term
1	English	3	6	9	9 (if you take only this course)
2	Math	3	6	9	18 (for two courses)
3	History	3	6	9	27 (for tree courses)
4	Humanities	3	6	9	36 (for four courses)
5	Biology (and lab)	4	8	12	48 (for five courses)

No magic number exists for how many hours you need to devote to your studies, but consider the formula introduced earlier. If you are taking a full load of courses (four or five a term) and the hours you have available for homework amounts to only five hours per week, you will likely have a problem completing your college requirements. Table 3.1 clearly shows that the more classes you take, the greater the demands on your time.

Most colleges consider a 12-credit hour schedule full time. Looking at Table 3.1, you can see that those 12 credit hours require a time commitment of 24 to 36 hours. If you're also planning on working a 40-hour-per-week job, then you must schedule 72 hours a week for school and work. That is the equivalent of having two full-time jobs.

That will leave you with 92 hours a week for everything else in your life. If you hope to get 8 hours of sleep per night (56 for the week), you will have only 36 hours remaining to fashion a life outside work and school.

If you can do it, great! If not, stop and reevaluate before you put yourself—and your friends and family—through a nightmarish schedule. If you are exhausted by the end of your week, remember that you, not your instructor, established the schedule.

A related strategy is to complete this exercise before you register for next term's classes. Recognize what your time constraints are before you commit to more classes than you will be able to handle. It's true that you can always withdraw from a class, but that can become costly in the end. It can also tarnish your transcript by giving the appearance of an individual who has difficulty completing tasks that he or she has started.

KEEPING TRACK OF TIME AND COMMITMENTS

After you understand how much time you need to devote to school and studies, you'll need a way to manage that time. A calendar—or even a simple piece of paper—will be effective if it helps you manage your time. Like your note-taking style, whatever you decide to go with, make sure it works for you and use it consistently.

Activity 3.3

Problems in Priority Management

Another strategy is to review some of the most common priority management problems facing students. Read the following list,* and check the ones that give you problems:

INTERRUPTIONS

- ○ Interruptions (phone calls)
- ○ Friends dropping by to say "hello"
- ○ Others requesting help
- ○ Meetings (school, organizations, work)
- ○ Other _____

ORGANIZATION

- ○ Assignments are too big to handle
- ○ Lack of planning
- ○ Procrastination (waiting until the last minute)
- ○ Overextended—too much to do
- ○ Too many unfinished projects/tasks—many incomplete activities
- ○ Unrealistic time estimates (expecting to finish a task in less time than it really takes)
- ○ Other _____

COMMUNICATION

- ○ Unclear instructions
- ○ Not listening carefully to instructor directions
- ○ Lack of needed information
- ○ Other _____

ATTENTION

- ○ Making careless mistakes so work has to be redone
- ○ Working on trivial things rather than important ones—don't prioritize well
- ○ Distracted by my cell phone
- ○ Other _____

BALANCE

- ○ Lack of balance—working too much
- ○ Lack of balance—playing too much
- ○ Inability to say "no" when someone asks a favor
- ○ Spending too much time on social networking sites
- ○ Other _____

EXPECTATIONS

- ○ Wanting my work to be perfect
- ○ Fearing failure
- ○ Other people's expectations
- ○ Other _____

RECREATION

- ○ Watching too much television or playing too many video games
- ○ Spending too much time text messaging or checking social media updates
- ○ Listening to too much music
- ○ Socializing
- ○ Other _____

ENVIRONMENT

- ○ Messy study space
- ○ No designated study space
- ○ Other _____

FAMILY

- ○ My sister/brother/children
- ○ My parents/roommate/family/spouse
- ○ Other _____

STRESS

○ Managing crises (emergencies, urgent events)

○ Feeling stressed or overwhelmed

○ Too many projects at the same time

○ Inability to make decisions

○ Other _____

OTHER

○ Other _____

*I would like to thank a former professor of mine, Dr. Elizabeth Winstead, for inspiring this list.

Review your choices. Is there one category into which most of your challenges fall? Or do you have problems in many categories? For example, do you find that most of your priority management problems are due to interruptions and attention issues? Or is a lack of organizational skills causing most of your problems?

Once you can focus on where and how the problems exist, it will be easier to address those challenges. Write your reactions here.

_____

Activity 3.4

Time-Wasters!

The R.E.D. Model (**R**ecognize Assumptions, **E**valuate Information, **D**raw Conclusions) provides a systematic way to approach critical thinking through the use of an easy-to-remember acronym.

Whereas Activity 3.3 helped you examine broad categories of priority management problems, this activity requires you to identify specific time-wasting items and who bears responsibility for them. You may be responsible for wasting some of your time, but some time-wasters come from other sources.

Time-Waster	Who Started This Time-Waster?	How Can I Control This Time-Waster?

What *conclusions* can you draw from your responses? Write your reactions here.

....

Activity 3.5

Adjusting to a College Schedule

Let's apply the R.E.D. Model to examine one of the organizational challenges you identified for yourself in Activity 3.3 or 3.4. Focus on your most significant challenge in priority management.

Write your challenge here: _____

Critical-Thinking Step	Application to Your Study Skills
Recognize assumptions	Reread the challenge you just wrote down. On a separate piece of paper, list the reasons you have that challenge. After you have listed your reasons, identify what is fact and what is fiction. That is, how do you know this assessment of your challenge is correct?
Evaluate information	Examine your organizational challenge from more than one perspective (point of view). Identify the reasons you have this challenge. Perhaps a family member or close friend can help you.
Draw conclusions	Based on your evidence, does your conclusion about your organizational challenge make sense? What is your plan to eliminate or minimize this challenge?

Three common tools for keeping track of priorities and managing time are the monthly calendar, the weekly calendar, and the daily to-do list. Each tool can be in a paper/book format or in the form of a digital calendar on your computer or electronic handheld device.

A **calendar** divides time into years, months, weeks, and days. It provides a way to track activities and commitments over time.

Monthly calendar. This format allows you to see up to four weeks at a time. You can easily spot conflicts, tests, personal commitments, and the like (see Figure 3.1).

Weekly calendar. A weekly calendar does not show the entire month at a glance, but it will allow you to enter more details for each day (see Figure 3.2). Some weekly calendars even provide space to schedule specific appointment times (say, a study group meeting).

Daily to-do list. You can become very detailed at using a daily calendar. A variation of this format is a simple to-do list (see Figure 3.3). Your list can be a single sheet of notebook paper. Write the date across the top. Down one side, list and number the items you need to do today. As you finish an item, cross it off. If you don't finish an item today, transfer it to tomorrow's to-do list. You probably will not check off every item every day. And there is nothing wrong with that! Simply progress toward your goals one task at a time. Move unchecked items to the next day.

Electronic calendar. Perhaps you are more comfortable with an electronic version of one of these kinds of calendars, as shown in Figure 3.4. It can provide the same tracking options but provide additional aids. A cell phone, for instance, provides calendar functions along with an alarm or "Alert" option that will audibly remind you that an item of note is on your calendar. This "Reminder" feature can be used as an excellent planning tool for people who are diligent about putting things on the calendar but then do not remember to look at the calendar.

Figure 3.1

	Monthly Calendar					
	Monday	Tuesday	Wednesday	Thursday	Friday	Sat/Sun
	March 1	2	3	4	5	6
						7
	8	9	10	11	12	13
						14
	15	16	17	18	19	20
						21
	22	23	24	25	26	27
						28
	29	30	31	April 1	2	3
						4

Figure 3.2

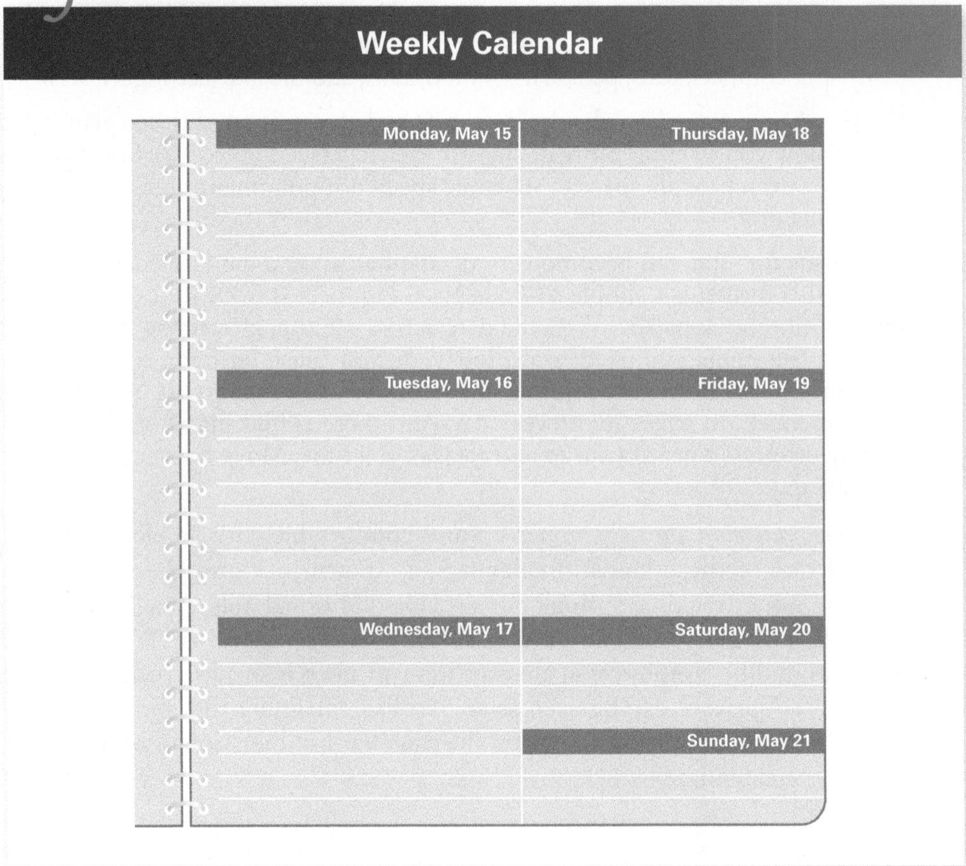

Weekly Calendar

Monday, May 15	Thursday, May 18
Tuesday, May 16	Friday, May 19
Wednesday, May 17	Saturday, May 20
	Sunday, May 21

Figure 3.3

Daily Calendar

Monday, May 15
7:00 a.m.
8:00
9:00
10:00
11:00
12:00 p.m.
1:00
2:00
3:00
4:00
5:00
6:00
7:00
8:00
9:00

Activity 3.6

Using Your Calendar to Keep Track of Assignment Progress

R E D

INFORMATION: For this activity, you will need to have all of your class syllabi in front of you, as well as your planner (in either paper or digital format). Every time you see an assignment and due date listed in a syllabus, enter that information on your calendar. Do this for all of your assignments in each of your classes. Specific items to look for include exams, term projects, reading assignments, quizzes, service learning projects, and lab visits.

CONCLUSIONS: How will using your calendar to track assignments help you be successful?

WHAT SHOULD YOU DO FIRST? ESTABLISHING PRIORITIES

OK, let's recap. You have an idea of where your time goes each week. You know how many hours are available for homework and studying. You even adopted a method for keeping track of your commitments. Now, you must determine what to do first, second, and so on. If you do not establish priorities (rank items by order of importance), you may end up spending time on minor tasks while ignoring the major projects that require much of your attention.

Figure 3.4

Electronic Calendar [PDA/cell phone screen]

Let's consider a few basic tips. After you have your list of things to do, make the following determinations:

- Which items must be addressed immediately? Studying for a quiz that will be given at 8:00 a.m. tomorrow has more immediacy than typing a research paper that is due two months from today.

- Which items are critical? You are scheduled to meet with your chemistry study group at noon today. But you just got word that the financial aid counselor wants to discuss your scholarship—also at noon today. Both are immediate. But the scholarship is critical to your continuing in college.

- Can you plan ahead? Using your syllabi and assignment pages, map out your entire semester. As you did in Activity 3.6, record on your calendar when each exam, quiz, and assignment is due. Then you will be able to see the "big picture"—and it will hold fewer surprises.

DOING A LOT OF STUFF ISN'T THE SAME AS MOVING FORWARD

Have you ever looked back on a very busy day and wondered why you didn't get more accomplished? "I don't know where the day went! I did a lot of stuff, but I seem further behind than I was at the beginning of the day!"

Do not equate "doing a lot of stuff" with making purposeful progress toward your goals. Look at your responses to Activity 3.2. In particular, examine your answers in column 3. Your "necessary" items are your stated priorities. Is the "stuff" you fill your life with connected to your priorities? Remember that if everything is a priority, then nothing is a priority.

SIMPLIFY

A major strategy for managing your priorities is to look at the "big picture," and then break down large tasks into small steps. Although seeing the big picture is necessary to find your direction, it might be a bit overwhelming. It might help you to break a big task or project into small, less intimidating steps. Then take one step at a time to complete the task. Activity 3.7 will help you apply this strategy to a classroom assignment.

Activity 3.7

Completing a Class Project

For the purpose of this activity, let's assume your assignment is to research and to write about the importance of social media to education. The assignment is due in three weeks.

Briefly jot down the steps you would take to complete the assignment. In other words, how would you manage your time in tackling this project? Days 1–3 and days 4–6 have been filled in to help get you started. Fill in the appropriate activities for days 7 through 21.

Days 1–3: Carefully read the assignment, and make sure I know exactly what I need to do for this paper. Note any special requirements and due dates the professor has listed. Look through the textbook for related information. Conduct an initial search of pertinent Internet sites. Perhaps there is someone I can talk to and help focus my thoughts.

Days 4–6: Go to the campus library with my list of topics. Ask a reference librarian to help guide me. Check out books and/or articles that may be of help. Start reading and taking notes.

Days 7–9:

....

....

Days 10–12:

....

....

Days 13–15:

....

....

Days 16–18:

....

....

Days 19–21:

....

....

ORGANIZATION AND PROCRASTINATION

> *The two rules of procrastination:*
> *(1) Do it today.*
> *(2) Tomorrow will be today tomorrow.*
> *—Author unknown*

"I'LL DO ALL OF THIS TOMORROW!"

All the tips, strategies, calendars, and campus resources in the world will do absolutely nothing if you don't take the first step toward putting them into action.

Procrastination—avoiding and postponing what should be taken care of now—can rob you of your time and derail your best intentions.

YOU CAN'T GET IT BACK—EVER!

Procrastinate enough and you will lose more than hours. Eventually those hours will stretch into days, months, and even years. To help you visualize this, here is a small challenge for you.

Find a blank copy of an annual calendar (or anything that can represent the months of the year and days in a month, similar to Figure 3.5) to complete this exercise.

Before you go to bed each night, place an X in the box that corresponds to the day on the calendar.* Once you have done that, realize that you can do nothing to remove that X. The day is gone—forever! You cannot get back what has passed. Are you satisfied with how you used your time for the day?

Let's relate that to your school term. If your instructor gives you two months to complete a term project, you have about 60 days to do the work. If you procrastinate and do nothing toward the project for the first 50 days, you have lost those days forever. And, obviously, you have only 10 days to complete the project.

This is a powerful reminder that today is the tomorrow you created yesterday. Procrastinate today, and your tomorrow will have more work and stress.

*Derek Lin, "Seize the Day." http://www.taoism.net/articles/seizeday.htm. (Accessed April 16, 2011.)

Figure 3.5

Today Creates Your Tomorrow

	1	2	3	4	5	6	7	8	9	10	11	12	13	14	15	16	17	18	19	20	21	22	23	24	25	26	27	28	29	30	31
1																															
2																															
3																															
4																															
5																															
6																															
7																															
8																															
9																															
10																															
11																															
12																															

WHY DO PEOPLE PROCRASTINATE?

Procrastinators may have various reasons for their behavior, but regardless, the habit is usually self-defeating. Procrastination is not synonymous with laziness. In fact, one psychologist suggests that procrastinators have energy to spare (Sapadin, 1999, pp. 10–20). It is just not focused in the appropriate direction.

Also, there is usually an excuse attached to why an assignment or task is not completed. Thus, the first step in dealing with your procrastination is to listen to your excuses and then develop a plan to refocus your efforts.

Table 3.2 provides an overview of six styles of procrastination, along with suggestions on how to fight these time-wasting behaviors.

Table 3.2 **Strategies to deal with procrastination**

Type of Procrastinator	Description	What Can You Do?
Perfectionist	You don't want to let yourself or others down. Everything you do has to be "just right." You end up postponing completion of a task by doing more work on it than is needed.	Change your thinking from everything *must* be perfect to everything will be as good as possible. Know the difference between *practical* and *ideal*. (This does not mean you have to settle for inferior work. It simply means you should allow yourself some leeway. Don't put pressure on yourself without reason.)
Dreamer	You have big plans and big ideas, but you never put them into action. You hope someone else will take care of the details for you.	Replace your dreams with *plans*. Develop *action steps*, and then follow them one at a time.
Worrier	You fear taking risks. So rather than do something different or challenging that may be risky, you avoid commitment and/or follow-through as long as possible.	Speak confidently about your abilities. Associate with people who are *positive* and will help you see your talents. Each week, take a little calculated risk (nothing foolish) to get used to stretching your abilities.
Crisis maker	You live for adrenaline rushes! You wait until the last minute to study or to complete a paper. The more pressure involved with a project, the better. You may even secretly like the attention this type of behavior brings. Unfortunately, as more projects stack up, you are not able to complete them satisfactorily.	Write assignment goals that include specific due dates that come *before* a course deadline—maybe two or three days before the due date. Use sports or some other activity to satisfy your adrenaline needs.
Defier	You don't see why your time should be affected by other people's demands (like class attendance or completing a written assignment).	Refocus. Ask yourself "What can *I* do?" and "What do *I* need to do?" rather than "Why do I have to do what *they* want me to do?" *You* made the choice to come to school, and *you* (probably) made the choice to take the particular class.

(continued)

Table 3.2 **Strategies to deal with procrastination (*continued*)**

Type of Procrastinator	Description	What Can You Do?
Overdoer	You don't know how to say "no." You don't want to disappoint people, so you take on too much, run out of time, and turn in a half-done or unsatisfactory project. You can do certain tasks very well, but you eventually run out of energy and crash. Ironically, then you *do* disappoint the very people you were trying to please, as well as yourself.	Learn that the healthiest word in the English language can very well be *no*. Reevaluate your goals. Before taking on too much, make sure your goals are being advanced. Obviously, there is a fine line between being self-centered and willing to help others. But if you are an overdoer, you probably crossed this line long ago and have failed to take proper care of your needs.

Source: Based on Sapadin, 1999.

ACTIVATION ENERGY

A **habit** is something we repeat with such frequency that it becomes an involuntary act. It seems as though we cannot help ourselves from doing it.

In the book *The Happiness Advantage: The Seven Principles of Positive Psychology That Fuel Success and Performance at Work*, Shawn Achor (2010) describes the concept of **activation energy**. He states that to "kick-start a positive habit" we need an "initial spark" to get us moving (p. 156).

Activity 3.8, the Two-Minute Drill, relates directly to activation energy. Those two minutes represent the initial spark needed to develop the habit of working with a tutor. As Achor (2010) states, "Lower the activation energy for habits you want to adopt, and raise it for habits you want to avoid. The more we can lower or even eliminate the activation energy for our desired actions, the more we enhance our ability to jump-start positive change" (p. 161).

In short, the less time or distance you put between you and a positive habit, the better chance you have of developing that habit. Reduce or minimize the obstacles, and increase the chances of doing the task. Sometimes, as depicted in Figure 3.6, a little extra effort and push is needed to get by or over the obstacle. Consider that extra effort as the activation energy that will get you closer to your goal.

Conversely, the more resistance you put between you and a bad habit, the better the chance to break that habit. Increase the obstacles in front of you, and reduce the chances of doing the task.

Think about it. If you want to develop the healthy habit of doing cardio exercise every day, you have to lessen the obstacles between you and the activity. If you have to drive to a gym that is 15 minutes away, you may find excuses for why you can't get to the gym. But if you decide you will start your exercise regimen by walking 30 minutes a day, maybe all you need to do is place your walking shoes by the door. It takes a moment to slip them on—and out the door you go.

Figure 3.6

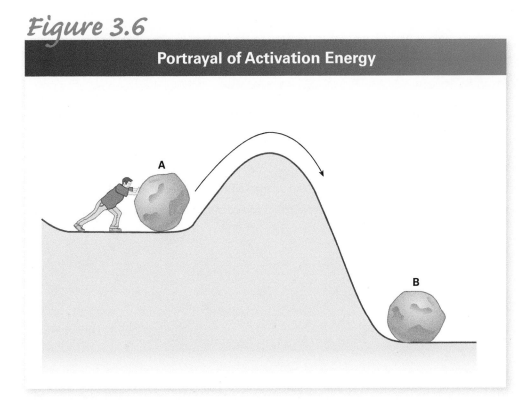

Portrayal of Activation Energy

You have lessened your activation energy. And you have pushed procrastination to the side.

JUST SAY "NO!"

As mentioned in Table 3.2, "no" can be a healthy word. Rather than overcommitting yourself, carefully evaluate your choices. Recognize any assumptions you have (such as "I have to do this because . . ."). Evaluate all the information that is before you. Then draw the appropriate conclusion about whether you should do it or not.

THE TWO-MINUTE DRILL!

Long-term goals can be intimidating. They are generally large, and the results are not realized until the distant future. These two factors (size and lack of immediacy) can be demotivators for some people. If that is the case with one of your goals, think smaller and more short term. Think of what you could do today—right now. Think of what you could do with just two minutes!

"Two minutes!" you might say. "What can I possibly do that would make any difference in just two minutes?"

Consider this example: A student has difficulty with math. He does his homework, studies for his tests, and even visits his professor. Still, this student is barely passing the course. A classmate suggested he work with a tutor in the student success center. Today, the student took two minutes to set up an appointment.

Now, the student still must follow through and keep the appointment. But he has taken the first step. He is now moving forward.

Activity 3.8

The Two-Minute Drill!

HELPING MARIE MAKE TIME FOR HER PRIORITIES

For this activity, let's help Marie (from the chapter-opening scenario) by modeling behavior for her. In this case, you will show her how to plan for the Two-Minute Drill.

Write one academic goal you have, and then write what you could do now (in two minutes) that would get you closer to that goal. Then consider a personal nonacademic goal. What could you do in two minutes to get closer to that goal?

Academic goal: ....

....

Two-Minute Drill to reach the goal: ....

....

Personal nonacademic goal: ....

....

Two-Minute Drill to reach the goal: ....

....

BACKWARD PLANNING

Another planning strategy is to plan backward. Suppose you have a test scheduled in one week. Start with the end product: walking into class prepared for the exam. Then work backward: How will you get to this point? Table 3.3 provides one option.

Table 3.3 Backward planning goal: To receive an A on the next biology exam

Day	Task
Thursday	Successfully take the biology exam (the result).
Wednesday	Briefly review major topics—no cramming necessary (☺).
Tuesday	Review vocabulary and potential exam questions.
Monday	Review your class notes again (reread).
Sunday	Review chapter questions in textbook; try to identify potential exam questions.
Saturday	Review class notes; review vocabulary and study guide sheets.
Friday	Review class notes; reorganize; write a brief summary of your notes; provide a descriptive title for your notes.
Thursday (the day you started)	Make sure all textbook readings have been completed.

ORGANIZATION AND SPACE

"The average executive wastes six weeks per year (one hour per day) searching for information in messy desks and files.

—*Wall Street Journal*

Once you set your priorities, examine your space. For the purposes of this section, space refers to those areas around you that relate to your studies outside the classroom: your home study area, your book bag or purse, and, if you have one, your car. The time that you spend searching your space for a book, notepad, or syllabus is time taken from the priorities you established on your calendar or to-do list.

HOME STUDY AREA

Whether you have a separate room dedicated to studying or just a small corner of a larger room, organize your space so it works for you. Here are some tips:

Workspace. The first thing to do is to identify an area that will be yours for schoolwork—a **personal study area**. Do whatever you can to clearly "mark your territory." Make sure others in your residence know this area is for your studies—not for stacks of laundry, not for someone else's personal items, and not for trash or miscellaneous items. Do whatever you can to establish your workspace in a quiet area that will be conducive to uninterrupted study time. This is your private work area.

© Shutterstock

Personal Storage Areas. For an organized and clutter-free workspace, you will need effective storage for your papers, books, supplies, and other items. Your **personal storage area** could include desk drawers, bookshelves, file boxes, plastic bins, or a file cabinet.

Whatever you use, follow these tips to help you stay organized:

- Develop a filing method. Desk drawers can be notorious agents of chaos. Avoid the urge to "toss and close" (toss an item in and then close the drawer). Designate specific drawers for specific functions. One may hold supplies such as pencils, pens, tape, and staples. Another drawer—or perhaps a file box or shelf—may be home to paper, envelopes, computer disks, and ink cartridges.
- Use file folders to organize papers. Create a file folder for each class. Clearly label the folder. You can keep a copy of the syllabus or assignment sheet here (as well as another copy in the notebook you carry to class each day). The folder can be a logical place to file returned papers or drafts of assignments. And then don't forget to "file the file folders." You can use a small file cabinet, a desk drawer, or a file-folder holder that sits on a corner of your desk.

- Use technology when available. Computer folders provide an efficient way to manage documents. Perhaps your computer already has a file folder labeled "My Documents." Within this folder, create a subfolder for each class you have. You may even desire to create separate folders for each major assignment or unit of material. You can do the same with most e-mail servers. Create a folder for each class, and then file correspondence with your instructor and classmates, as well as any papers you submit. Also, file any comments you receive from your instructor. Whatever works for you, use it. Be sure to back up all your document files on a disk or flash drive.

- Create a message center to hold important notices. This can be as simple as a small wall-mounted cork board on which you tack important reminders. Or you can use a chalkboard or laminated wall poster to record important dates and tasks.

Activity 3.9

Evaluate Your Home Study Area

For this activity, move beyond your current classroom and examine where you study. Is your home study area well planned? How efficiently does it fulfill its intended purpose? Use the following scale to rate it.

1. On a scale from 0 to 5, rate the features of your home study area. A rating of 0 indicates the feature does not exist in your study area. A totally efficient and effective feature of your study area will rate a 5. Circle the numbers that most closely apply to you:

My workspace	0—1—2—3—4—5
My filing system	0—1—2—3—4—5
My drawers for supplies	0—1—2—3—4—5
My computer files	0—1—2—3—4—5
My e-mail files	0—1—2—3—4—5
My message center	0—1—2—3—4—5
Other: _____	0—1—2—3—4—5
Other: _____	0—1—2—3—4—5

2. Based on your ratings, how efficient and effective is your home study area? What can you do to improve it?

WHAT CAN YOU DO IF STUDY SPACE IS NOT AVAILABLE WHERE YOU LIVE?

Perhaps the suggestions just discussed are impossible to put in place, given your living situation. In that case, check with your campus or community library. Perhaps you can use a small study room or section of the library for your quiet area.

AVOIDING REPETITIVE STRAIN INJURIES

In addition to being responsible for the academic integrity of your work, you must be responsible for the health and condition of your body. Although hours sitting at a computer workstation may not appear to be demanding, they can have a debilitating effect on your body.

Repetitive strain injuries (RSIs), which are also called repetitive stress injuries, commonly occur among people who spend long hours typing at a keyboard and staring into a computer monitor. As the name implies, the injury results from repetitive (continual) motion or action. Typing at a keyboard for a prolonged period, for instance, has been cited as a cause of carpal tunnel syndrome (CTS). The repeated keystroke activity can lead to swelling of the thumbs and wrists, if care is not taken.

Various sources have provided checklists of activities that can minimize the risk of RSIs (for example, see Marxhausen, 2005). Perhaps your school library has information about the proper positioning of your monitor, keyboard, and chair to reduce eyestrain and muscle fatigue (see Figure 3.7).

Also remember to take appropriate stretch breaks and eye breaks. Simply standing up and walking away from the computer screen for a couple of minutes can reduce fatigue.

PERSONAL PORTABLE STORAGE AREA

Whether you use a book bag, purse, or some other item to carry your books and supplies to class, the item should be both effective and efficient for your needs. For instance, a book bag can be an effective tool for carrying a number of books,

Figure 3.7

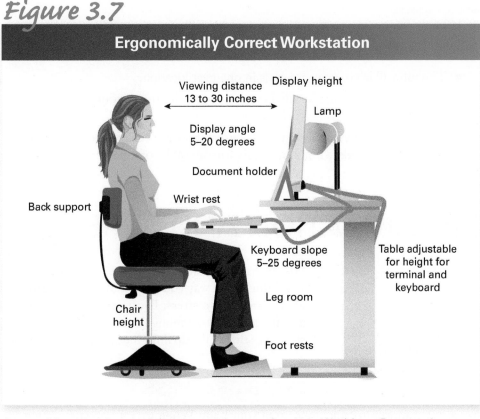

Ergonomically Correct Workstation

Viewing distance 13 to 30 inches

Display height

Lamp

Display angle 5–20 degrees

Document holder

Back support

Wrist rest

Keyboard slope 5–25 degrees

Table adjustable for height for terminal and keyboard

Leg room

Chair height

Foot rests

Source: Library of Congress (Integrated Support Services, Workforce Ergonomics Program). "Ergonomics and VDT Use." Computers in Libraries 13 (May 1993). From a flyer prepared by the Library of Congress Collections Services VDT Ergonomics Committee, 1991–1992.

notebooks, supplies, and assignments. But if finding any one of these things from the deep recesses of the bag proves time consuming and frustrating, then perhaps the manner in which you are using the bag is not efficient. Make sure that any tool, such as a calendar or book bag, serves your purposes:

- Type of bag. Consider using a bag that has a couple of compartments. Many book bags have two main compartments, plus a small zippered area in front of the bag and possibly others on one or two sides. The main compartments can be used to hold books, notebooks, assignments, and a laptop computer. The smaller compartments work well for pens, pencils, and other supplies, as well as keys, cell phones, computer disks, or digital handheld devices.
- Identification. Have some form of identification attached to your bag, in case you ever leave it in a classroom or somewhere else. Providing your name and school e-mail address is probably enough information.
- Nightly review. Each night, empty the book bag to make sure you have not overlooked an important piece of paper that you shoved into the bag earlier in the day. Once you complete this, pack the bag for the next day. Place it where you will not forget it in the morning when you leave for class.

CAR

Has your car become a mobile storage area? Has the trunk become a "black hole" that has swallowed up books and important papers? Do you need a shovel to clear out the backseat?

If you use your car as a storage area, consider placing a plastic or vinyl tub (with a lid) in the trunk. This will accomplish three things:

- The tub will keep your materials in one neat location.
- The lid and the plastic or vinyl construction will protect your material in case the trunk leaks.
- When you place valuables in the backseat, they are easily visible to would-be thieves. The trunk, while not totally invulnerable, offers a bit more security.

ORGANIZATION AND STRESS

There is more to life than increasing its speed.
—Mohandas K. Gandhi, political leader and activist

Disorganization—whether in the way you manage your time or the way you keep your work and storage areas—can create stress. Because stress is emotionally and physically draining, it makes sense to develop strategies that will help limit the stressors in your life.

TYPES OF STRESS

Stress can compromise the integrity of your body. When we refer to stress, we typically describe how our bodies react to external and internal pressures. Physiologically, stress represents a time of extreme arousal in the body. Blood pressure can rise, the heart and pulse beat more rapidly, the body can perspire, and clear thinking may become more difficult.

Psychologists generally recognize two types of stress: distress and eustress. *Distress* is what we usually refer to when using the word stress. It is considered bad stress or pressure. For instance, suppose a student has just received a letter from the financial aid office saying she is in danger of losing her aid because her grade-point average has fallen below the criterion. Without financial assistance, she will not be able to remain in school. Her heart begins to beat quickly, and she feels flushed and sick to her stomach.

Eustress is positive, or good, stress or pressure. For example, imagine that it is graduation day. This is what you have worked so hard to achieve. Your family and friends are in the audience. As your name is called and you get up to cross the stage and get your diploma, your heart is racing—but your chest is full of pride!

Stress can move us to action. But continual exposure to stress can lead to physical ailments or emotional trauma—both of which will compromise the integrity of your body.

STRESS SIGNALS

Stressors differ from person to person. Pay attention to your body. It will give you clues when something is wrong. Some of the more common signals include the following ("Understanding Stress," n.d.):*

- Cognitive symptoms, such as being anxious, having memory problems, and worrying at an unusually high level
- Emotional symptoms, such as irritability, moodiness, and a sense of isolation
- Physical symptoms that include headaches, rapid breathing, and chest pain
- Behavioral symptoms that appear as anger, changes in eating habits, and abuse of alcohol or drugs

STRESS-REDUCING SUGGESTIONS

As with stress signals, stress-reducing strategies are individualistic. What works for one person may not work for another. Table 3.4 provides a few of the most common healthful and legal suggestions. Some other strategies, while they may reduce stress in the short run, have unhealthy consequences in the long term:

- Drinking alcohol to excess
- Abusing drugs
- Promiscuous sexual activity
- Smoking
- Binge eating

*This list is not meant to be diagnostic. Seek professional assistance as needed.

Table 3.4   **Stress-reducing suggestions**

Develop a support network.	Reinterpret situations in a positive light (reframe).
Examine your belief system.	Take a break and relax.
Exercise regularly.	Take breaks for peak performance.
Get a good night's sleep.	Engage in healthy recreation.
Learn to say "no" if saying "yes" will overwhelm you.	Concentrate on your breath—slower, deeper, and longer.
Limit your intake of caffeine (a stimulant).	Practice guided imagery.
Maintain a sense of humor.	Meditate or pray.
Maintain realistic expectations.	Talk with a trusted friend or mentor.

Source: Based on Posen, April 1995.

Activity 3.11

How Do You Handle Stress?

1. List the healthy strategies you have used in the past to deal with stress.

....

....

2. Which strategy or strategies do you tend to use the most and why?

....

....

3. If you have engaged in any unhealthy stress-reducing strategies, what can you do to replace them with healthier choices?

....

....

Chapter SUMMARY

Organized people respect their time. They know it is a precious resource, and they refuse to waste it. Having an organized workspace will be a positive impact on your personal time. Being organized will also help create a calmer, more manageable environment. And that, in turn, will reduce stressors.

As you apply the tools outlined in this chapter for managing your priorities and space, remember that planning does not translate into rigidity. You can be efficient and effective and still be spontaneous.

Before leaving this chapter, keep the following points in mind:

■ You cannot control time. You cannot create time. However, you can effectively use time for your benefit.

■ The way you use time reflects what you value in life. What you spend your time on indicates your priorities.

■ The more classes you take, the more demands you have on your time. That sounds simplistic, but many students fail to look at the "big picture" when planning a semester.

■ Procrastination can rob you of your time and derail your best intentions.

■ Organize your personal and portable spaces outside the classroom.

■ Organizing time and space will help to limit the chaos and stress in your life.

CRITICALLY THINKING
What Have You Learned in This Chapter?

. At the beginning of this chapter, you read about Marie. She has taken a full load of classes—and she is not coping well.

Let's apply what you learned in this chapter to help Marie. However, before you dive into Marie's problem and propose your solution, take a moment to think about the main points of the chapter.

Review your notes from this chapter and also the key terms, chapter learning outcomes, boldface chapter headings, and figures and tables. For instance, consider how the chapter learning outcomes may be used to help Marie.

■ Develop a written schedule that provides at least two hours of study time for every hour scheduled in the classroom.

■ Use and evaluate at least one priority management tool (a calendar or planner).

■ Develop a weekly to-do list that ranks your tasks in order of importance.

■ Identify at least three types of procrastination and a strategy to deal with each.

■ Describe how applying organizational skills can help you balance your life's demands.

© Shutterstock

TEST YOUR LEARNING

Now that you have reviewed the main points of this chapter, reread Marie's story. Pretend that you are Marie's mentor. Using the R.E.D. Model for critical thinking, help Marie critically review her concerns.

R

Recognize Assumptions:

Facts: What are the facts in Marie's situation? List them.

....

....

Opinions: What opinions do you find in this situation? List them here.

....

....

Assumptions: Are Marie's assumptions accurate?

....

....

....

E

Evaluate Information:

Help Marie compile a list of questions that will help her make the most appropriate decision?

....

....

What emotions seem to be motivating Marie at this time?

....

....

Is anything missing from Marie's thought process?

....

....

Do you see any confirmation bias?

....

....

....

D

Draw Conclusions:

Based on the facts and the questions you have presented, what conclusions can you draw?

....

....

What advice do you have for Marie? What solutions do you propose?

....

....

Based on your suggestions, do you see any assumptions?

....

....

Finally, based on what you know about using critical thinking, problem solving, and priority management, what plan of action do you suggest for Marie?

....

....

....

Information LITERACY

4

By seeking and blundering, we learn.
—Johann Wolfgang von Goethe, writer

CHAPTER LEARNING OUTCOMES

By the time you finish reading this chapter and completing its activities, you will be able to do the following:

- Use multiple types of information sources to help you make an educated decision about a challenge confronting you.

- Explain and use the four steps an information-literate person follows when doing research.

- Use a search engine to locate information.

- Critically evaluate a source of information for accuracy, authority, objectivity, currency, and scope.

- Explain and practice one strategy for responsible behavior for each of the following: e-mailing your professor; receiving and sending text messages; and participating on a social networking site.

- Create an appropriate online profile that will impress an employer.

The Case of JAYNE

Jayne is close to graduation and has begun applying for jobs. She has diligently built a portfolio that shows examples of her talents and skills. The campus career center has helped her develop a dynamic résumé. She just completed a workshop on interviewing strategies. "I am ready to tackle the job market," she recently told her advisor. While she has a solid academic record and an impressive portfolio, she is concerned about something that is not reflected in her college transcript or résumé.

Last week, one of her professors did a presentation on "digital tattoos." They are not the kind of tattoos that people put on their skin but the kind that mark people on the Internet.

Jayne constantly uses social media sites. She "tweets" regularly, updates her social networking site hourly, and posts photos and videos of her

© Shutterstock

Key Terms

Academic integrity
Blogs
Citation
"Digital tattoo"
Information literacy
Interlibrary loan
Keyword search
Online profile
Plagiarism
Reference librarian
Search engines
Social media
Status updates
Surfing the Web
Texting
Wikis
World Wide Web

INTRODUCTION Chapter

Have you ever considered how much information is produced worldwide in one year? One study (Lyman & Varian, 2003) discovered these intriguing facts:

- Instant messaging accounts for 5 billion messages per day.
- Each month, the average U.S. Internet user spends 74 hours, 26 minutes at work and 25 hours, 25 minutes online at home. Americans use the Internet to send e-mail (52%), get news (32%), find information (29%), surf the Web (23%), do research for work (19%), check the

outings with friends on a regular basis. She always says, "I only share this stuff with people I am 'friends' with. So, there is no harm, because they would never do anything to hurt me. Anyway, I can always delete items I don't like. And if someone 'tags' me in a photo, I can always 'untag' that photo. No big deal at all."

Now Jayne is reconsidering. Her professor shared news stories of how employers today use Internet searches to find out about applicants. He even showed the class how a few clicks on a popular search engine could turn up photos and tweets—things Jayne thought were private on the Internet. While she has not done anything illegal or unethical, she is concerned that an employer will view her photos and words out of context and that that could have a negative impact on her job hunting and future career.

CRITICALLY THINKING
about *Jayne's* situation

You are Jayne's career counselor. What strategies would you suggest for her to follow?

weather (17%), and send instant messages (14%) (Pew Internet and American Life Project).

- Enough new information is produced annually to create a 30-foot-high pile of books for each person in the world.

- Ninety-two percent of this new information is not in print form. Most of it can be found on hard disks. Print accounts only for 0.01 percent of all new information.

- Even though print accounts for a minimal amount of the stored information, each person in North America uses an average of nearly 12,000 sheets of paper per year. That is about 33 sheets per day per person.

- The amount of information stored on disks, film, and paper doubled from 1999 to 2002. In less time than it would take a student to complete an undergraduate degree, the amount of available information worldwide increased by 100 percent!

Also, consider what author Erik Qualman (2010) has found in his research:

- Half the world's population is under 30 years of age, and 96 percent of them have joined social networking sites.
- As of 2003, the World Wide Web (WWW) contained 17 times the volume of information found in the print collections of the Library of Congress. And the Web continues to grow.
- There are more than 200,000,000 blogs in the world.
- Some universities no longer issue e-mail addresses to their students.

Because there does not appear to be any slowdown in this phenomenal explosion of and access to information, a number of challenges present themselves. For instance, just because information is increasing in volume does not mean it is increasing in quality. How can you separate the credible from the absurd?

Moreover, having too much information can be overwhelming. What can you do when you find hundreds or thousands of possible sources in researching a term paper? How will you know which sources have the best information? Or, more practically, what is the most effective way to trim the vast number of sources to a workable few?

But being information literate goes beyond knowing how to ferret out the best research for a term paper. With social media sites such as Facebook exploding in popularity, understanding how to use these sites appropriately—in ways that benefit you—has become critically important. That includes knowing the best ways to communicate and protect your privacy and dignity online.

This chapter will not only explore strategies that will help you efficiently and effectively locate, evaluate, and use the vast storehouse of information around you, but it will also teach you how to effectively navigate the world of social media.

Activity 4.1

Reflecting on Your Current Level of Information-Literacy Skills

Before you answer the items that follow, reflect on your current level of information-literacy skills. Think of how well (or poorly) you have used these skills in the past.

As you do in completing all of the reflective activities in this book, you should answer from your heart. This exercise is not meant for you to answer just like your classmates or to match what you may think the instructor wants to see. Take your time to give a respectful and responsible general accounting of your experiences with information-literacy skills. A truthful self-assessment now will help you build on skills you have while developing those you lack.

For each of the following items, circle the number that best describes your typical experience with information-literacy skills. Here is the key for the numbers:

0 = never, 1 = almost never, 2 = occasionally, 3 = frequently, 4 = almost always, 5 = always

When considering your past successes and challenges with information literacy, how often . . .

1.	Did you understand what information you needed to locate to complete a project?	0	1	2	3	4	5
2.	Did you know where to look for information to complete your project?	0	1	2	3	4	5
3.	Did you evaluate information you found for accuracy?	0	1	2	3	4	5
4.	Were you able to find enough appropriate information to complete a project?	0	1	2	3	4	5
5.	Were you able to determine whether the information you found was well rounded and objective?	0	1	2	3	4	5
6.	Were your projects completed responsibly and honestly, according to the standards of academic integrity?	0	1	2	3	4	5
7.	Did you protect (and not give out) your personal information on social media sites, chat rooms, or blogs?	0	1	2	3	4	5
8.	Did you maintain your integrity and dignity when communicating with social media?	0	1	2	3	4	5

Add up your scores for items 1 through 8. Divide by 8. Write your answer here: ....

Using the key provided to explain each number (0, 1, 2, 3, 4, 5), complete this sentence: When it comes to information literacy, I _____ use information, technology, and social media in an effective manner.

Based on your answers, what insights have you gained about your experiences with information literacy?

....

....

WHAT DOES IT MEAN TO BE AN INFORMATION-LITERATE PERSON?

"Research is what I'm doing when I don't know what I'm doing.
—Wernher Von Braun, rocket physicist

Being information literate will help you successfully complete the requirements for your degree or certification. But it also involves much more.

On the way to your diploma, you will become exposed to viewpoints that will challenge your currently held beliefs and values. Where will you find the information to support your viewpoints? How will you know if a classmate or an instructor is presenting accurate conclusions? And once you leave your school and enter the world of work, how will you know how to access, judge, and use information to help you advance in your chosen career field? If you do not know how to use information, then its value diminishes.

Twenty years ago, an information-literate student knew how to find information in the library's card catalog, locate bound books on the shelves in the library's reference room, and operate a microfilm or microfiche machine in the library's documents room. Although these resources are still available and valuable, as a student of the twenty-first century, you need to know how to navigate hundreds, thousands, and even millions of pages of bound and digital resource material. Additionally, once you have found the information, you need to know how to evaluate it before you decide whether to use it.

People who do not know how to access (or who choose not to access) the incredibly rich storehouse of Internet resources put themselves at a great disadvantage. They will be illiterates standing alongside the information highway, watching those who know how to use the tools pass them by at a rapid pace.

At the very least, students today need a working knowledge of computers and how to connect to and communicate on the Internet. If cost creates barriers, find the computer lab on your campus and ask how you can get a free e-mail account and Internet access. Colleges and universities offer courses about how to effectively access and use information. Some schools offer online tutorials to instruct students in how to make sense of the maze of available information. Does your school offer an information-literacy course? Are students at your institution required to pass an information literacy test?

Text messaging, social networking sites, and e-mail provide a number of opportunities to stay in touch with families and friends. A social networking site such as Facebook, MySpace, LinkedIn, or Twitter can let anyone correspond with hundreds, thousands, or millions of people in an instant. And with a couple of keypad entries, your cell phone will let you send a text message.

As with any technology or time-saving device, however, opportunity costs are involved with social networking. For example, while social networking sites keep us connected, they can be a serious drain on time. Do you know how to maximize your time on such sites while not jeopardizing your academic and personal priorities? Do you know when it is appropriate to send and receive text messages? And do you know how to protect your privacy when posting comments and personal profiles?

As noted in the chapter introduction, the amount of available information has exploded, and all indications are that the explosion will continue well into the future. Not only is there an abundance of information, but there are also a variety of locations to find information. Libraries, blogs, commercial websites, government publications, service organizations, political action committees, status updates on social media sites, and professional organizations are but a few of the disseminators of information.

FOUR STEPS TO COMPLETING AN ASSIGNMENT IN AN INFORMATION-LITERATE MANNER

Research is the process of going up alleys to see if they are blind.
— Thorstein Veblen, economist and sociologist

Today's complex informational system creates challenges. The key is to know not just where to look for information but also how to separate the good from the bad, the informative from the misleading. An information-literate person can "recognize when information is needed and [has] the ability to locate, evaluate, and use effectively the needed information" (Association of College and Research Libraries, 2006). These four facets of **information literacy**—knowing what information you need, where to find it, how to evaluate it, and how to use it properly—are illustrated in Figure 4.1.

Figure 4.1

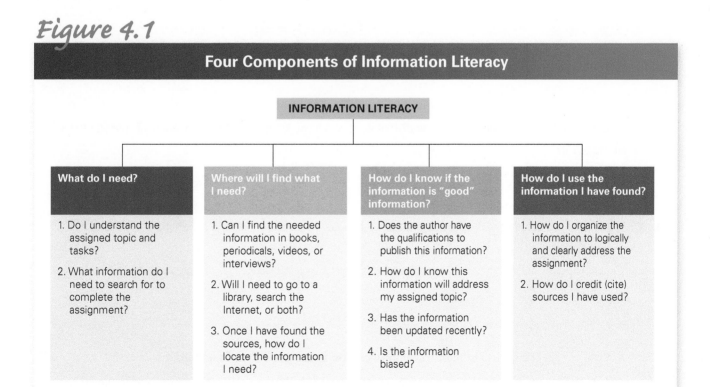

Four Components of Information Literacy

INFORMATION LITERACY

What do I need?	Where will I find what I need?	How do I know if the information is "good" information?	How do I use the information I have found?
1. Do I understand the assigned topic and tasks?	1. Can I find the needed information in books, periodicals, videos, or interviews?	1. Does the author have the qualifications to publish this information?	1. How do I organize the information to logically and clearly address the assignment?
2. What information do I need to search for to complete the assignment?	2. Will I need to go to a library, search the Internet, or both?	2. How do I know this information will address my assigned topic?	2. How do I credit (cite) sources I have used?
	3. Once I have found the sources, how do I locate the information I need?	3. Has the information been updated recently?	
		4. Is the information biased?	

The R.E.D. Model (**R**ecognize Assumptions, **E**valuate Information, **D**raw Conclusions) provides a systematic way to approach critical thinking through the use of an easy-to-remember acronym.

While the thought of information literacy may be intimidating at first, consider that you have been doing this sort of thing for years. When you looked for information about a computer or a car, when you prepared a report for a class or your boss, and when you analyzed information about a political issue, you were using information-literacy skills. Activity 4.2 asks you to use the information literacy skills you currently have. You can practice your R.E.D. Model skills, as well.

Activity 4.2

Building on Your Information-Literacy Skills

Think of a time when you bought a piece of technology. It might have been a cell phone, a television, a laptop computer, or a personal portable digital audio player.

For the purpose of this exercise, let's assume you want to purchase a cell phone. You would like one that provides reliable service for a reasonable price, but you are confused as to which phone represents the best value. Applying the four basic facets of information literacy, answer the following questions:

1. What assumptions do you have about the product you are considering? For example, do you have an opinion that a certain brand name is the best? Can you identify any fiction in your assumption? What do you know are the facts?

   ....

   ....

2. What information do you need to know before you can buy a cell phone?

   ....

   ....

3. How will you find the information you need?

   ....

   ....

4. How will you evaluate the information you find? That is, how will you know a reliable and reasonably priced product when you see it?

   ....

   ....

5. Once you have evaluated all of the literature about cell phones, how will you use the information to come to a conclusion?

   ....

   ....

In its simplest form, information literacy involves four steps:

1. *Know what information is needed.* This requires reflection before starting your search.

2. *Access the needed information.* This requires time to responsibly seek out pertinent information.
3. *Evaluate the information that is located.* This requires responsible action to judge the effectiveness of the information found.
4. *Use the information that has been found and evaluated.* This requires time to reflect on the appropriate use of the information retrieved.

Each step builds on the previous step. If you miss one step, the information you gather can be seriously flawed.

Step #1. KNOW WHAT INFORMATION IS NEEDED

Knowing what information is needed is a basic but often rushed step. Before digging through the library or surfing the Internet, be sure you understand what to look for.

Take, for example, the following assignment, which could be given in a history class:

Write a 10-page paper identifying and explaining five major consequences of World War II. The sources you use must include at least five books, three periodicals, and two nonprint sources. The paper is due two weeks before the final exam. The paper will be worth 25 percent of the final course grade.

By asking yourself a few simple questions, the nature of the assignment becomes clear:

- What do I need to do?
    - ☐ *Write a 10-page paper*
- What is the topic?
    - ☐ *Identify and explain five consequences of World War II*
- What types of source material must be used?
    - ☐ *At least five books*
    - ☐ *At least three periodicals*
    - ☐ *At least two nonprint sources*
- When is the paper due?
    - ☐ *Two weeks before the end of the term* (You can enter this on your calendar.)
- How much is this assignment worth?
    - ☐ *Twenty-five percent of the final course grade* (In other words, this is a major part of your grade for the entire term.)

Activity 4.3

Practical Application: What's the Assignment?

Using an assignment from one of your classes, answer the following questions. These initial steps require a relatively small investment of time and energy and will help maximize your efforts to efficiently find appropriate source material.

1. What is the exact wording of the instructor's assignment? Write it here, and then highlight the key words in the assignment.

....

....

2. What task(s) do you have to complete? Is a required length and format specified?

....

....

3. What is the exact topic? Can you state specifically what you need to write or speak about? This is critical, as it will guide you in the step of finding the needed information.

....

....

4. What specific types of sources are called for? Are you required to use class notes, the textbook, databases, the Internet, or other sources?

....

....

5. When is the paper due? How much time do you have to complete this assignment? (Put it on your personal planning calendar.)..

6. How much is the assignment worth? Is it a major portion of your grade for the course?..................................

Step #2. ACCESS THE INFORMATION

Once you know what topic you will research, you will be ready to find pertinent information. One question guides this part of the process: Where can you locate the source material?

The traditional library: A campus-bound building. Ease and accessibility make the Internet a remarkable tool. It can be accessed from virtually anywhere, and it connects to millions of sites. At times, however, you may need to or wish to do it the more traditional way: by walking into a library, talking with the librarians, and using the reference materials there. Once you enter your campus (or community) library, you will find the following:

- **Online catalogs and databases.** Libraries have electronic catalogs of their holdings, which can be accessed in much the same manner as when you use an online search engine. Once you find the call numbers for the materials, you can physically examine the books, photos, charts, and videos on the library shelves.
- **Reserve.** This material is usually held on a shelf behind the circulation desk. This shelf is where an instructor might place a copy of an article or book he or she wants the class to read. The material may be restricted just to library use.
- **Reference librarian.** Sometimes, nothing can replace real human contact! The **reference librarian** will help you navigate the library's holdings. If you are having a difficult time getting started—knowing what keywords to use in your information search, for instance—this person will be ready to introduce you to various search strategies and direct you to the most appropriate databases.
- **Interlibrary loans.** Perhaps you have found a book that would be a perfect source for your term paper, but it is in a university library on the other side of the state or nation. And it is not available in e-book form. Librarians can

arrange for the book to be sent to your campus library. Once your request is received by the library holding the material you want, the **interlibrary loan** will arrive on your campus within a matter of days.

The World Wide Web library: The 24/7 Internet. If you were looking for information quickly and did not care about its quality, you could locate a dizzying array of information with only a few clicks of a computer mouse. However, ease does not always equal quality.

Apply your R.E.D. Model for critical thinking here, and you will have a better chance of separating the fact from the fiction—the good from the bad. The key is to know not just where to look for information but also how to differentiate the credible from the misleading.

Today, you have the option of being able to search a collection that is far more immense than any single library. The **World Wide Web** (or the Web, for short and the www. found in most Internet addresses) is the connection or link to an array of digital books, articles, nonprint sources, and personal communications so vast that, until recently, it was considered out of the reach of the common person. The Web is one of the various information resources the Internet allows us to access. When accessed effectively, this information brings power to the hands of the users. But unfocused use of this vast resource results in a huge waste of time.

Consider the following guidelines to maximize your time:

- **Know how and why to use the Internet.** Once connected to the Internet, your computer can access a virtually endless supply of information. You could "surf the Web" for hours, days, or even months and not exhaust the information available. Therein lays a potential calamity for the uninformed or unfocused user.

  "Surfing the Web," as the activity is known in popular usage, has come to describe an aimless ride through cyberspace, following one link to another without much thought or direction. Although this can be entertaining (and may uncover useful information), it does not help a college student who has multiple classes, a job, and a number of research papers to complete in a short time.

  Not all information on the Internet is created equally. Some websites provide expert and scholarly analysis, while others post inflammatory personal opinions with little substance and support. Some sites promote particular products, services, or causes (Riedling, 2002, p. 72). At the very least, be aware of what the sites represent and how their information will affect your research.

- **Use search engines.** Literally billions of pages of information can be found using the Internet. How can anyone find anything in such a cyber pile of material? Without an effective method or strategy to help your search, this would take the better part of your college career to complete!

  The use of **search engines** provides the strategy to move mindless Web surfing to a clearly focused ride. Use search engines for on-campus collections found in the library, or use them on the Internet to assist in gathering pertinent information from the many databases on the World Wide Web. Search engines speed the search process by allowing you to find material related to the area of your research instantaneously.

  The Internet offers a variety of search engines. You possibly have already used some of the following: www.google.com, www.yahoo.com, www.altavista.com, www.bing.com, www.dogpile.com, www.lycos.com, and www.ask.com.

One cautionary note: While search engines provide a wonderfully useful tool, once you find information through a search engine, you still have to determine its credibility. Databases tend to control for accuracy with peer reviews and the like. But they hold a large amount of material. Libraries typically subscribe to a number of these. Usually, a password is required to access a library's database. Once again, the reference librarian will prove invaluable by helping you obtain the password and recommending the best databases to use based on your topic.

Activity 4.4

Using a Google Images Search to Help Jayne

Most times, search engines are used to find written words. You type in a search word or phrase, and up pops a listing of websites with information on that subject. Did you know that you can do the same kind of search for images?

For this activity, open up Google's homepage. Look for the word *Images*. (At this writing, it is found in the upper-left-hand section of the homepage.) Click on that link, and then go to the search box in the middle of the screen. Type in a celebrity's name. See the photos that appear. Type in your name. What appears? Type in the name of a college event (maybe a weekend football game). What appears?

■ What insights did you get from doing this simple search?

....

....

■ How might this information help Jayne (from the chapter-opening situation) with her dilemma?

....

....

Just like people, search engines have unique appearances. Some open with a page full of columns, colors, and information. Others prefer a more minimalist approach, showing a few basic links on the homepage.

Which is best will depend on your personal preferences. Do you like a site that looks clean and neat but requires you to dig down a few "layers" by clicking through one, two, or three pages to get what you want? Or would you prefer a site that provides a lot of information with a variety of links right on the homepage?

You will find some sites very easy to navigate, but others will seem a maze of sensory overload. Besides preferring a certain look of a site, you will come to prefer a site based on the good fortune you experience each time you search for information.

■ **Conduct keyword searches.** Whether you search for information from your campus library or conduct an Internet search from your personal computer, one of two things usually happens: Either you find very few sources, or you quickly turn up hundreds if not thousands. In the first instance, you may be frustrated by the lack of pertinent material. But in the second instance, you will find so much information that you will be overwhelmed.

Exploring the holdings of your campus library or the Internet can be maximized with a **keyword search,** in which you use a word or phrase to help you find material on your topic. This type of search can uncover books, periodicals, and nonprint materials.

For example, let's say you type in *consequences of World War II* for a keyword search, and your search turns up 24 possible sources. At this point, you might narrow your search by typing in cold war. This time, your search of the campus library catalog turns up 408 "hits," or possible results, which include information in all formats. This means that this particular library collection—the Florida State College at Jacksonville college library—holds 408 sources in print or nonprint format. The point is that with a more refined search (more precise wording), the number of hits you get may increase.

Applying a few simple strategies will allow you to narrow or broaden your computer search. These strategies will work with a campus library system or on the World Wide Web:

- **Effective and efficient searching.** One such strategy based on *Boolean logic* allows you to broaden or narrow your search using one of three words: *AND, OR,* or *NOT* (Riedling, 2002, pp. 28–32). (Some search engines or databases require that these connector words be typed in uppercase letters.) Using *OR* will expand your search to turn up as many hits as possible (see Figure 4.2). However, the connector words *NOT* and *AND* will limit the number of hits received on a topic; they are valuable to use if your initial keyword search turned up more sources than you wanted (see Figures 4.3 and 4.4).

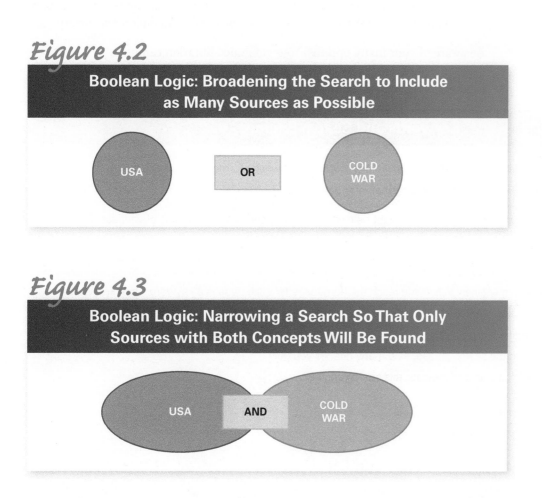

Figure 4.2

Boolean Logic: Broadening the Search to Include as Many Sources as Possible

USA   OR   COLD WAR

Figure 4.3

Boolean Logic: Narrowing a Search So That Only Sources with Both Concepts Will Be Found

USA   AND   COLD WAR

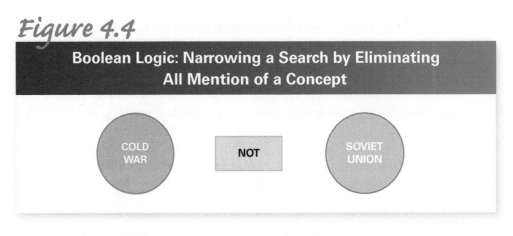

Figure 4.4

Boolean Logic: Narrowing a Search by Eliminating All Mention of a Concept

■ **One more effective strategy.** The use of quotation marks (" ") is another strategy that may help limit your search to a particular series of words and in that particular order. For instance, if you conducted a keyword search using *consequences of World War II*, your hit list would include all source material that contains any of those words. But if you placed quotation marks around the words ("*consequences of World War II*"), your search would uncover only sources with those words in that exact order.

There is a downside, however, to a keyword search: If your keywords are not broad enough, you may miss a significant portion of information. To compensate, you may wish to look for additional subject headings. (These can be found in the library's online catalog.) For instance, other subject headings that may relate to the topic of the Cold War include nuclear weapons, foreign relations—Soviet Union, world politics—1945 to 1989, Cuban Missile Crisis, and diplomatic history.

Be aware of your many options. Your reference librarian can help.

Activity 4.5

Keywords and Search Engines

In Activity 4.3, you performed step 1 of information literacy: determining what information you need to find. This activity gives you practice in step 2: accessing that information.

1. Return to Activity 4.3. List five keywords that might help you find information about the topic of your assignment.

....

....

2. Choose two of the search engines. When you reach the homepage for each, type in a keyword. Then answer the following questions for each search engine.

a. Name of search engine: _____

  1. Once you typed in the search phrase, how many hits did you get?..

  2. How easy or difficult was it to navigate this search engine?

    ....

    ....

    3. What kind of information did the initial hits page provide, and how helpful would this information be in guiding your search?

    ....

    ....

  b. Name of search engine: _____

    1. Once you typed in the search phrase, how many hits did you get? ....

    2. How easy or difficult was it to navigate this search engine?

    ....

    ....

    3. What kind of information did the initial hits page provide, and how helpful would this information be in guiding your search?

    ....

    ....

3. Finally, of the two search engines used, which one did you find to be most beneficial? Why?

....

....

Step #3. EVALUATE THE INFORMATION

Once you locate information on the Internet, you might get caught up in the natural tendency to use it immediately. After all, wasn't that the purpose of the search in the first place?

Yes, it was, but another step remains: evaluating the information. How do you know if the information is credible? On the Internet, there is no guarantee of a "consistent and reliable" peer-review process (Riedling, 2002, p. 61).

When evaluating information, consider these four criteria (Riedling, 2002, p. 62):

1. **Accuracy and authority.** Is the site precise and expert? What experience (credentials) does the author have? Is there a sponsoring site or organization? What do you know about that organization?
2. **Objectivity.** Is the site evenhanded and impartial? Is the material factual, unbiased, and in-depth? Is the coverage balanced? Is the site full of advertisements, or is it scholarly?
3. **Currency.** Is the site up to date and current? Is there a copyright date? (This indicates ownership; it does not indicate credibility or accuracy, however.) Has the site been recently updated, or is the information old? Are there references (bibliography and footnotes, if appropriate)?
4. **Scope.** Is the range of coverage small or vast? What is the breadth and depth of the site? That is, does it provide an in-depth review of the topic, or is it a superficial overview with broad, general statements?

Activity 4.6

How Do You Know If Internet Information Is Accurate?

The following is an excerpt from an e-mail that saw fairly wide distribution in the late 1990s. The excerpt was found online in an About.com article about so-called urban legends.

Using the R.E.D. Model, examine this e-mail (available online at http://urbanlegends.about.com/library/weekly/aa120298.htm). Circle each fact. Put a box around each statement of fiction. Place a question mark (?) over information you are not sure about. After you have completed your review, write a short response that identifies the assumptions found in the e-mail—or in your own thinking. Then draw a conclusion: Is this an accurate accounting of what could have happened?

Will Black Voting Rights Expire in 2007?

We are quickly approaching the 21st Century and I was wondering if anyone out there knew what the significance of the year 2007 is to Black America? Did you know that our right to vote will expire in the year 2007? Seriously! The Voters Rights Act signed in 1965 by Lyndon B. Johnson was just an ACT. It was not made a law. In 1982 Ronald Reagan amended the Voters Rights Act for only another 25 years. Which means that in the year 2007 we could lose the right to vote!

Does anyone realize that Blacks/African Americans are the only group of people who still require PERMISSION under the United States Constitution to vote?!

In the year 2007 Congress will once again convene to decide whether or not Blacks should retain the right to vote (crazy, but true). In order for this to be passed, 38 states will have to approve an extension.

Activity 4.7

Evaluating a Website

ARTICLE ABOUT EMPLOYER INTERNET SEARCHES

The Internet provides a wealth of information. But some sites are not very accurate or credible. This short activity will help you review the Internet with a critical eye, incorporating the four criteria of accuracy, objectivity, currency, and scope.

For this activity, open a search engine and conduct a search for an article about employers using the Internet to gather information about applicants. Once you have settled on an article, read it and complete the following items.

1. What is the common name of the site? (This is usually found on the homepage.)

....

....

2. What is the exact URL? This is the address (location) of the site. It will typically begin with http:// or http://www. (Note: When entering a URL, be sure to type it exactly. If only one character is incorrect, the site may not be located.)

....

....

3. What main point is the article attempting to prove? List three facts the article presents. Are any assumptions identified?

....

....

4. *Accuracy and authority*: Can you rely on the information you find on this site?

   a. Who is the author of the site?

....

....

   b. What evidence is provided on the site that the author is qualified to publish this material?

....

....

   c. What are the author's credentials? Include any affiliations (e.g., university professor, government agency). If none are listed, state that.

....

....

   d. What is your opinion of this author's credentials? Why do you or don't you trust this site?

....

....

5. *Currency:* Is the article current? When was it last updated? _____

6. *Scope:* Explore some of the links of this site. A link takes you immediately to another page (or another place on the same page) when you click your mouse on it. What types of links exist?

....

....

7. *Objectivity:* Discuss one of the links in detail. Is the information biased or slanted in any way?

....

....

8. Would you recommend this site to other students with the same career interest? Why or why not?

....

....

9. Briefly summarize what you learned from this site.

....

....

10. What questions do you still have about this topic? Who could help you with these questions?

....

....

Step #4. USE THE INFORMATION

Is information power? Contrary to popular belief, it is not power. It is the application (use) of information that can bring power.

Regardless, information must be used responsibly, and it must be conveyed in a clear and convincing manner. If you deliver a classroom presentation, write an analysis of a current event, or describe the features of a new video game; what and how you communicate the information will have an impact on how it is received.

Consider the history term paper described earlier in the chapter. Let's assume you had to complete that paper as an actual assignment. You put in a number of hours figuring out exactly what you were going to research; you found appropriate information in the library, on the Internet, or both; and then you determined what information was suitable for your final product. At this point, keep one question in mind: Do you want to waste all of your quality effort with a hastily crafted paper that looks like it was thrown together in the wee hours of the morning?

The presentation—how you use your information—is critical. No matter how much you may know, the impact of your knowledge will be minimal if the information is not clearly and thoroughly presented. At a minimum, do the following:

- Provide the final product in the form required by the instructor: length of the paper, cover page, illustrations, bibliography, and so forth.

- Ask someone you respect to critically review your paper, evaluating the organization and content of the presentation as well as grammar and spelling. Ideally, this should be someone who is a better writer than you.

- Before you turn in your final product, be sure that what you have written reflects what the instructor asked for.

THE SOCIALNOMICS REVOLUTION

"The Internet's greatest strength—rapid and cheap sharing of information—is also its greatest weakness."

—*Erik Qualman, author*

© H. Armstrong Roberts/ClassicStock/Almay

Information literacy has traditionally been concerned with ensuring students can find their way around the library and Internet for research purposes. Today, those skills still remain important for a college student. But a new dynamic has presented itself: the world of social media.

SOCIAL MEDIA: Consumer-Generated Information

Growing up in the 1950s and 1960s, I watched TV. Oh, I did other things young kids usually do. I played ball, rode my bike, hiked in the woods, did my homework (I actually did!), went to school, and did my chores to earn an allowance (about 50 cents a week, thank you). But I also watched a lot of television. Mostly "sitcoms," old movies, and sporting events.

In those days and through most of the last part of the twentieth century, media was produced by them and consumed by us. Clay Shirky (2010) points out in his book *Cognitive Surplus: Creativity and Generosity in a Connected Age* that media in the twentieth century was mostly a "single event" (p. 22): passive viewing. The producers of media were the "professionals" (p. 42) We sat in front of the TV and consumed what they sent into our households. Yes, we might yell out answers while watching one of the growing numbers of game shows, but no one really heard us.

© CJG Technology/Alamy

In this model, television watchers had two roles: (1) Find the media by searching through a handful of channels, and (2) watch what they found. The same for newspapers of the day. Delivered to our doorstep, they provided us with the news they thought to be important. We read the news that the publishers produced. Radio and movies provided more of the same.

Wow, how times have changed! In the groundbreaking book *Socialnomics: How Social Media Transforms the Way We Live and Do Business*, Erik Qualman (2010) describes the **social media** revolution we have witnessed and continue to witness. No longer do we have to wait passively for the news to reach us. We—all of us—can now be the producers. In short, social media is the phenomena that allows for consumer-generated media. It has fundamentally transformed the way we live, relate with friends and family, conduct business, and go to school.

TYPES OF SOCIAL MEDIA

> *People asking "Where do people find the time?" aren't usually looking for an answer; the question is rhetorical and indicates that the speaker thinks certain activities are stupid.*
>
> —*Clay Shirky, author*

Social networking sites enable millions of people to share information with friends and strangers around the world. Let's examine a couple of the most popular technologies and sites.

TEXT MESSAGING

Text messages are brief and usually sent from cell phone to cell phone. You might see them referred to as SMS (short message service). **Texting** is used for reasons that range from inane ("What's up?") to significant (colleges sending emergency notifications to their students).

For speed, a certain online jargon of abbreviated words has developed. For instance, "bff" means "best friend forever," and "lol" means "laugh out loud."

Does your college have an emergency texting notification system? Are you registered with it?

To grasp how fast this service has grown, consider these statistics ("USA Text Messaging Statistics," 2009):

- 203 million Americans text.
- 2.5 million text messages are sent each day in the United States.
- On average, cell phones are used more for texting than placing phone calls.

SOCIAL NETWORKING SERVICES

A few of the most popular social networking sites and applications are Facebook, MySpace, LinkedIn, Skype, Wikipedia, Twitter, and Renren (a Chinese site). Whereas texting allows people to stay in touch with quick messages, most social networking sites allow individuals to share so-called profiles about themselves. The user can be as detailed or as brief as desired about the intimate details of his or her life. (And therein lies a potential problem—more later.)

Sites like Facebook and MySpace are used for personal networking—friends connecting with old friends and new acquaintances. At the beginning of 2011, Facebook had 500 million registered users from around the world, and 70 percent of all Facebook users were outside the United States (Facebook press room, n.d.). These users were on Facebook more than 700 billion minutes per month. Statistics such as this show that social media has become a major player in the modern pop and business culture. Social media sites are becoming more visible in corporate America, as well. One study by Patterson (2009) found that 59 percent of leading retailers have a "fan page" on Facebook, including Best Buy, Wal-Mart, Toys R Us, and Kohl's.

BLOGGING

In recent years, the Web has seen an explosion of Web log sites known as **blogs**. Early in the Internet age, a Web log was literally a listing of websites about a particular topic. Today, blogs are written pieces posted on websites. They usually include the opinions or observations of the writer (known as the blogger) about a topic. Often, the blogger will include visuals or links to support his or her thoughts.

Think of blogs as similar to what you might find in the editorial section of the local newspaper. In some cases, blog sites may be used internally by an organization to distribute information and generate discussion. More often, a blog contains personal opinions by anyone who wishes to post on the Web ("Global Availability," 2005).

Approach the information on such sites with a "user beware" mindset. Traditional publishing (especially scholarly journals and textbooks) requires that other professionals in the field review a manuscript for credibility and accuracy. There is no such requirement for a blog. Granted, having a professional review does not automatically make a source good. But understand that a blogger can immediately post any material he or she wishes—with or without supporting evidence.

MICRO BLOGGING

Microblogs, such as Twitter and LinkedIn, allow for short updates. There is typically a character limitation; that is, the user can only type so many letters and symbols.

Again, these sites are wildly popular. After five years of operation, Twitter reached 1 billion tweets per week. And it continues to grow at a rate of about 460,000 new accounts per day ("Twitter Statistics," n.d.).

SKYPE

Skype allows users to hold audio and video calls from computer to computer. It is used by friends and families for staying in touch with loved ones around the world, by corporations for sharing information, and by students for completing class assignments. Generally speaking, computer-to-computer "calls" are free. A slight fee is charged for computer-to-landline calls.

Skype can be used to bring distant experts into a meeting that is held halfway around the world. It is a wonderful tool for collaboration.

GLOBAL COLLABORATION

Wikis are sites that allow people to log on and become content contributors. Wikipedia is probably the most commonly known and used wiki. Articles are posted and revised online by multiple people. Wikis offer another valuable resource for groups to create, share, and store documents online.

With Google Docs, a person can house documents online for remote access when away from his or her home computer. The documents can be shared with groups for review and editing.

YOUTUBE

This video-hosting site is the second-largest search engine in the world (Qualman, 2010). Users can create "channels," save their favorite YouTube videos, and upload videos they have created. YouTube is a free service that gives everyone the chance to become a movie maker, actor, or producer.

A video that "goes viral" is wildly popular, according to Internet jargon. One of YouTube's most-watched videos is "Charley Bit My Finger—Again." This cute, 55-second clip of two young brothers has been viewed 300-plus million times at the time this book was published.

EFFECTIVE AND RESPONSIBLE WRITTEN COMMUNICATION IN THE INTERNET AGE

Learn as much by writing as by reading.
—Lord Acton, historian and writer

There is absolutely no question that social media has revolutionized our world. As with any game-changing technology, social media has changed our lives forever. Social media sites, applications, and technologies allow us to do more with a more diverse group of people in a shorter period than ever thought possible. We can communicate faster with more people about a wider range of topics. We can add our opinions with a few keystrokes. We have become both consumers and producers.

With these advancements, however, come considerations for responsible use. It is easy to get caught up in the speed and convenience of the technology and lose our good sense. This section will take a quick look at how to be a meaningful participant in this communication revolution and still maintain our integrity, dignity, and privacy.

APPROPRIATE COMMUNICATION: Just Because It's Fast Doesn't Mean It's Appropriate

Probably the best advice I have heard for online communication came from a former student of mine. Kim, an engineer and business owner, offers this valuable advice:

> *Talk to people online as if they were sitting in front of you. In this world, you never know when you will meet someone on the street, in a business meeting, or in a coffee shop. If you say something inappropriate, there will be repercussions. Simply stated: If you would not say something face-to-face, then don't say it online.* (Mihalik, 2011)

If you post an inflammatory comment at 2:30 a.m. and think better of it at 9:00 a.m., it's too late. The post has been out there and may already have been forwarded to other people. In short, you will have lost control of your post. One educator put it this way: "Think before you send. Posting is like a bullet. Once it is out of the chamber, you can't bring it back" (Budd, 2011). Socialnomics author Erik Qualman (2010) simply states, "You need to act as if your mother is watching you."

In the following sections, you will find a few basic tips for communicating effectively in the Internet age. We will look at some of the tools and review privacy and civility considerations.

EFFECTIVE E-MAIL COMMUNICATION*

E-mail has revolutionized communication. As long as an Internet connection is available, one person can instantaneously contact another on any continent at any time. Information can be rapidly accessed and just as quickly passed along to another location. E-mail communication is quick, paperless, and free. (There have been limited discussions, however, about charging for e-mail use, primarily to cut down on spam.) E-mail is also faceless and open to abuse. Therefore, remember to observe e-mail netiquette (the rules of behavior for using the Internet).

Takeaway: Especially in e-mails to professors or perspective employers, be polite, get to the point, and, above all, be grammatically correct. Do not use text lingo. It is a quick way to lose credibility with your audience.

Table 4.1 provides a brief list of e-mail dos and don'ts that information-literate people observe. Remember that your professor is not your buddy. Write to him or her with respect. That includes using a salutation ("Hi, Professor" for instance) and a closing ("Thank you").

*This section based on Piscitelli (2011), p. 201.

Table 4.1 E-mail dos and don'ts

E-mail *Dos*	E-mail *Don'ts*
Do follow rules of grammar, punctuation, and capitalization in all e-mails. An e-mail represents you in cyberspace.	Don't type in all capital letters (the equivalent of SHOUTING!).
Do be courteous.	Don't send inflammatory notes.
Do respect the privacy of your e-mail recipients. If you use a distribution list, put the names in the "blind copy" (bcc) space when composing your e-mail. Everyone will receive the e-mail, but no one's e-mail address will be displayed for others to see and use.	Don't abuse distribution lists, and don't send spam. You may think the latest joke or inspirational story is great, but the 50 people in your address book may not have the same taste. You could also be sending someone a computer virus.
Do use it for business and school purposes to collaborate on projects.	Don't indiscriminately give out personal information. Beware of "phishing" schemes. They are e-mails that come unsolicited and ask for personal information, such as birthdates, passwords, and Social Security information.
Do choose an e-mail address or screen name that portrays a respectful self-image. What you think is a cute e-mail or screen name may be perceived in a negative way: "foxylady," "spoiledrotten," "studpuppy," and "Uwannabeme" may sound creative and adorable, but they do not impart the image of a serious student or potential employee. Quick test: Would you be pleased to have your username called out by the professor in class or by an employer's secretary as she called you in for a job interview?	Don't compromise your dignity or integrity.
Do use clear language. Judiciously use emoticons (symbols used to represent emotions, such as a "smiley face") to indicate the emotion behind a statement if the wording is not clear. (Better still, if the wording is not clear, rewrite or eliminate the passage altogether.)	Don't be sarcastic. The facial expressions behind an e-mail cannot be seen, so your words must speak for themselves.

Activity 4.8

Critically Thinking about Information Literacy Skills

Read the e-mail below. Circle all of the inappropriate items and errors it contains. Then compare your findings with a classmate. Finally, retype the e-mail in a more appropriate and professional manner.

TO: Professor@college.edu

FROM: littlesexyoneforsure@collegestudent.edu

Subject: HELP!!!!!!!

Yo, prof

there was trouble on the bridge my alam did not go off and I got in late last night. what did i miss in class. i have not completed my homework; PLEASE GIVE ME EXTRA TIME I DO NOT WANT TO FLAIL THIS CLASS!!!!!!!!!!!!

please respond ASAP--I AM WAITING BY MY COMPUTER NOW. lol

© PhotoAlto/Almay

RESPONSIBLE TEXTING

For many people, e-mail has given way to texting: sending short messages from cell phone to cell phone. Even though e-mail remains a popular tool in today's communication toolbox, it is, by some accounts, less popular with the texting generation. Some colleges and universities have reconsidered whether to provide e-mail addresses to incoming first-year students.

As with any activity, texting has both benefits and costs. While it allows for instantaneous connection, it also has had a negative impact, as text lingo has slowly crept into formal correspondence. Texting has also caused more classroom and business meeting distractions, as people believe they need to be constantly connected to others.

Takeaway: Be mindful of where you are. Just because a text message can reach you at any time or any place does not mean that you have to answer it immediately. In class, be considerate of your classmates and your instructor. You may find the subject matter or presentation boring, but that does not give you license to distract others. When your cell phone rings or you fumble to read or send a text, everyone around you is affected.

Call it what you want to—dependency, addiction, or self-absorption—but negative habits are being created that may carry into the business world. Know how to use the technology—but don't let it use you. See Table 4.2 for a brief listing of texting benefits and drawbacks.

Table 4.2 Text messaging benefits and costs

Benefits of Text Messaging	Costs of Text Messaging
It's quicker than having a full phone conversation.	The social connection of speaking with a live person is lost.
You may be able to text when making a phone call is not possible.	The ease of texting makes irrelevant and time-wasting messages more prevalent.
You can respond to a text when you want; your response does not have to occur at the time you receive the text message.	Sometimes texting creates a false immediacy—the belief that the text message must be answered immediately, no matter what the circumstance.
Your phone-call minutes may be more expensive than texting minutes (depending on your plan).	Unless you have a plan for unlimited texting, texting can be a budget buster for some people.
Texting is private; people nearby cannot hear your "conversation," as they might with a phone call.	Texting during classes or meetings or church services (or . . .) is an inappropriate habit. It is distracting and rude.
Texting provides a visual representation of a message.	Text lingo/abbreviations may have an adverse effect on formal writing skills.

POSTING APPROPRIATE STATUS UPDATES

Status updates are like mini-blogs. People post short messages about things they have just done or are about to do. They can convey meaningful messages, funny anecdotes, or questions. They may include photos or videos or website links.

At times, status updates can be trite and inappropriate. Again, remember that you are creating an online persona—one that a future employer or graduate school may find. A quick Internet search will find postings about inappropriate photos or updates that landed teachers, parents, and students in embarrassing situations and sometimes led to legal difficulties.

Takeaway: Update responsibly. When posting photos, ask yourself, "Am I OK with anyone seeing this photo?" Even if only your "friends" will see it, remember that they can forward it to other people. And that photo can possibly be downloaded by another person. If someone is taking photos at a party, that person may post the photo on his or her site and "tag" you in the photo. Yes, you can "untag" the photo but you cannot "unsend" the photo.

Show courtesy for other people. Before posting photos of them, ask for their permission. In short, protect your privacy and that of others. While the Internet is a wonderful tool, it also attracts its share of predators. Avoid giving out private information indiscriminately.

TWEETING WITH A PURPOSE

Twitter (and other microblogs) provide a useful networking service: a 24/7 message board. And tweets are short. Even so, tweeting can take up a lot of time—both sending and receiving.

Takeaway: Implement these strategies to make your tweet communications more meaningful:

- Make your messages stand out. Is it important to tweet that you don't like standing in line at the post office? Create tweets that have value. Maybe you can tweet a heartfelt message for the day or send helpful advice to college students. Share something that will positively catch attention and make a difference in the world.
- Don't rant, and don't cuss.
- Remember that your feed is public.
- As of March 2006, all tweets become part of the Library of Congress digital collection—even the embarrassing ones!

SOCIAL MEDIA AND PRIVACY CONCERNS:
Common Sense Is Not Always Common Practice

You might have heard people talk of a "digital footprint." The implication is that no matter what we do online, we leave an impression. Like footprints on the beach, you leave a trace of your visit.

That is true enough. But as we discussed earlier, your online presence leaves more than a footprint in the sand. Footprints can be washed away by an incoming tide. Removing your digital presence is not so easy, however. Instead of a digital footprint, consider the metaphor of a **"digital tattoo."** It conjures up a more permanent presence. Yes, a tattoo can be removed, but at what cost and scarring?

Erik Qualman (2011) cautions us to assume that whatever we post will be seen by everyone. He relates a story about an ad agency employee who mistakenly posted a tweet that contained an expletive. The employee thought it would be OK, since it was his personal account. Unfortunately, he inadvertently posted the offensive tweet on the Chrysler Twitter account: the automotive giant for whom his company was working. Oops! The mistake cost the employee his job, and it lost the account for his former employer (Qualman, 2011).

The online digital tattoo you create can be found anywhere by anyone. It consists of everything you post about yourself and everything you write in response to someone else. It contains all the photos, videos, music, and poetry that you post or link to say something about who you are. In short, when you create your digital tattoo, you actually create an online reputation.

Activity 4.9

How Big Is Your Digital Tattoo?

It is becoming increasingly common for employers to do Internet searches on job applicants. Find out what an employer would find out about you by doing your own search of yourself. See what (if anything) is circulating on the Web about you. Here is a quick activity to help with that search:

1. Go to www.google.com. Type in your name for a Web search. See what comes up. Is there anything surprising?
2. Once again, go to the upper-left-hand corner. This time, click on "Videos." What appears on the screen? Are there any videos of you? Anything surprising?

All social media users need to familiarize themselves with the privacy settings of the sites they use to protect their personal information. The best precaution is to avoid posting compromising information. Discretion is important. You have control over how much or how little you post on your profile. You also have control over the messages you post. Unfortunately, some individuals seem to put commonsense aside and post all types of photos, videos, messages, and rants. In doing so, they create a less-than-favorable digital tattoo. Again, when posting information about yourself, ask this question: "Would I be pleased to see this same information posted on the front page of the local newspaper for all of my friends, family, and faculty to view and read?"

Since employers can access social networking sites, what you or someone you know posts could very well be career suicide (Masnjack, 2006). Even National Football League teams are using social media to get information on prospective draftees ("NFL Prospects," 2009).

CREATING AN APPROPRIATE ONLINE PROFILE

Online sites allow a user to post an online profile. Think of the word profile, and you may think of the outline of a person or thing. While a profile does not show every feature, it provides a general representation of what the person or thing looks like.

This is, in essence, what an **online profile** does. It is usually a short representation of you for others to see. Think of it as an online identity. The user generally can post as much or as little as he or she decides. A profile is a brief introduction of yourself to all people who view your site. It can include information about your likes, dislikes, education, travels, career, desires, relationships, and residence. You can also post a photo. But as stated earlier in the privacy section, a little commonsense will take you a long way.

How do you want yourself portrayed? Classy? Sassy? Funny? Goofy? Professional? People can read your profile and think, "I would like to meet that person. I would like to get to know more about him," or they can think, "What a piece of work that guy is!" My guess is that you want to present yourself in the best possible way.

Here are a few pointers:

- Be honest. Your profile should reflect integrity and dignity.
- Be grammatically correct when using any public forum and especially if you are posting to a professional network, such as LinkedIn. Remember that a majority of employers now search for and access your online profile(s) and may use this information when making hiring decisions.
- Be appropriate in photos. Do you really want your photo to be one that looks like you have been at an all-night party? Think digital tattoo.
- Be considerate. Your profile is not the place to offend the sensibilities of other people. Remain civil in your post.
- Be appropriate in words. This goes beyond being grammatically correct. Type a rough draft and read it. Ask yourself, "Is this how I really talk? Would I be impressed hearing this?" A former student had this great advice: Make your profile sound like you if you were carrying on an appropriate face-to-face introduction. Would you really walk up to someone and say, "I don't do this often. Actually, this is my first time. I am coming off a bad relationship. I am a bit lonely and depressed . . ." Really—would you say that? Would you want to hear that as an introduction? Be natural, and be appropriate (Mihalik, 2011).
- Think of your mentor. Would he or she be proud to read your profile—and would he or she proudly say, "I know that person!"

Activity 4.10

Create an Appropriate Online Profile

As you know from the chapter-opening scenario, Jayne has concerns about her online identity. This is your chance to help Jayne by showing her what is appropriate.

On a separate piece of paper, type a brief (no more than 100 words) profile of yourself. What information is important to include? What should you leave out? What is your idea of an appropriate online profile?

SOCIAL NETWORKING: Positive Habits

Just like any tool, social media tools can be used for ill purposes without proper monitoring, discipline, and prioritization. If you use technology in a disciplined manner, you can access information and build networks that will help you get what you want and what you need.

Table 4.3 **Social networking: Use your time wisely**

Positive Habit	Strategy to Build the Positive Habit
Build meaningful connections with friends.	Manage your contact/friend list.
Stay in contact with your friends anywhere in the world (part 1).	Do people really want to know that you are having your tires changed? Rather than trivialize your life, write about positive and significant events.
Stay in contact with your friends anywhere in the world (part 2).	Manage your usage of the social sites. Check it once in the morning and once in the evening, for instance. And set a reasonable amount of time—say, no more than 30 minutes each time.
Keep undivided attention on your studies during study time.	If you have homework to do, do not access your social network until you have completed the assignment. Shut off your e-mail, your text messaging, and your social networking site. Access them as a reward for yourself. Remember your priorities.
Protect your privacy.	Keep your profile/status/personal information professional. While you can be playful and show a sense of humor, you should understand that it may be possible for anyone to find the "digital tattoo" (traces of information) you leave.

Table 4.3 lists a few of the positive consequences of using social networking sites, along with strategies to enhance those results and to eliminate the time drain of unhealthy social networking habits. In fact, there have been reports of people signing off from their social sites because what started as a way to stay in contact has become an uncontrollable drain on their time.

If you use a social networking site, evaluate how you use it. Are you using it to help you manage and advance your priorities, or have you allowed it to take control of your time? Remain disciplined, and focused on your priorities.

The following exercise is offered as a tongue-in-cheek review, but completing it may be an effective way for you to examine your social networking usage. Perhaps you can even add some items yourself.

Activity 4.11

Critically Thinking about Information Literacy Skills

You may be addicted to a social networking site if you . . .

- Update your status/profile multiple times each day.
- Constantly change your profile/site photo.
- Have to access your site by phone when you are away from your computer.
- Have "friends" whom you have never met.
- Get up in the middle of the night to go to the bathroom—but have to check your site to see if anyone has left a message for you.

- Feel it is necessary to tell anyone, at anytime, what you are doing at that moment.
- Cannot start your homework until you check your social networking site.
- Spend more time on your site than you do on your homework.
- Have to check your site numerous times throughout the day, including while in class or at work.

For more information on Internet addiction, see Stiles (2009), along with various YouTube videos.

1. Can you add any other items to this list?

2. How do you measure up? Do you have an addiction to a social networking site?

TRANSITIONING TO FORMAL COMMUNICATION (WITH YOUR INSTRUCTORS)

Social media sites provide practice for composing and relaying communication, even if in an abbreviated format. You have heard of people being bilingual or even bicultural—people who can easily and effectively move from one culture to another. They understand the rules and expectations in both worlds, and they can thrive in either one.

The same holds true for your written communication. You may be able to knock out hundreds of text messages in a short period of time. You may type in all lowercase letters, use text lingo, and not use salutations or closings in correspondence with your closest friends. That will probably be accepted (and maybe even expected).

But when you are communicating with instructors, employers, graduate school admission representatives, or a government representative, the rules are different—and you will need to make the necessary transition. In short, your professors still have traditional writing expectations. As English teachers have told students for years, "You have to know your audience."

Consider these simple strategies:

- Your instructor (or boss, or dean) is not your "friend." Keep the communication professional.
- Use proper grammar. Use a spellchecker. Depending on what you are writing, have someone proofread it for you.
- Be respectful of the person's time. Get to the point. Consider using bullet points (•) to outline information for quick reading.
- Fully identify yourself: first and last name plus any other identifier that may help the reader know who you are and why you are communicating.
- Avoid telling the reader you need him or her to do something "as soon as possible" (ASAP!). You may have an emergency, but that does not make it the reader's emergency. Obviously, real emergencies exist at times and need to be dealt with appropriately and expeditiously. But if everything is always an emergency, then nothing is an emergency.
- A polite thank you is always appreciated.

YOUR ENGLISH PROFESSOR KNOWS BEST

Walk into most any English professor's office, and you will find the walls and bookcases lined with every conceivable text on writing style, techniques, strategies, and the like. The purpose of this section is not to teach you how to write. (You will receive that instruction from competent English instructors.) The intent is to introduce and reinforce a few basic writing strategies that will help with your formal writing assignments and essay exams.

WRITING DECISIONS*

Before you write anything, you need to know why you are writing. From content to writing style, know what your instructor expects from your efforts. For instance, you will, at one point or another in your college career, be asked to write an essay that is descriptive, narrative, comparative, or argumentative. Some essays focus on how to do something, while others concentrate on describing cause and effect.

Some of the basic decisions that a writer must make (for either a short essay or longer research paper) include determinations about the following:

- The topic
- An opinion on the topic
- Supporting evidence for the opinion
- The audience for whom the writing is intended (may be the instructor)
- The organization of the paper
- The individual who will proofread the essay (besides you)

LOOK AT YOUR T.O.E.S.: The Basic Components of an Essay

Let's use a memory strategy to help you better organize an essay. T.O.E.S. is an acronym that will help you remember the main components of a basic essay. Your essay must have a Topic, an Opinion, supporting Evidence, and a Summary.

Activity 4.12

Practice with Your T.O.E.S.

1. Complete the following:

(Topic)	Give the name of one of your best friends—just the name.
(Opinion)	State an opinion about that person.
(Evidence)	List three facts that support your opinion about this individual.
(Summary)	Write a one-sentence summary.

*This section based on Piscitelli (2008), pp. 146–156.

2. Do the same exercise again, but this time, convince someone of something you should be allowed to do.

T: (What do you want to do?) ....

O: (Why should you be allowed to do it?) ....

E: **1.** ....

    2. ....

    3. ....

S: ....

3. Organize an answer to a textbook or lecture question.

T: ....

O: ....

E: **1.** ....

    2. ....

    3. ....

S: ....

WHAT CAN YOU DO ABOUT WRITER'S BLOCK?

Even the best-prepared student will encounter writer's block at times. Even a well-tuned car won't leave the driveway unless the battery is cranking. When your "writing battery" is drained, ask yourself the following questions to get moving again:

- Can I relate this (the topic) to anything else?
  - □ Connect the topic to your textbook or a class discussion—or even to a current event.
- Can I form any groupings or make any connections?
  - □ Sometimes, it is helpful to reorganize the material you have. Doing so may help you see the material in a new way.
- What are the consequences of this issue?
  - □ If your topic is to evaluate why something or someone is important, you may wish to consider for a moment the consequences if this thing or person were not present.
  - □ Is this good/positive or bad/negative?
  - □ Looking at an issue from a simple plus/minus perspective may help you see it in a new light.
- Do others really care about it?
  - □ Who might be most affected by this particular topic?
  - □ How do I feel about it?
  - □ If you can make a personal connection to the topic, it may be easier to generate ideas.
- How does this fit with a "bigger picture"?
  - □ Generally, your topic will be a smaller piece of a larger issue. Recognizing this may help you generate some connections and new thoughts.

EVALUATING IT: How Do You Know If You Have Written an Acceptable Essay?

Use the checklist in Activity 4.12 to assess the quality of your essay. Avoid the temptation to hand in an assignment just to turn something in. It should be reflective of thought and diligence.

Activity 4.12

Post-Writing Essay Checklist

Sometimes, it is difficult for us to see our own mistakes. We either miss them or do not recognize them as errors. To us, they look right. We may spend so much time with a particular assignment that we miss errors that are readily apparent to others. These are reasons that another set of eyeballs can help notice and eliminate some common errors.

You can use the following checklist to review your own paper. But have a classmate or study partner use it as a guide to review your paper before you submit it to your professor:

1. Did you correctly interpret the instructions?
   ☐ Did you understand each important word in the prompt?
2. Does your paper have a clear introduction (main idea)?
   ☐ Is there a topic?
   ☐ Is an opinion presented?
   ☐ Did you present a brief "road map" of how you will prove your argument?
3. Is all of your support relevant to the topic and the opinion? Always ask yourself, "Why is this fact or paragraph important? How does it support the purpose of the paper?"
4. Is your evidence based on support, or is the essay full of unsubstantiated glittering generalities? For instance, don't say "The government was in lots of trouble." Rather, be more specific and state "The central government was weak, because it lacked the power to tax and control commerce."
5. Does the paper follow a logical path?
   ☐ Do subsequent paragraphs connect with the information introduced in the first paragraph?
6. Have you checked your grammar and sentence structure?
   ☐ Do subjects and verbs agree?
   ☐ Are you using the correct words to express your thoughts?
7. Are your writing style and wording appropriate for your audience? That is, is the presentation suitable for the person(s) who will read the paper? As a rule, most school assignments should not use slang.
8. Is the essay neat (penmanship, typing format, errors neatly corrected)?
9. Have you cited all your sources?
10. Have you read your paper aloud? Listen to your words and sentences. This can be an effective way to hear grammatical errors. Even if you do not know all the grammatical rules, you probably know when something sounds wrong!
    ☐ Do the sentences flow? Do they make sense? (This method is most effective when a study partner reads the paper.)
11. And in the category of "Simple things often get overlooked," make sure your name is on the paper.

Congratulations! You have completed a thorough and well-prepared paper.

RESPONSIBILITIES OF THE INFORMATION AGE

Real integrity is doing the right thing, knowing that nobody's going to know whether you did it or not.

—*Oprah Winfrey, entrepreneur*

ACADEMIC INTEGRITY

When students or professors exhibit academic integrity, they have completed their work (research, writing, and homework) in a respectful, responsible, and honest fashion. Violations of academic integrity are not new. Ever since schools have existed, students have looked for shortcuts to completing assignments or taking exams. If anything is new, it's that technology makes plagiarizing easier. Cheating has moved into cyberspace, whether it involves copying material from a website and directly pasting it into one's own paper (without proper citation) or buying a paper from any of the various Internet "dot-com paper mills."

Colleges and universities are rising to the challenge. At the very least, violations of academic integrity typically result in failure for the particular assignment. But the punishments can and do become more severe. Students can fail a course, be suspended for a term, or be expelled from school. Some schools have created a grade that reflects failure due to violation of academic integrity. (For example, see "Academic Integrity Policy," 2006.)

> Locate and read your school's academic integrity policy. What are your responsibilities? What possible punishments can a student receive for violating the academic integrity policy?

AVOIDING PLAGIARISM

Students—and all researchers and authors, for that matter—have an obligation to respect the sources used in their research. Researchers must adhere to a code of **academic integrity**. Whether you conduct research to write a book or complete an English class assignment, certain standards of behavior are expected. This includes providing credit when using the words and ideas of other authors.

Such credit is called a **citation**. It generally consists of the author's name, the title of the publication, the publisher's name, the place and date of publication, and the page numbers from which the material came. If the material being credited was obtained from the Internet, the URL (www.) will be needed.

When a writer, researcher, or student takes another's words or ideas and does not give credit, a theft of intellectual property has been committed. **Plagiarism** is the dishonest representation of someone else's work as your own. When writing a paper and submitting work, it is your responsibility to provide appropriate citations to your sources. Simply put, give credit to an author for his or her thoughts, and you will avoid plagiarism.

Here are some basic guidelines for avoiding plagiarism (Procter, 2006):

- Whether you use another person's exact words or just his or her ideas, give credit. Do this as soon as you use the words or ideas. Even a paraphrase of a work (putting someone's idea into your words) must be cited. Remember that quotation marks must be used when using another person's exact words.
- When in doubt, cite.

- Cite facts you use to support an argument.
- Common knowledge does not need to be cited. This includes statements such as "George Washington was the first U.S. president"; "Pearl Harbor was bombed by the Japanese"; and "Mickey Mantle played for the New York Yankees."
- Cite the opinions of others you use to build your own argument. Do not pass off someone else's opinion as your own.
- While doing research, be sure to include all necessary bibliographic data in your notes.
- Check with your professors about the appropriate citation (documentation) style to use.

Chapter SUMMARY

Before leaving this chapter, keep the following points in mind:

- The information explosion has increased the availability of information, and it has also increased the types and locations of the information.
- Information literacy requires a person to know what information to look for, how to find that information, how to judge the information's credibility and quality once it has been found, and how to effectively use the information once it has been found and evaluated.
- Locate and use school resources that will sharpen your information literacy skills.
- Academic integrity demands a strict code of conduct (moral expectations) that governs the manner in which students and professors do research and behave in class.
- Your e-mails, texts, posts, and blogs represent you in cyberspace.
- When you create an online profile, be mindful of your privacy and dignity. Remember that if you post it on the Internet, it will become public.

CRITICALLY THINKING

What Have You Learned in This Chapter?

At the beginning of this chapter, you read about Jayne. She was about ready to graduate and enter the job market. She had her portfolio together but was concerned about how her "digital tattoo" might affect her employment search.

Let's apply what you learned in this chapter to help Jayne. However, before you dive into Jayne's problem and propose your solution, take a moment and stop and think about the main points of the chapter.

Review your notes from this chapter and also the key terms, chapter learning outcomes, boldface chapter headings, and figures and tables. For instance, consider how the chapter learning outcomes may be used to help Jayne:

© Shutterstock

- Using multiple types of information.

- Explain and use the four steps of information literacy.

- Use a search engine to locate information.

- Critically evaluate a source of information for accuracy, authority, objectivity, currency, and scope.

- Explain and practice one strategy for responsible social media behavior.

- Create an appropriate online profile.

TEST YOUR LEARNING

Now that you have reviewed the main steps of the information literacy process, reread Jayne's story. Pretend that you are Jayne's career advisor. Using the R.E.D. Model for critical thinking, help Jayne critically review her concerns.

Recognize Assumptions:

Facts: What are the facts in Jayne's situation? List them.

Opinions: What opinions do you find in this situation? List them.

Assumptions: Are Jayne's assumptions accurate?

Evaluate Information:

Help Jayne compile a list of questions that will help her make the most appropriate decision.

What emotions seem to be motivating Jayne at this time?

Is there anything missing from her thought process?

Do you see any confirmation bias?

Draw Conclusions:

Based on the facts and the questions you have presented, what conclusions can you draw?

What advice do you have for Jayne? What solutions would you propose?

Based on your suggestions, do you see any assumptions?

Finally, based on what you learned about information literacy, what plan of action do you suggest for Jayne?

Motivation and GOAL SETTING

5

We have too many high-sounding words, and too few actions that correspond with them.

—Abigail Adams, First Lady of the United States

CHAPTER LEARNING OUTCOMES

By the time you finish reading this chapter and completing its activities, you will be able to do the following:

- List and briefly describe the major motivating force in your life.

- Identify a motivational barrier and at least one strategy to overcome it.

- Create a goal statement that includes what you want to do, how you will do it, why you will do it, and when you will accomplish it.

- Evaluate your locus of control.

The Case of DOMINIC

Ever since Dominic could remember, he wanted to attend college. Yes, there were people—including his teachers—who had encouraged him, but something deep inside him had kept pushing him forward. He knew he needed a college education to make a good life for himself.

After the first day of classes, Dominic smiled and said to himself, "I'm here. I've achieved my dream to go to college!"

Recently, Dominic's adviser and his study skills instructor have started to ask about his long-term goals and the steps he has planned to achieve those goals. Dominic has never given that much

© Shutterstock

Key Terms

Action steps
Excuse
Extrinsic motivation
Goal
Intrinsic motivation
Locus of control
H.O.G.s
Motivated learner
Motivation
Motivational barriers
Persistence
Strategy
Values

Chapter INTRODUCTION

College has been and will continue to be a series of learning experiences. You have had to find your classes, buy books, get a parking decal, locate the campus library, fight for a parking space, tackle assignments, and maybe fit in with a new roommate. At times, it might feel like you are moving in a cloud of dust. You might say, "Who has time for strategies? I'm just trying to survive!"

This chapter will examine what motivates you to achieve your goals.* When you establish a goal, you are actually planning a strategy to obtain

*This chapter based on Piscitelli (2008), pp. 26–41.

thought. Yesterday, he told a friend, "If I come to class, pass my exams, and make it to the next term, isn't that good enough? I don't see the need for writing goals. It seems like a complication."

Lately, though, Dominic has found it more difficult to remain focused. His direction seems fuzzy, and his motivation seems faltering. Procrastination has crept into his life, and he is falling behind in his studies. Earlier today, he confided to his study skills instructor, "I know I have to stay motivated and remember why I am here. But staying motivated and focused on where I am going has become increasingly difficult."

CRITICALLY THINKING
about *Dominic's* situation

You are Dominic's study skills instructor. What strategies would you suggest for Dominic to follow?

what you desire. Whether you achieve the goal depends in great part on how effectively you plan and carry out your strategy.

Corporate leaders use the word strategy often. One company develops a strategy to market and sell computers directly to customers. A textbook publisher revises its strategy to sell more books and experiences to college students. Automobile manufacturers constantly refocus their strategies to put drivers (buyers) in their vehicles.

MyStudentSuccessLab

MyStudentSuccessLab (www .mystudentsuccesslab.com) is an online solution designed to help you 'Start strong, Finish stronger' by building skills for ongoing personal and professional development.

Every successful business must have a **strategy**—a plan of action—that simply and clearly places it in an advantageous position in the marketplace. The corporate strategy is all about making winning choices and using available resources to bring about success. The same holds true for the college student. Having a well-developed plan—your strategy to reach your goal—will help you make choices that effectively use the resources you have.

Motivation goes to the heart of your **values**—the things that are important to you. Your values determine what you want to accomplish by the end of this term—or even by the end of this week. What do you want to gain from college? Or asked another way, why are you here (college), and what drives you to remain here?

If you are like most people, you have not reached every goal you have set. You can probably produce a long list of reasons this has happened. Maybe one of the goals you set was not a strong enough force in your life to become a priority—and a reality. You might blame the people you have associated with. You might even point fingers at external events over which you had no control. But when all the excuses for not achieving your dream have been exhausted, the most accurate question to ask is this one: What am I doing to get what I want?

Once you know why you are in college, it's time to focus on what you need to do. What steps do you need to take to achieve your goals, and when will you take those steps? Once you establish academic goals, how will you stay motivated to make them become realities?

As you move toward your goals, it will be helpful to establish checkpoints to help you assess your academic choices and priorities along the way. In addition to measuring progress toward achieving each goal, you will want to reflect on its appropriateness. Ask yourself some more questions: Is the goal I established still right for me? Is this what I want to do? Is it healthy for me? Goals should be energizing, not emotionally draining (Piscitelli, 2011, p. 56).

Activity 5.1

Reflecting on Your Current Level of Motivation and Goal-Setting Skills

Before you answer the items that follow, reflect on your current level of motivation and goal-setting skills.

As you do in completing all of the reflective activities in this book, you should write from your heart. This exercise is not meant for you to answer just like your classmates—or to match what you may think the instructor wants to see. Take the time to give a respectful, responsible general accounting of your experiences with motivation and goal setting. Doing a truthful self-assessment now will help you build on skills you have while developing those you lack.

For each of the following items, circle the number that best describes your typical experience with motivation and goal-setting skills. Here is the key for the numbers:

0 = never, 1 = almost never, 2 = occasionally, 3 = frequently, 4 = almost always, 5 = always

When considering your past successes and challenges with both motivation and goal setting, how often:

		0	1	2	3	4	5
1.	Did you establish a specific goal that can be quantifiably measured?	0	1	2	3	4	5
2.	Did your goals have an established end point—a date for completion?	0	1	2	3	4	5
3.	Did your goals have specific action steps?	0	1	2	3	4	5
4.	Were you motivated to do something just because of the extrinsic reward you would receive?	0	1	2	3	4	5
5.	Were you motivated to do something because of how it made you feel inside?	0	1	2	3	4	5
6.	Did you expect what you did would affect what happened to you?	0	1	2	3	4	5
7.	Did you establish goals that made you stretch—that were not easy to attain?	0	1	2	3	4	5
8.	Were you able to identify a motivational barrier and then do something to overcome it?	0	1	2	3	4	5

Add up your scores for items 1, 2, 3, and 7. Divide by 4. Write your answer here: _____

Using the key provided to explain each number (0, 1, 2, 3, 4, 5), complete this sentence: When it comes to goal setting, I _____ establish clearly stated specific goals that make me stretch and grow.

Add up your scores for items 4, 5, 6, and 8. Divide by 4. Write your answer here: _____

Using the key provided to explain each number (0, 1, 2, 3, 4, 5), complete this sentence: When it comes to motivation, I, _____ am aware of what motivates me and how to take charge of my motivation.

Based on your answers, what insights have you gained about your experiences with organization?

MOTIVATION

> *Ability is what you're capable of doing.*
> *Motivation determines what you do.*
> *Attitude determines how well you do it.*
> —*Lou Holtz, football coach and television sports analyst*

Motivation moves you to act on or toward something. It can come from within you, or it can be the consequence of some outside force that drives you forward.

Actually, you do not need this book or a college instructor to tell you what motivation is. Before you ever set foot on your college campus, you were driven by desires—and you acted on those desires. For instance, one of those desires was to attend college. You made choices and took actions to make that happen. And here you are, just as you wanted to be. Motivation provided the fuel, the energy, to move toward your goal: to go to college.

WHERE DO YOU FIND MOTIVATION?

Motivation varies from person to person depending on the opportunities, challenges, tasks, activities, and life experiences he or she faces. An athlete's love for sports may motivate her to get to practice early and remain late. A student who did not do as well on a reading quiz as he would have liked pushes himself to improve by 10 points on the next quiz. Maybe you know a single parent who attends school at night, works a full-time job during the day, is the treasurer for her child's school PTA—and awakens early each day to study for her college classes.

These are motivated individuals pursuing their goals. But what creates the drive to accomplish these activities? Where does the drive come from?

EXTRINSIC AND INTRINSIC MOTIVATION

Motivation comes from within you (**intrinsic motivation**) or from some source outside you (**extrinsic motivation**). The single mother who is a student may be moved intrinsically, extrinsically, or both. Table 5.1 provides a glimpse into her motivations.

Table 5.1   **Intrinsic and Extrinsic Motivation**

	Why? Intrinsic Motivation	**Why? Extrinsic Motivation**
Attends school at night	She has always wanted to be the first in her family to get a college degree. She has always loved reading and learning. They give meaning to her life.	The only way she can advance in her job and get a pay raise is to have a college diploma.
Works a full-time job	She loves her job and would like to become a supervisor some day.	She has a child to raise and rent to pay each month.
Serves as treasurer for her child's school PTA	She is able to plan activities that will benefit the children of the school. It gratifies her to watch the children laugh and play with new playground equipment that the PTA was able to purchase.	She was told volunteer work would look good on her college application.
Awakens early each morning to study	She loves the classes she is taking and thirsts for as much knowledge as she can retain.	She has to maintain a C average if she wants to keep her financial aid.

Obviously, this single mother is driven by a variety of factors. Whether they are intrinsic or extrinsic, they bring her closer to her goal of college graduation.

Let's make this a little more personal. Think about the beginning of this school term. Your professors outlined course expectations in their syllabi. Whether you have adhered to those requirements has been up to you. Do you attend class regularly because you enjoy the lectures, discussions, and classmates (intrinsic motivation) or because you know that attendance counts toward your grade (extrinsic motivation)?

Consider that even if you do something for extrinsic reasons, it is connected to what you want intrinsically. Take the previous example. If you go to class because it counts toward your grade, the grade is extrinsic. However, the fact that you consider a grade valuable is tied to your intrinsic motivation. Perhaps it represents the value you place on your work ethic, or maybe the grade is a reflection of how you view yourself. Something inside you moves you to want that grade (Piscitelli, 2011, p. 60).

CHARACTERISTICS OF A MOTIVATED LEARNER: Can an Individual Learn to Be Motivated?

If you understand what makes up motivation, you can more effectively evaluate your behavior—and begin to make changes, as needed. Let's review one model that breaks the behavior of **motivated learners** into five distinct parts (VanderStoep & Pintrich, 2003, pp. 40–41):

1. Motivated behavior always involves making a choice. Maybe spending time in a college classroom means you cannot work as many hours at gainful employment, and consequently, you will take a pay cut while pursuing your studies. But you still came to college for some reason. In short, you were motivated to make this choice.
2. A motivated person will put forth effort to achieve a goal. He or she is not waiting for the goal to happen. The motivated individual chooses to make the goal happen.
3. The motivated individual exhibits **persistence**. Simply put, this student has the trait known as "stick-to-itiveness." He or she can stick with a task until it has been completed.
4. Motivated learners critically think about what they are doing. If they write an essay, they think about the topic, think about the outline, and think about the final product. They engage the topic. Like people who are engaged to be married, engaged students choose to be committed to their work.
5. Finally, if the preceding four characteristics—choice, effort, persistence, and engagement—are all present, the student will have a connection to a product. There will be some form of achievement—a movement closer to a goal (see Figure 5.1).

© iStockPhoto

Figure 5.1

Components of Motivation

ACHIEVEMENT

CHOICE — EFFORT — PERSISTENCE — ENGAGEMENT

FLEXIBLE YET FOCUSED

If your final result is not what you had hoped for, it doesn't necessarily mean you lacked motivation. It may indicate that it's time to reevaluate your choices and then recommit your efforts. Flexibility is important. You can't control everything that will happen in college (or in life). Remain focused on your journey, and allow yourself the flexibility to make adjustments along the way.

Activity 5.2

Self-Monitoring Check: Are You a Motivated Learner?

Reflect on a time you were committed to something. You may have been an athlete on a team, a member of a club, an officer in student government, a musician at a recital, or playing a role in some other activity on which you worked diligently.

1. Exactly why were you committed to the task? What characteristics of motivation (choice, effort, persistence, engagement, and/or achievement) were present?
2. Who helped to keep you moving toward your results? Was someone or something else driving you (extrinsic motivator), or did some force within you (intrinsic motivator) drive you forward?
3. What did you do to maintain your level of commitment over time?

OVERCOMING MOTIVATIONAL BARRIERS

For the moment, imagine that you cannot control the external forces that stand between you and what you would like to achieve. Whether it's an instructor's expectations, an uncaring employer, or the state of the economy, we'll put those factors aside for now. Instead, your target for this section will be those things you can control—that originate within you. Those things are **motivational barriers**.

Attitude. Think of something you have had difficulty staying motivated to achieve. Maybe you have not been able to get to the gym as often as you would like each week.

Or perhaps you have not lost the weight you had hoped to shed this year. Listen to your words (Miller, 2005, pp. 44–47).

Consider these statements:

- "I *hope* to lose weight."
- "I will *try* to lose weight."
- "I *think* I will be able to lose weight."

What do you notice about these statements, especially the italicized words? Compare them with the following statements:

- "I *will* lose weight."
- "I *shall* lose weight."
- "I *pledge* to lose weight."

These statements present more forceful and more positive sentiments. There are no wishy-washy thoughts. Using this language of action states the point (the goal) in a very definite manner.

Suggestion: Listen to your words. They might very well reflect your attitude or commitment level. Your attitude reflects your perceptions about an issue. It is often (but not always) reflected in your behavior. Are you using the language of commitment or the language of doubt and uncertainty?

In fact, state and make the following pledge to yourself: When it comes to motivation, I will eliminate the word *try* from my vocabulary.

That's right! Get rid of those three letters. Think about the times people have told you they would try to do something. "I will try to stop by your house" or "I will try to get to the gym tomorrow" or "I will try to study more this week." Face it: Merely trying lacks commitment. Used enough, the word *try* will become an easy excuse—and a path to unachieved goals. Do you want friends who will *try* to help you or friends who will actually help you? Are you satisfied with a professor who will *try* to be exciting in class or a professor who is exciting in class? Would you pay a mechanic who *tried* to fix your car—but did not? How about an employer who promises to *try* and pay you! Rather than be indecisive, be decisive and move forward boldly and with purpose.

Mental Paralysis. Think of a ping-pong game. Two contestants paddle a small ball back and forth over a table net. One player makes an incredible shot, but the opponent makes a masterful return. Back and forth the game goes. Eventually, one player will win.

Sometimes, our minds engage in a ping-pong game of sorts when we encourage ourselves to accomplish something. Let's call the two opponents *Yes* and *But*. Every time *Yes* presents a reason to move forward with an action, *But* skillfully returns with a reason to stay put. Back and forth the exchange goes. While *Yes* makes good attempts, the exchange can become tiring and nothing is accomplished. *But* has been too persistent and eventually stops the progress. Here is what such a "match" might sound like:

- "Yes, I need to study more for my math exam."
- "But, I really don't have any more time to devote to that class."

- "Yes, I know that time is an issue. Still, I really must devote more time to math class."
- "But, I never have been any good at math. The extra time won't help anyway!"
- "Yes, I guess I'm just destined to be a poor math student."

In this exchange, the person ended up talking himself right out of the commitment. As a professor of psychology once said, "The word *but* functions like an eraser, negating the motivation that went before—and nothing happens" (Miller, 2005, p. 46).

Suggestion: Erase the word *but* from your motivational vocabulary before it erases your motivation.

Commitment. Sometimes, the initial excitement to do something fades away quickly. Maybe it is difficult to maintain motivation because you lack passion for what you want to accomplish. For instance, perhaps you committed to play intramural sports with your friends. After two weeks of practice, however, you are not excited about continuing. When you examine the issue, you recognize that you participated only because you did not want to disappoint the friends who were going to play. You also have noticed that to devote time to the sport, you have had to stay up much later each night to complete your homework and have had to give up some hours from your part-time job. After careful analysis, you decide the intramural sport is not where you need—or want—to invest your energies.

Suggestion: Revisit why you are committed to do something. If you can honestly say that the cost in time, effort, or emotion is more than you are willing to pay, then maybe you should look for another road to follow. Once again, pay attention to what you say— what words you use. If you continually hear yourself saying "I can't do . . . ," perhaps you really are saying "I won't do . . ." whatever needs to be done. The word *can't* can become another excuse—and when combined with *try* and *but*, it can be deadly to motivation and goal attainment. "I *can't* get to the tutor. I *try*—but just *can't!*"

That sounds like the excuse it is, even though it sounds better than "I won't go to the tutor. I did not make an appointment, so I just won't go." While that second statement sounds harsh, it may be close to the truth. Remember, either you *do* something or you *do not*. To say you *tried* might make you feel better, but it will not get you closer to your goals.

Are You in the Way? At times, you might create your own obstacles. Sometimes, for example, two motivators might conflict with each other. For instance, perhaps you have pledged that you will earn a 3.5 *grade-point average (GPA)* this term. In addition, you have pledged to work at your part-time job as many hours as you can to save money for a car. You are motivated by the high GPA, and you are motivated by the money to buy a car. Working to get one might have a negative effect on reaching the other.

Suggestion: Examine your motivators. If one seems to have a harmful effect on another, you might want to rethink what you want to do. Or perhaps look for alternatives. For instance, maybe you could work more hours on the weekends, leaving school nights for homework. Do not work at cross-purposes with yourself.

BUT, I MIGHT FAIL!*

We have all heard stories of people—famous and not so famous—who failed miserably but were able to rebound from the depths of despair and achieve success. It may be hard to find the benefits in failure when it happens, but they are there.

Consider some of these famous failures ("Famous Failures," n.d.):

- Award-winning actress and comedienne Lucille Ball was dismissed from acting school.
- Early in the Beatles' career, a record company rejected them because it did not like their sound and thought "guitar music was on its way out."
- Future NBA Hall of Fame basketball player Michael Jordan did not make his high school basketball team.
- Long before Thomas Edison became a famous inventor, a teacher told him he was stupid.
- A newspaper fired Walt Disney because he lacked creativity.

Life is full of risks—and failed attempts. Just because you fail at something does not make you a failure. It simply means you failed at that attempt. If Michael Jordan had never rebounded from his high school failure, think of the basketball and athletic genius the world would have missed. As cliché as it sounds, the only failure in a failure is the failure to get up and do it again.

Think of what might have happened if the following individuals had not gotten up again after falling short ("Fifty Famously Successful People," 2010):

- R. H. Macy started and failed at seven businesses before finally hitting it big with his store in New York City.
- Actor Harrison Ford was initially told he "didn't have it what it takes to be a star."
- Author Stephen King's first book received more than 30 rejections.

So, the next time you do not achieve what you want and consider quitting, think of what the world might miss if you do not persevere toward your dream! Think of our ongoing question: What are you doing to get what you want?

UNDERSTANDING EXCUSES

To handle your excuses, you must first understand what they are and why you make them. When you use an **excuse**, you attempt to explain a particular course of action you have taken to remove or lessen responsibility or blame for a result. Generally, excuses can be traced to fears of the unknown, insecurities about the future, or a perceived inability to handle a present situation. As stated earlier, when we make excuses, we tend to fall back on try, but, and can't to explain why we did not take action and move forward.

Again, what we say becomes what we do.

*This section based on Piscitelli (2011), pp. 63–64.

GOAL SETTING

> *To accomplish great things, we must dream as well as act.*
>
> *—Anatole France, poet*

WHAT IS A GOAL?

The first part of this chapter looked at what drives a person to a destination. Now, let's turn our attention to that end point—to the goal your motivation moves you toward.

Generally, people think of a **goal** as a place they want to reach. The "place" can be academic ("I want an A in history"), it can be personal and nonacademic ("I will run and finish a five-mile race"), or it can be community oriented ("I will help paint the community center").

We all have goals of one kind or another. They can be simple, short-term goals, like cleaning a room, or they can be more complex long-term destinations, like becoming qualified for a particular career.

Activity 5.3

Critically Thinking about Your Motivation and Goal-Setting Skills

R E D

The R.E.D. Model (**R**ecognize Assumptions, **E**valuate Information, **D**raw Conclusions) provides a systematic way to approach critical thinking through the use of an easy-to-remember acronym.

Let's apply the R.E.D. Model to your ability to stay motivated to reach your goals. Activity 5.2 may be helpful for this activity.

List a best practice (something you do well) that you use to stay motivated. Then answer the questions that follow.

Critical-Thinking Step	Application to Your Motivation and Goal-Setting Skills	Your Explanation (here or on a separate piece of paper)
Recognizing Assumptions	Examine your motivational best practice from more than one *perspective (point of view)*. How do you know this is one of your best practices?	
Evaluating Information	Explain specifically (give an example) how this best practice has helped you in the past.	
Drawing Conclusions	How can your best practice help you reach one of your academic goals?	

WHY DO YOU NEED GOALS? CONVERTING FANTASIES TO DREAMS—AND DREAMS TO REALITIES

Almost everything you have done in your life has connected directly to goal setting. For instance, have you ever done any of the following?

- Tried out for an athletic team?
- Decided to play a musical instrument?
- Saved your money to buy someone a gift?
- Taken certain high school courses so that you could apply to college?
- Filled out an application for a summer job?
- Asked someone for a date?

If you have done any of these things or other things similar to them, you have engaged in goal setting. Because you have a history on which to build, what follows should not be intimidating. Consider this example:

> Perhaps when you were a child, you picked up a basketball and started to throw it toward a basket. A few years later, you found yourself on a community basketball team. By that time, you had been playing basketball in the local park for five or six years. You knew how to dribble the ball, pass it, and toss it through the hoop.
>
> You had the basic skills, but your new team coach still provided instruction. He or she built on your skill base. Most likely, you did not adequately learn some of those previous skills. Maybe your body was in the wrong position when shooting a jump shot. The coach gave you some advice. Sometimes, it was just a little tweak here or there. In the end, you became a much better all-around ball player (Piscitelli, 2011, pp. 65–66).

That's the idea with the rest of this chapter. Don't forget what you have learned, but be open minded enough to examine and use some new strategies. In other words, respect your experiences while taking on the responsibility to build new experiences.

Goal setting allows you to focus your sights on something you want to achieve, make a plan, and finally move toward that result. Effective goals, whether long term or short term, address the *why, when,* and *how* of our lives. If your goals lack these components, then they will turn out to be daydreams or mere fantasies.

H.O.G.S: Huge, Outrageous Goals

In the book *Built to Last,* Jim Collins and Jerry I. Porras (2002, pp. 93–94) describe what they refer to as "BHAGs." In their research on successful companies, they found that companies that set big, hairy, audacious goals consistently outperformed their competition. In other words, these companies did not settle for making goals they could easily reach. They set goals that required effort to attain.

The same holds true for your personal goals. If you continually set goals you can easily reach, you may never know the joy and exhilaration of stretching yourself to new heights. You may not reach the potential you are really capable of fulfilling.

When setting your goals, think of the acronym **H.O.G.** (An *acronym* is an abbreviation formed by the first letters of a group of related words. You can use acronyms as memory tools.) Set a *huge, outrageous goal*. This does not mean to establish a goal that is impossible to reach. Think of it more as a reminder not to settle for something less than your best effort. If you aim high and take the appropriate action steps, you will move farther than you may have thought possible. Yes, you may stumble. You may even fail to achieve a particular goal. Aim low (the easy way), and you will hit your mark every time—and more than likely never achieve your potential.

While it is good to have ambition and potential, without initiative, those other qualities may never be realized. Stretch! Take the initiative to set a huge outrageous goal—and move toward the potential you have.

Activity 5.4

Helping Dominic with His Goals

In the chapter-opening story about Dominic, you read that he could not remain focused on what he needed to do—the important things for his college success. He was scattered in his thinking and becoming discouraged. Completing this activity will allow you to model a strategy for Dominic.

Reflect on one of your current goals. It can relate to one of your classes, a campus club of which you are a member, your current job, or some other part of your life.

1. State the goal.

   ....

2. Why do you have this goal? Why is it something you want to do?

   ....

3. When do you wish to accomplish this goal? (What is the date for completion?)

   ....

4. How will you accomplish this goal? That is, what resources will you need to achieve your goal?

   ....

5. How will you know when you have accomplished your goal? What, specifically, will have happened?

   ....

6. Is this a huge, outrageous goal (H.O.G.)? Explain your answer.

   ....

7. Finally, here is a question that many people ignore: How do you know that this is the correct goal for you to pursue now? Does the goal move you toward an emotionally satisfying result?

   ....

   ....

LONG-TERM GOALS NEED SHORT-TERM ACTIONS

Goals go beyond the classroom. In fact, goals address many issues in life. Figure 5.2 gives a broad overview of categories of goals.

The four main categories of goals, which are shown in the middle tier of Figure 5.2, can be classified as *long-term goals*. They are large goals that will be accomplished in the future. They will not be reached in a day or two. In the case of career goals, years will be required.

Figure 5.2

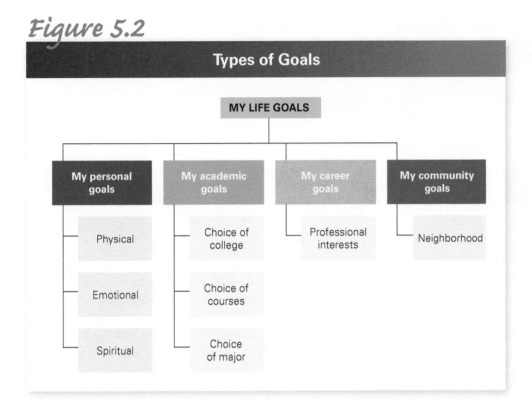

Types of Goals

MY LIFE GOALS

My personal goals	My academic goals	My career goals	My community goals
Physical	Choice of college	Professional interests	Neighborhood
Emotional	Choice of courses		
Spiritual	Choice of major		

You may have heard a classmate say "My long-term goal is to be rich—and my short-term goal is to get an A in my math class." While getting rich may definitely be admirable for your friend, he or she has a lot of ground to cover between getting an A in math and amassing riches for life. For our purposes here, let's consider an A in math as the long-term goal for this term—and that may move you a step closer to your dream of being rich.

WHAT DOES A CLEARLY STATED GOAL LOOK LIKE?

The questions in Activity 5.4 provide a glimpse into the parts of a goal. (For a more detailed discussion, see Wilson [1994], pp. 4–9.) A useful goal—as opposed to a mere fantasy—must provide the means to help you reach your desired destination (see Figure 5.3).

The first step to reach your challenge involves developing a clear *goal statement*— a concrete step to make your dreams become reality. A clearly stated goal has the following six properties:

1. **A clear goal is written.** This is the step in which you state precisely what you want to achieve. Once it has been put in writing, it becomes an affirmation of intent. Put it where you will see it every day. Some people find the process of actually writing a goal awkward and a waste of time. Nevertheless, this is a valuable exercise as you develop the habit of establishing long-range plans.
2. **A clear goal must be specific and measurable.** Exactly what will be accomplished? Saying "I want to have a better English grade" is admirable, but it is incomplete. How do you define *better*? If your current grade is a D, would you be satisfied with a D+ (which, after all, is better than a D)? By *how much*

Figure 5.3

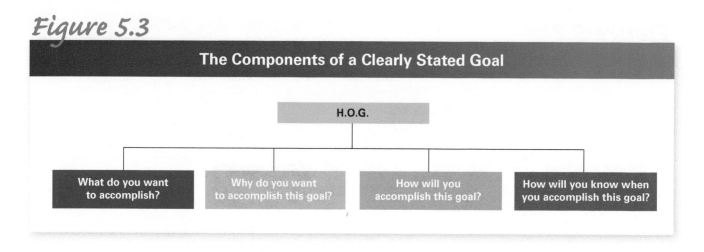

do you wish to raise your grade? By *when*? How will you know when you have achieved the goal? Write in concrete terms so that you clearly know when you have achieved the goal. Here is a much clearer statement: "I want to get a B in my English class by the end of the semester." There is no doubt as to what you want to accomplish. You have also identified the time frame in which you want to accomplish the goal.

3. **A clear goal has to be realistic.** It should be challenging, yet attainable. Saying you will raise your English grade from an F to an A by the end of the week is not realistic. Challenge yourself, but do not frustrate yourself. Refer to the discussion earlier about H.O.G.s.

4. **A clear goal must have a practical "road map."** Know where you are going, how you are going to get there, and when you plan on arriving. Aimlessly wandering toward a goal will waste your valuable time. Simplify the goal by dividing it into manageable, bite-size **action steps**. In other words, once you have set a long-range goal, identify the action you need to take to achieve that goal.

Move toward your goal with specific, measurable, and responsible action steps. Rather than tackle too much at once, establish manageable and action-oriented steps. For many people, taking a bite-size move forward is not as overwhelming as heading toward a more complex and long-range goal. These action steps get a person moving in the right direction.

Second, taking specific action steps will help you mark your progress, step by step, toward your ultimate goal. If one of your academic goals is to get an A in your English class by the end of the term, an action step may be to find a study group, to attend tutoring sessions, or to visit the professor once a week with specific questions.

5. **A clear goal anticipates potential problems and obstacles.** Your goals will not be immune to twists and turns of the road. Don't become paranoid or obsessive about potential problems, but do anticipate some of the problems you may encounter. If you do, obstacles will less likely surprise you—or be as demoralizing.

An activity I do with my students and audiences around the nation will emphasize this point. I pose the question "Who has a goal to have more money in life?" Most people raise their hands. Whether it is to pay for a college education, to pay off a debt, or to purchase a needed item, most people do want to have *more* money. I call a couple of people to the front of the room, and I place dimes in their hands. I tell them they have just reached one of their life goals. They now have *more* money than when they came into the room that day. The obvious point is that they were not thinking about a dime. They were thinking of hundreds or thousands of dollars. And here's the moral of the story: Be specific with your goals.

6. **A clear goal has built-in incentives.** Even though you want to reach a point where your goals are intrinsically motivating, you should recognize (and enjoy) your achievements. Provide appropriate rewards for yourself as you make progress. In fact, establish a schedule of incentives (rewards) that coincide with your "bite-size" action steps. After doing all of your homework, perhaps you could reward yourself with a pizza or a recreational activity. When you get that hard-earned A, treat yourself to a movie with friends. The reward should provide you with a little "fuel" (motivation) to keep plugging away toward your goal.

TIPS ON DEVELOPING YOUR ACTION STEPS

- Once you have identified a goal, identify the most important step you can take to move toward it—right now. Doing so requires you to prioritize your steps.

- Make a commitment to take this important step as soon as possible. Can you do it tonight? Tomorrow?

- Be diligent, but be flexible. That is, treat your goals and their action steps with respect, but understand that you may need to make adjustments. As the Dalai Lama has said, "Remember that not getting what you want is sometimes a wonderful stroke of luck"—as you will be forced to look in a new direction.

- Be willing to ask for help. The three Fs—friends, family, and faculty—can be wonderful resources.

Here is an example of a "road map":

Goal:	To Get an A in Math by the End of the Semester.
Action Steps:	Carefully read the instructor's course description, assignment page, and any other handout.
	Complete all assigned homework.
	Correct and rework any problems marked as incorrect on homework or tests.
	See the instructor at least once a week for extra help—for a second explanation or a chance to work additional problems.
	Find a study group.
	Participate in class.
	Get A's on all the tests.

Activity 5.5

Establishing Action Steps to Reach Your Long-Term Goals

For this exercise, determine a long-term personal goal *and* a long-term academic goal for one of your courses. Then, for each long-term goal, identify two specific action steps that will take you closer to the bigger goal. As the term implies, these will be *action-oriented movements* toward your destination.

Remember to keep the goals measurable. State them in terms that will allow you to know when you have achieved them.

1. Personal goal: ....

Action steps to reach the personal goal:

1. ....

2. ....

What incentive or reward will there be for you to reach this goal?

....

2. Academic goal: ....

Action steps to reach the academic goal:

1. ....

2. ....

What incentive or reward will there be for you to reach this goal?

....

In any study skills book, you will find suggested steps to follow in goal setting. And incorporated into these plans you will usually find all (or most) of the previously mentioned six properties of a clearly stated goal. One model, for instance, uses the acronym SMART (Meyer, 2004). That is, goals need to be specific, measurable, attainable, realistic, and tangible.

Use whatever works for you.

Activity 5.6

Identifying Clearly Stated Goals

Dominic, from the chapter-opening story, has asked you to review the following list of personal goals. Put a check (✓) in the circle next to each item you think clearly states a goal and an X in the circle next to each item you think is not very clear.

- ○ I will do better in school by the end of this term.
- ○ I will raise my math average by at least one letter grade.
- ○ I will write something worthwhile in English class.
- ○ I need to remember more stuff.
- ○ I want my instructors to like me.
- ○ I will be able to write a clear thesis statement for every essay I am assigned.
- ○ I will study more effectively by appropriately rewarding myself each time I move closer to my goals.
- ○ I will be nicer to my family.
- ○ I will become a better friend.
- ○ I will become healthier by doing at least 30 minutes of aerobic exercise four days per week.

Take a moment and write what is wrong and what is right with each of the goals you just reviewed. *Pick one of the poorly written goals, and make it better for Dominic.*

What advice do you have for Dominic to be successful at achieving his goals? Briefly write down specific action steps here.

....

....

....

....

OBSTACLES, MISSTEPS, AND DETOURS

Think about your favorite movie or novel for a moment.* Can you remember the hero or heroine? That person likely started at a certain point in his or her life and ended at another at the conclusion of the story. In most novels and movies, the final scene represents some type of success or progress for the main character. However, that achievement does not occur without twists and turns of the plot. Those adventures—or misadventures—keep you turning the pages of the book or sitting in your seat watching the screen.

As the hero or heroine makes progress toward a particular goal, an obstacle presents itself and thwarts him or her from the goal. To continue requires gathering his or her thoughts, refocusing, and then moving ahead toward the goal. This continues until the final scene. Plotting the journey of the lead character would look more like the up-and-down path you see in Figure 5.4 than a straight line.

Figure 5.4

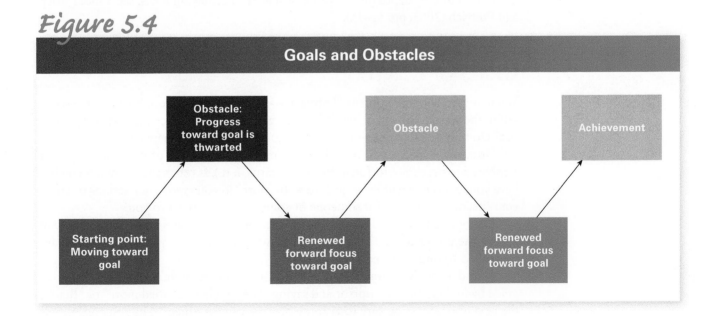

*For a more in-depth discussion of this movie/novel analogy, see Beck [2001]. Pay particular attention to her discussion of the change cycle.

Just like the hero or heroine, you, too, will probably have missteps along the way. Goals are set in the *real world*. Problems, unforeseen circumstances, and "bad luck" are also part of the *real world*. Expect them, plan for them, but keep moving toward the desired result.

Here are some common obstacles to achieving goals:

- **Not expecting mistakes.** If you expect to move along without any glitches and one occurs, you may become so dejected that you will give up. For instance, when planning the steps to finish a term paper, leave flexibility and "breathing room" for an unexpected detour, like a computer malfunction. Being prepared for missteps and wrong turns will make you better able to handle them. They still won't be pleasant, but you will be able to remain focused in dealing with them.

- **Blaming obstacles for your lack of abilities.** Sometimes, an obstacle is beyond your control. Sometimes, it happens because you have never worked toward this type of goal before. You might become frustrated with a particular instructor's teaching style, or the content of a course may stretch you beyond your previous knowledge and experience. It can become too easy to say "I'm stupid" or "I don't *do* history!" Skill levels can change. Each time you enter a classroom, you bring your *old skills* to a *new situation*.

- **Not changing your environment.** If you want to increase your biology grade by one letter grade by the end of the term, you may need to change your study environment. Or maybe the study group you work with is not right for you. Take stock of where, when, and how you are doing things, and then make a well-planned move. It may mean having to make choices about when and where to meet with your friends. Learn to say no if saying yes to a particular situation will compromise your goals. Refer to the sections earlier in this chapter called Commitment and Are You in the Way?

For a more in-depth discussion of obstacles to achieving goals, see VanderStoep and Pintrich (2003, pp. 32–35).

LOCUS OF CONTROL

You may face one more potential obstacle—one that springs from how you see yourself in the world. Do you believe that your actions can influence the way things turn out? Do things just happen to you, or do you cause things to happen?

How you answer questions like these reflects your **locus of control**, a concept attributed to psychologist Julian Rotter (Mearns, n.d.). It refers to how much you believe your actions can affect your future. In short, do you *expect* your actions to affect your life, or do you *wait* for someone or something to happen to you?

A simplified description of locus of control is the *focus of one's power*. Do you believe the power to control events resides within you, or do you believe events are controlled by outside forces?

A student with an *internal* locus of control, for example, explains a poor test grade by looking into the mirror and saying "I should have studied more" or "Before the next exam, I will be sure to visit my professor in his office." The responsibility is placed on that student's shoulders *by that* student. On the other hand, a student who is more apt to blame the teacher exhibits an *external* locus of control. Statements such as "That teacher is not fair" or "How could I possibly do well when the teacher

Figure 5.5

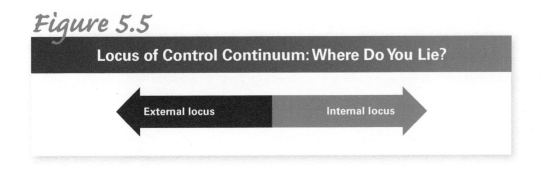

covers so much material each class period?" characterize a student looking to assign responsibility elsewhere.

Generally speaking, a person's locus of control can be internal and external. That is, there will be situations in which you exhibit an internal locus of control and times you are more external. Refer to Figure 5.5. As with any continuum, few people are found on either extreme. Most of us fall somewhere in between. But upon reflection, we notice that we tend to lean to one end or the other.

Are you a person who generally takes responsibility for his or her actions? Or are you someone who is more apt to blame someone else? Use this information to heighten your awareness.

Recognize that we all face times when *other people* (external) have significant influence or control over what we will or will not do. For instance, the college or university sets the final exam schedule, and the students must adjust their own schedules to meet those dates.

So, here is the point: Pick what you can have an impact on, and then address it. You must be able to make realistic assessments of what is within your ability to change—and what is not. Too often, we attempt to fix what we cannot, should not, or will not. First, identify the *what* and the *why*. Make a realistic assessment of *where* to go and *what* steps to take.

Ask yourself these four simple questions:

- *What* happened?
- *Why* did it happen?
- *Where* do I go from here? (Think of this as your goal.)
- *What* is my first step? My second step? (Think of these as your action steps.)

Activity 5.7

Identifying Locus of Control

Read the following scenario, and then identify and explain whether the person exhibits an external or internal locus of control:

Natasha has missed a number of math classes lately due to child care difficulties. She recently missed two quizzes—and the instructor does not allow makeup quizzes. She fears that her grade may be severely reduced as a result.

Yesterday morning, Natasha went to the instructor's office. She said, "I know it is my responsibility to get to class and take the quizzes on time. But my babysitter is no longer available. I think I have a new person lined up. Is there any extra credit I can do to make up for the lost points on those two quizzes?"

1. Did Natasha exhibit an internal or external locus of control? Briefly explain your answer.

....

....

....

2. How can this knowledge benefit you?

....

....

....

W.I.N.: Do You Know What's Important Now?

Successful athletic coaches motivate their student athletes. When their players confront a difficult choice, coaches often instruct them to follow the principle of W.I.N.—What's Important Now. So, every day, take some step toward your goal, no matter how small or seemingly insignificant. Ask yourself, What's important now for me to achieve my goal? Once you have identified the step, then act on it. If you do not make progress toward your goal, no one else will.

Activity 5.8

Fix What?

R
E
D

Let's say you wish to raise your English grade by 20 points. What's the first thing you have to do? You must understand why you are not doing well. That is, before you can fix the problem, you have to know what the problem is. This is a basic step for critical thinking and problem solving.

For this activity, pick a class (or something in your life outside school that needs fixing/changing). Write your subject here:

I need to fix/change ....

Assumptions: Now, briefly explain how you know this change is needed. What specific facts tell you that you need to change or fix something? Write them here:

....

....

....

Evaluating information: Here comes the tricky part. From the following list, choose the items that may be connected to your problem. Check as many as apply, and at the end, briefly explain your selections.

- ○ Teacher
- ○ Parent
- ○ Student
- ○ Friend
- ○ School administration
- ○ Government
- ○ Boss
- ○ Spouse
- ○ Girlfriend/Boyfriend
- ○ Society
- ○ Other (specify) ....

- ○ Some combination (specify) ....

Explanation: ....

....

....

Conclusion: Finally, look at what items you checked. What is your connection to each one? Can you, in fact, make an immediate impact on each item you checked? Or are some more long term and therefore not of help right now? For instance, you may believe you are doing poorly this term because you have to take required courses you have no interest in taking. Well, that may be the case. Nevertheless, you probably aren't going to change the school's requirements by the time the semester ends.

Goal: Based on the critical thinking you did in the previous item, write a goal that addresses what you need to fix or change. ....

Chapter SUMMARY

This college term will pass quickly—and another will approach just as quickly. The weeks ahead will require you to complete academic work, focus on planning, have a strong knowledge of yourself, and apply strategies to take responsibility for your time and behavior (an *internal locus of control*). In the end, it will be up to you to stay motivated, set goals, and set your course for success. You control your fate.

Keep the following points in mind as you move with determination through your semester:

- Motivation is the driving force moving you toward your goals.

- Goals provide purpose and meaning to life. They can help energize you to reach the destination by keeping the end in focus.

- Action steps need to be specific, measurable, and responsible.

- Goals are set in the real world—and problems, unforeseen circumstances, and bad luck are also part of the real world. Expect them, and plan for them.

- Effective goals are written, specific, measurable, realistic, and have an end point—a date for which to strive.

- Your locus of control influences whether you believe life will just happen to you or that you will be able to influence what happens.

CRITICALLY THINKING
What Have You Learned in This Chapter?

Let's apply what you learned in this chapter to help Dominic from the chapter-opening scenario. However, before you address Dominic's problem and propose a solution, take a moment to think about the main points of the chapter.

Review your notes from this chapter and also the key terms, chapter learning outcomes, boldface chapter headings, and figures and tables. For instance, consider how the chapter learning outcomes may be used to help Dominic:

- List and briefly describe the major motivating force in your life.

- Identify a motivational barrier and at least one strategy to overcome it.

- Create a goal statement that includes what you want to do, how you will do it, why you will do it, and when you will accomplish it.

- Evaluate your locus of control.

© Shutterstock

TEST YOUR LEARNING

Now that you have reviewed the main points of this chapter, reread Dominic's story. Pretend that you are Dominic's study skills instructor. Using the R.E.D. Model for critical thinking, help Dominic critically review his concerns.

Recognize Assumptions

Facts: What are the facts in Dominic's situation? List them.

Opinions: What opinions do you find in this situation? List them.

Assumptions: Are Dominic's assumptions accurate?

Evaluate Information:

Help Dominic compile a list of questions that will help him make the most appropriate decision.

What emotions seem to be motivating Dominic?

What, if anything, is missing from his thought process?

Do you see any confirmation bias?

Draw Conclusions:

Based on the facts and the questions you have presented, what conclusions can you draw?

What advice do you have for Dominic? What solutions do you propose?

Based on your suggestions, do you see any assumptions?

Finally, based on what you learned about using critical thinking, motivation, and goal setting, what plan of action do you suggest for Dominic?

Learning 6 STYLES

It's what you learn after you know it all that counts.

—*Attributed to Harry S Truman,*
33rd President of the United States

CHAPTER LEARNING OUTCOMES

By the time you finish reading this chapter and completing its activities, you will be able to do the following:

- Identify the preferences of your particular learning style.

- Develop practical strategies to use your learning style in class.

- Develop practical strategies to use your learning style in your life outside class.

- Apply your knowledge of multiple intelligences to develop strategies for academic success.

The Case of ALLEN

Allen is a happy and well-adjusted first-year college student. He reads his assignments, attends class, participates in all discussions, and studies for all of his exams. Unfortunately, his grades are not what he would like them to be.

On the suggestion from an adviser, Allen recently took a learning-styles assessment. Although the assessment did not reveal anything new, it reinforced that Allen was a visual learner and that he preferred a quiet and well-lit study area.

© Shutterstock

Key Terms

Attention
Auditory learning preference
Environmental factors
   (affecting learning)
Intelligence
Kinesthetic learning
   preference
Learning preference
Learning style
Multiple intelligences
Read/Write learning
   preference
Visual learning preference

Chapter INTRODUCTION

Imagine this: You walk into a doctor's office and announce, "Doc, I don't feel well. Can you give me a prescription?" Any reasonable doctor would first need to know some specifics: What are your symptoms? What medications are you taking? To what drugs are you allergic? In other words, the doctor would have to recognize you as an individual patient with characteristics that make you distinct and separate from other patients in the waiting room.

The same goes for study skills. While your instructor and textbook will introduce you to a variety of study skill strategies, you will need to

Allen knows that one of his current problems is that all of his professors lecture with very few visual aids. Some do not even use PowerPoint. He is having difficulty staying focused in class. After about 10 minutes of a lecture, his mind wanders, and so he misses notes and important points.

Allen's grades are beginning to suffer, and he is becoming discouraged. He is considering switching to all online classes to fix the situation.

CRITICALLY THINKING
about *Allen's* situation

You are Allen's adviser. What strategies would you suggest that he follow?

concentrate on the ones that best fit your individual learning style. Simply put, be mindful of how you learn, and be willing to examine and make adjustments to what you have done in the past. Just because you have developed the habit of studying this way or that does not mean that way is best for you.

If we are honest with ourselves, we will likely admit that many of our habits are not productive in terms of accomplishing tasks. We do things a certain way, well, because that is how we have always done them.

MyStudentSuccessLab

MyStudentSuccessLab (www .mystudentsuccesslab.com) is an online solution designed to help you 'Start strong, Finish stronger' by building skills for ongoing personal and professional development.

I am your constant companion.
I am your greatest helper or your heaviest burden.
I will push you onward or drag you down to failure.
I am completely at your command.
Half the things you do, you might just as well turn over to me,
and I will be able to do them quickly and correctly.
I am easily managed; you must merely be firm with me.
Show me exactly how you want something done, and after a
few lessons I will do it automatically.
I am a HABIT!

—**Author unknown**

The main goal of this chapter is to help you become a more mindful learner. Rather than do things because that is how you "have always done them," you will be asked to dig deeper and discover strategies that will help you process the information you receive each day efficiently and effectively. You will benefit the most when you concentrate on those strategies that best fit your learning style. Question old habits, build on what works, and embrace new strategies.

Activity 6.1

Reflecting on Your Learning Style

As you do in completing all of the reflective activities in this book, you should write from your heart. This exercise is not meant for you to answer just like your classmates—or to match what you may think the instructor wants to see. Take the time to give a respectful and responsible general accounting of your experiences with your study environment and how you prefer to learn (verbally, visually, or with movement). Conducting a truthful self-assessment now will help you build on the insights you already have while developing those you lack.

For each of the following items, circle the number that best describes your *typical* experience. Here is the key for the numbers:

0 = never, 1 = almost never, 2 = occasionally, 3 = frequently, 4 = almost always, 5 = always

When considering your past successes and challenges with learning, how often:

1.	Did you notice that a classroom lecture—when it was accompanied with photos, video, or a PowerPoint presentation—either positively or negatively affected your ability to understand the material?	0	1	2	3	4	5
2.	Did you notice that directions—when they were given verbally, without any visuals—affected your ability to understand the message?	0	1	2	3	4	5
3.	Did you notice that when you were allowed to do something physically with material, like create a picture or model of it, it had an impact on your learning?	0	1	2	3	4	5
4.	Did you notice that the amount of lighting in a room either positively or negatively affected your ability to study or pay attention?	0	1	2	3	4	5

5.	Were you aware of how the temperature of a classroom or study space had an impact on how well you focused on the topic at hand?	**0**	**1**	**2**	**3**	**4**	**5**
6.	Did you perform better when the instructor clearly mapped out the exact steps you had to follow to complete a task?	**0**	**1**	**2**	**3**	**4**	**5**
7.	Did you notice the effect that eating or not eating a meal before an exam had on your performance?	**0**	**1**	**2**	**3**	**4**	**5**
8.	Did you notice how background noise helped or hindered your concentration?	**0**	**1**	**2**	**3**	**4**	**5**

Add up your scores for items 1, 2, 3, and 6. Divide by 4. Write your answer here: _____

Using the key provided to explain each number (0, 1, 2, 3, 4, 5), complete this sentence: When it comes to how I receive and understand information, I _____ am aware of my learning preference (for taking in or giving out information).

Add up your scores for items 4, 5, 7, and 8. Divide by 4. Write your answer here: _____

Using the key provided to explain each number (0, 1, 2, 3, 4, 5), complete this sentence: When it comes to how environmental factors affect my learning, I _____ am aware of these factors.

Based on your answers, what insights have you gained about your experiences with identifying and using your learning style?

....

....

PROCESSING INFORMATION

> *If keeping someone's interest in a lecture were a business, it would have an 80 percent failure rate.*
> —John Medina, author and molecular biologist

Brain researchers have found that the more closely we pay **attention** to something, the better chance we have of learning it. While that sounds obvious, remember that when we pay attention, we tend to concentrate on the topic, issue, or event that is before us. Studies suggest that it is not uncommon for people to mentally "check out" somewhere between 10 and 15 minutes from the start of a lecture.

Think of the implications for you. When you are attentive and engaged—that is, when you pay attention and take an active part in your course work—the chances for success increase significantly. John Medina, author of *Brain Rules: 12 Principles for Surviving and Thriving at Work, Home, and School*, has stated, "The more attention the brain pays to a given stimulus, the more elaborately the information will be encoded— and retained. . . . Whether you are an eager preschooler or a bored-out-of-your-mind undergrad, better attention always equals better learning" (2008, p. 74).

So, in simple terms, pay attention to the instructor, and you will have a better chance of remembering the material. However, what is simple is not always easy. You could make a great argument that "It is up to the instructor to make the class interesting enough to pay attention to." But there are things you can do to help yourself concentrate in class and beyond.

LEARNING STYLES*

One way to become an engaged student is to know as much as possible about the way you learn—and then apply that knowledge to your academic tasks. When people examine their **learning styles**, they attempt to understand the characteristics or traits of how they learn. In other words, they look at what factors affect how they learn.

You may have heard someone say that she is a *visual learner* (learns by seeing photos or pictures, for instance). Another might claim to be an *auditory learner* (he has to hear something to understand it). Or some of your friends may have mentioned how **environmental factors** affect them. For instance, the following environmental factors can affect learning:

- Lighting (how the room is illuminated)
- Sound (how much silence or noise surrounds us)
- Temperature (how cool or hot the room is)
- Comfort of furniture (how soft, hard, or firm the chair is)
- Structure of time and/or task (how much time you have to sit in the classroom or in a group)
- Ability to move about (how much movement you can have while in the classroom)
- Peer interaction (who you work with during the class)

LEARNING PREFERENCES

Your **learning preference** is one part of your learning style. It refers to the manner in which you process (take in and put out) information. Students typically have a particular preference that helps them best understand the material being presented.

Although the material in this section just scratches the surface of a large body of research, it will provide an opportunity for you to think critically about how you best process your course materials.[†] Generally, you will hear about

---

*This section based on Piscitelli (2011), pp. 89–90.

[†]A great deal has been written about learning styles. The intent here is to provide a brief overview. This chapter uses the VARK instrument to help you examine your preference for using information—part of a learning style. You may also wish to examine the following sources: Nancy Lightfoot Matte and Susan Hillary Henderson, *Success, Your Style: Right- and Left-Brain Techniques for Learning* (Belmont, CA: Wadsworth, 1995); Rita Dunn and Kenneth Dunn, *Teaching Students Through Their Individual Learning Styles: A Practical Approach* (Reston, VA: Reston, 1978); Roger G. Swartz, *Accelerated Learning: How You Learn Determines What You Learn* (Durant, OK: EMIS, 1991); and James Keefe, *Learning Style Handbook: II. Accommodating Perceptual, Study and Instructional Preferences* (Reston, VA: National Association of Secondary School Principals, n.d.).

three particular preferences: auditory, visual, and kinesthetic. A fourth preference, read/write, is part of the VARK Questionnaire, which you will use later in this chapter.

Auditory Learning Preference. Some individuals can *listen* to a verbal explanation of a task and then carry out the assignment successfully. These students receive auditory (oral) directions and translate them into a product. They prefer taking in and putting out information using their sense of hearing. Many times, these are verbal individuals. They may find group discussions enjoyable, and they probably have a talent for explaining (or at least attempting to explain) things to others.

Visual Learning Preference. Other students must see something before processing it effectively. For example, if these students had to set up a new high-definition, flat-screen television, they would find it very helpful to have diagrammed instructions about what to do. They would benefit from seeing colorful lines and arrows showing how to connect the various wires and cables to the high-speed cable box, as well as the speakers to the television. The use of such visual aids enhances their ability to learn. If they receive only oral instructions, the process will be more difficult for them to complete. Students who gravitate to this type of learning tend to respond well to videos, photos, PowerPoint slides, and graphic illustrations.

Kinesthetic Learning Preference. Other people work best by moving, handling, or manipulating objects. A student who is better able to understand a biological principle by physically *doing* a laboratory experiment learns in a kinesthetic (or body movement) manner. This student might get more out of a lesson if he or she were able to go on a field trip to see and touch rock formations, rather than simply read about them from a geology textbook. Similarly, for this student, a role-play activity may hold more interest than a lecture. Athletic competition is another example of a kinesthetic activity. Active physical engagement may tend to keep this type of learner focused and on task.

Read-Write Learning Preference. This is one of the VARK preferences. People with this preference for learning do well reading textbooks, magazines, blogs, and class handouts. They also tend to feel comfortable taking notes and writing essays (Fleming, 2001–2009a). As the name implies, these people are comfortable *reading and writing* during the learning process.

HOW DO *YOU* LEARN?

The activity that follows gives you the chance to use a learning preference inventory: the VARK Questionnaire (Version 7.1). Once you have completed the VARK instrument, you will have your profile of the four preferences for taking in and putting out information: *visual, auditory, read/write,* and *kinesthetic* (Fleming, 2001–2009b). Some people have a strong preference for one of these learning modalities, and others have a preference for more than one.

Again, think of a *preference* as something you would select to do—a choice that you would make. In the case of your learning preference, it is a way you choose to work. There is no right or wrong preference. There is *your* preference.

Activity 6.2

The VARK Questionnaire (Version 7.1): How Do I Learn Best?

For each item, choose the answer that best explains your preference, and circle the letter next to it. **Please circle more than one** if a single answer does not match your perception. Leave blank any question that does not apply.

1. You are helping someone who wants to go to your airport, town center, or railway station. You would:

   a. draw or give her a map.
   b. tell her the directions.
   c. write down the directions (without a map).
   d. go with her.

2. You are not sure whether a word should be spelled 'dependent' or 'dependant.' You would:

   a. see the words in your mind and choose by the way they look.
   b. think about how each word sounds and choose one.
   c. find it in a dictionary.
   d. write both words on paper and choose one.

3. You are planning a holiday for a group. You want some feedback from them about the plan. You would:

   a. use a map or website to show them the places.
   b. phone, text, or e-mail them.
   c. give them a copy of the printed itinerary.
   d. describe some of the highlights.

4. You are going to cook something as a special treat for your family. You would:

   a. look through the cookbook for ideas from the pictures.
   b. ask friends for suggestions.
   c. use a cookbook where you know there is a good recipe.
   d. cook something you know without the need for instructions.

5. A group of tourists wants to learn about the parks or wildlife reserves in your area. You would:

   a. show them Internet pictures, photographs, or picture books.
   b. talk about or arrange a talk for them about parks or wildlife reserves.
   c. give them a book or pamphlets about the parks or wildlife reserves.
   d. take them to a park or wildlife reserve, and walk with them.

6. You are about to purchase a digital camera or mobile phone. Other than price, what would most influence your decision?

   a. Its having a modern design and looking good.
   b. Hearing the salesperson tell me about its features.
   c. Reading the details about its features.
   d. Trying or testing it.

7. Remember a time when you learned how to do something new. Try to avoid choosing a physical skill (e.g., riding a bike). You learned best by:

   a. diagrams and charts—visual clues.
   b. listening to somebody explaining it and asking questions.
   c. written instructions (e.g., a manual or textbook).
   d. watching a demonstration.

8. You have a problem with your heart. You would prefer that the doctor:

   a. showed you a diagram of what was wrong.
   b. described what was wrong.
   c. gave you something to read to explain what was wrong.
   d. used a plastic model to show what was wrong.

9. You want to learn a new program, skill, or game on a computer. You would:

   a. follow the diagrams in the book that came with it.
   b. talk with people who know about the program.
   c. read the written instructions that came with the program.
   d. use the controls or keyboard.

10. I like websites that have:

    a. interesting design and visual features.

    b. audio channels, where I can hear music, radio programs, or interviews.

    c. interesting written descriptions, lists, and explanations.

    d. things I can click on, shift, or try.

11. Other than price, what would most influence your decision to buy a new nonfiction book?

    a. It looks appealing.

    b. A friend talks about it and recommends it.

    c. You quickly read parts of it.

    d. It has real-life stories, experiences, and examples.

12. You are using a book, CD, or website to learn how to take photos with your new digital camera. You would like to have:

    a. diagrams showing the camera and what each part does.

    b. a chance to ask questions and talk about the camera and its features.

    c. clear written instructions with lists and bullet points about what to do.

    d. many examples of good and poor photos and how to improve them.

13. Do you prefer a teacher or a presenter who uses:

    a. diagrams, charts, or graphs?

    b. question and answer, talk, group discussion, or guest speakers?

    c. handouts, books, or readings?

    d. demonstrations, models, or practical sessions?

14. You have finished a competition or test and would like some feedback. You would like to have feedback:

    a. using graphs showing what you had achieved.

    b. from somebody who talks it through with you.

    c. using a written description of your results.

    d. using examples from what you have done.

15. You are going to choose food at a restaurant or cafe. You would:

    a. look at what others are eating or look at pictures of each dish.

    b. listen to the waiter or ask friends to recommend choices.

    c. choose from the descriptions in the menu.

    d. choose something that you have had there before.

16. You have to make an important speech at a conference or special occasion. You would:

    a. make diagrams or get graphs to help explain things.

    b. write a few key words and practice saying your speech over and over.

    c. write out your speech and learn from reading it over several times.

    d. gather many examples and stories to make the talk real and practical.

	a)	b)	c)	d)
Please count your choices (the number of times you marked each letter. Place your answers to the right.)	**Visual**	**Aural**	**Read/Write**	**Kinesthetic**

CALCULATING YOUR PREFERENCES. Once you have determined your preferences, visit the VARK website (www. vark-learn.com) and study the "Helpsheets" to find learning strategies for each of the preferences. Finally, reflect for a moment on the Helpsheet for your preference. How will you use this information today?

PRACTICAL APPLICATIONS

Instruments such as the VARK can provide important insights that allow you to use your critical-thinking skills. For instance, if you have difficulty in the classroom (say, paying attention), apply what you have learned about VARK preferences to your studies. The problem might be related to whether you have been handling information in the most effective manner *for you*. If you are a visual learner but never play to that strength, you might be making things harder for yourself.

Let's assume, for example, you have to study for a quiz on the branches and functions of the nervous system. If your preferred method for learning is auditory, you could recite the information aloud to yourself in an attempt to hear and "burn" the concepts into your memory. You could also record the information into a digital recorder and then play it back.

If, however, you learn best with the read/write preference, you could read your class textbook, review your class notes, and then write a brief outline or summary of the material.

You could just as well draw up a diagram of the nervous system and physically label it as a warm-up activity for your in-class quiz. Such a study approach would encourage you to use various preferences. Drawing a diagram and then labeling the particular parts engages more of the brain than just staring at a piece of notebook paper with terms written on it. It also allows you to work kinesthetically (drawing and physically labeling the diagram) and visually (looking at the diagram and the labels). Table 6.1 (p. 139) provides additional strategies to use your preferences to maximum success.

For the remainder of this chapter (as well as this book and this school term), refer to your VARK preferences. Use them to help you process, organize, and understand the vast amounts of information you will receive. Moreover, do not forget to use your problem-solving skills when you encounter academic challenges. If, for example, you end up with a professor whose teaching style is at odds with your learning style, first acknowledge that the difference exists, and then come up with a plan that draws on your strengths (Piscitelli, 2011, p. 94).

Activity 6.3

Critically Thinking about Your Learning Styles

R **E** **D** The R.E.D. Model (**R**ecognize Assumptions, **E**valuate Information, **D**raw Conclusions) provides a systematic way to approach critical thinking through the use of an easy-to-remember acronym.

For this activity, concentrate on how you can use the preference information you identified for yourself in the VARK Questionnaire (Activity 6.2). Apply the R.E.D. Model to your learning preference.

Critical-Thinking Step	Application to Your Learning Preference	Your Explanation (Here or on a Separate Piece of Paper)
Recognizing Assumptions	Based on your experiences, how do you know the VARK Questionnaire has (or has not) accurately identified your preference?	
Evaluating Information	Clearly state what your particular learning preference is, according to the VARK. Explain specifically (give an example) how this preference has shown itself in your school experiences.	
Drawing Conclusions	Based on the evidence before you, does your conclusion about your learning preference make sense? How do you believe the VARK assessment of your learning preference connects to your academic progress? That is, how can this assessment help in school and in your world outside school? What insights have you gained about your learning preference?	

Activity 6.4

How Do You Learn Best?

Reflect on the various ways you process information. Then answer the following questions

1. *Auditory*: Describe a recent class situation in which you understood the material by *hearing* the explanation. You really "got it"! Rate how often this happens on a scale of 1 (almost never) to 5 (almost always). Explain why you think you did or *did* not get it.

    Rating: ....

    Explanation: ....

    ....

2. *Visual*: Describe a recent class situation in which you understood the material by *seeing* the explanation. Maybe the instructor used a video, model, or interactive website. Whatever she used, you really "got it"! Rate how often this happens on a scale of 1 (almost never) to 5 (almost always). Explain why you think you did or did *not* get it.

    Rating: ....

    Explanation: ....

    ....

3. *Kinesthetic*: Describe a recent class situation in which you understood the material by *physically doing something*. Maybe it was a science lab, or maybe you had to construct a project. Whatever happened, you really "got it"! Rate how often this happens on a scale of 1 (almost never) to 5 (almost always). Explain why you think you did or did *not* get it.

    Rating: ....

    Explanation: ....

    ....

4. *Read/write*. Describe a recent class situation in which you understood the material by both *reading* and *writing*. Maybe it was reading your class notes and then writing a one-paragraph summary. Whatever happened, you really "got it"! Rate how often this happens on a scale of 1 (almost never) to 5 (almost always). Explain why you think you did or did *not* get it.

    Rating: ....

    Explanation: ....

    ....

5. *Environment*: Describe the environment (climate, lighting, ventilation, sound) in which you learn the best.

    ....

    ....

    ....

MAKING LEARNING-STYLES INFORMATION WORK FOR YOU

It is one thing to *know* how you learn best, but it is quite another to *use* that knowledge. When we actively learn, we listen, view or manipulate information, *and* then we process that information. That is, we *use* it in some way.

Table 6.1 provides questions and suggestions to apply learning-style information to your academic success. As you read these suggestions, think back to the chapter-opening situation about Allen. Would any of these suggestions help him solve his problem?

MULTIPLE INTELLIGENCES*

Whereas *learning style* looks at, among other things, our preference for taking in and putting out information, **intelligence** refers to our ability to use information to solve problems—to use the information for practical purposes. *Learning style* looks at ways we feel comfortable using information. *Intelligence* examines what we do with that information.

Think of it this way: Intelligence is the *what*, and learning style is the *how*. When we use our intelligence, we reason, solve problems, and use a set of skills to interact with our environment. That is *what* we do. We do those things with our hearing, sight, and touch—our learning style. That is *how* we do it.

*This section based on Piscitelli (2011), pp. 94–96.

Table 6.1 **Make Learning Styles Work for You**

If You Show a Preference for . . .	Then Ask Yourself . . .	A Few Suggestions Include . . .
Auditory learning	How can I use verbal cues to help me understand my class work?	• Sit as close to the instructor as possible to make sure you hear all that is said. • Record lessons (with instructor knowledge). • Record yourself as you describe your notes. Then play back and listen. • Join a study group. • If available, use the audio notes of your textbook located online. • Find and download a podcast that relates to the material the instructor presented in class.
Visual learning	How can I use visual aids to help me understand my class work?	• If available, use the visual aids on the textbook's online website. • Perhaps your instructors have posted PowerPoint presentations or outlines on their websites; if so, print them out. • Change your note-taking strategy by drawing more diagrams and flowcharts. • Find online videos that relate to the class lesson for the day.
Kinesthetic learning	How can I use movement to help me understand my class work?	• If possible, construct a model of your class material. • Perform a skit, role-play, or debate that uses the main ideas from the lesson. • If it helps, move, walk, or pace while you learn new concepts.
Read/write learning	How can I use print material and my writing skills to help me understand my class work?	• Read textbook introductions, key terms, chapter learning outcomes, and summaries to help focus your attention on the key points. • If there are activities in the chapter, write answers and review them.
Structure and clear explanation	How can I more formally structure my assignments?	• If your instructor's instructions sound vague, stop by his or her office and ask for clarification. • Join a study group to help you organize your thoughts. • Ask a classmate for his or her interpretation of the assignment instructions. • Use textbook organizers, like key terms, chapter learning outcomes, and summary sections.
A quiet study environment	How can I minimize noise so that I can concentrate more on my studies?	• If you do not have a quiet space at your residence, block regular time on your calendar to work in the campus library. • Be mindful of eyestrain, which can be caused by certain types of lighting.
A brightly lighted study area	How can I have the best lighting for my studies?	• Buy a small desk light for your study area. • When possible, read outdoors in sunlight.

Harvard professor Howard Gardner did pioneering research in the area of **multiple intelligences**. He maintains that the traditional manner of measuring intelligence (IQ) with a single number is misleading. It leads us to believe that there is only one intelligence. According to Gardner in his breakthrough book *Frames of Mind: The Theory of Multiple Intelligences* (1983), we have eight different intelligences to pick from when solving problems. Many of us, though, use only two or three of them. Just think of what you will be able to do once you tap into as many of the eight intelligences as possible.

And who knows whether more intelligences will be identified? Researchers have investigated a ninth intelligence: spiritual or existential. It refers to the ability to connect with nonphysical or metaphysical stimuli. But for our purposes, we will look at the first eight intelligences.

THE EIGHT INTELLIGENCES

Gardner maintains we all have at least a trace of each intelligence. Some of the intelligences may be highly developed, and some a little less developed. Here is Gardner's list, with a brief explanation of each category and possible connections to life choices (Armstrong, 1994):

- **Linguistic intelligence ("word smart"):** You are good with the written word. You can express yourself with language. Occupations that might rely on this intelligence include writer, speaker, lawyer, and teacher.
- **Logical-mathematical intelligence ("number smart"):** You can think abstractly and solve problems. Logic and order are strengths for you. You understand cause and effect. You can analyze material. Numbers do not scare you. Occupations include scientist and mathematician.
- **Spatial intelligence ("art smart"):** You can visually re-create your world. A clear sense of direction is involved, too. Occupations include sculptor, painter, and anatomy teacher.
- **Bodily-kinesthetic intelligence ("body smart"):** You have coordinated control of your own body. You have a strong sense of learning by movement or action. You can effectively use your hands, fingers, and arms to make something. Occupations include athlete, actor, and dancer.
- **Musical intelligence ("music smart"):** You have the ability to use the major components of music (rhythm and pitch). You can recognize patterns and use them effectively. Occupations include musician and dancer.
- **Interpersonal intelligence ("people smart"):** You understand the moods and motives of the people you associate with. If you are to deal effectively with other people, you must be skilled in this intelligence. Occupations include teacher, politician, and salesperson.
- **Intrapersonal intelligence ("me smart"):** You draw strength and energy from within yourself. You understand yourself and can apply that knowledge in real-life situations to produce the best results. You understand what is good for you. You know who you are and what you can do. You know what to get involved with and what to avoid. Occupations include independent-type positions, such as researcher and entrepreneur.
- **Naturalistic intelligence ("nature smart"):** You can understand, explain, and relate to things in the natural world around you. You have a unique ability to classify and separate items based on their characteristics. Occupations include botanist, zoologist, archaeologist, and environmentalist.

Figure 6.1

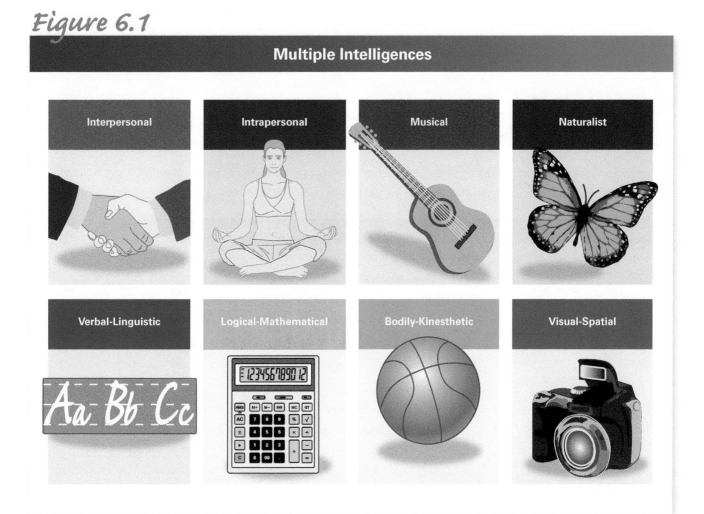

Figure 6.1 provides a visual view of the multiple intelligences.

In the interest of full disclosure, there are critics of Gardner's theory. For one critical review, see Ferguson (2009). Gardner actually responded to one critic in an article he co-authored with Seana Moran (2006).

HOW CAN YOU USE THIS INFORMATION TO ORGANIZE YOUR STUDIES?

At times, you will learn well by visual means, and other times, auditory techniques will be more productive. There will be times when your "word smart" intelligence stands out above all the others, and other times when you will exhibit great spatial capabilities ("art smart"). Or perhaps individual work might be your normal routine, but a study group can be appropriate when working with a troubling concept.

The point is to understand what works best *most of the time*. Then, use that knowledge to adapt to the situation in which you find yourself.

All students can benefit from tapping into multiple intelligences when learning class material. That means if you have a tendency to understand your textbook readings or class lecture notes primarily through your linguistic intelligence, you may benefit by reprocessing the same information with your interpersonal (study group) or spatial intelligence (model). Doing so will help your brain to develop a stronger connection with the information. And you will have a better chance to "hardwire" the pathways in your brain that will help you remember what you are learning. Think of nursery rhymes that children learn. They usually internalize them by using more than one intelligence: reading, singing, moving, and interacting with others.

Activity 6.5

Using Multiple Intelligences to Help Allen

The following table suggests two study strategies to use with each intelligence. Add a third strategy that might work (or has worked) for you. Again, consider what strategies might be appropriate for Allen (from the chapter-opening scenario).

Multiple Intelligence	Practical Suggestions for Your Academic Success
Linguistic intelligence ("word smart")	**1.** Use a note-taking summarizing strategy. **2.** Text message, establish a Facebook poll, or tweet a friend about your homework assignment. **3.** ....
Logical-mathematical intelligence ("number smart")	**1.** Construct a chart or pie graph to help you analyze the material. **2.** Apply your newly learned information to a situation or problem you have. **3.** ....
Spatial intelligence ("art smart")	**1.** Use an informal flowchart format for note taking. **2.** Use colored highlighters for your notes and textbook reading. **3.** ....
Bodily-kinesthetic intelligence ("body smart")	**1.** Move around when you study. Change study locations. **2.** If appropriate, draw or build a model to represent the material you want to understand. **3.** ....
Musical intelligence ("music smart")	**1.** Listen to background music while studying (as long as you can still concentrate on the study material). **2.** Put the class notes into a rhyme, rhythm, or beat. **3.** ....
Interpersonal intelligence ("people smart")	**1.** Find study groups that will help you master the class material. Maybe you can develop a virtual study group using Facebook or some other type of social networking service. **2.** Tutor a classmate. **3.** ....
Intrapersonal intelligence ("me smart")	**1.** Before you start to work, meditate, pray, or quietly reflect about the assignment you have to complete. Perhaps you could write a brief journal entry for yourself. **2.** Find a quiet place to study. **3.** ....
Naturalistic intelligence ("nature smart")	**1.** Study or read outside. **2.** Classify your study material into categories of similar characteristics. **3.** ....

Chapter SUMMARY

In this chapter, you thought about *how* you learn and *what* you can do with your particular learning preferences. You have examined the importance of taking control of your learning process. As each week on campus passes, you will begin to notice what *is* working for you and what is *not*. You will know where your challenges lie and what strengths you can draw on to meet them.

Before leaving this chapter, keep the following points in mind:

- Learning style examines the factors that influence how you process information.

- Learning preference addresses how you take in and put out information.

- According to the VARK Questionnaire, there are four preferences for taking in and putting out information: visual, auditory, read/write, and kinesthetic. Various factors—from the classroom setting to the manner of presentation by the teacher—will affect different people differently.

- Your preference for receiving and using information will not necessarily reflect the style of the person sitting next to you in class. It is your preference.

- The theory of multiple intelligences looks at what skills you will use to reason and solve problems in your environment.

CRITICALLY THINKING
What Have You Learned in This Chapter?

Let's apply what you learned in this chapter to help Allen from the chapter-opening scenario. However, before you look into Allen's problem and propose your solution, take a moment to think about the main points of the chapter.

Review your notes from this chapter and also the key terms, chapter learning outcomes, boldface chapter headings, and figures and tables. For instance, consider how the chapter learning outcomes may be used to help Allen.

- Identify the preferences of your particular learning style.

- Develop practical strategies to use your learning style in class.

- Develop practical strategies to use your learning style in your life outside class.

- Apply your knowledge of multiple intelligences to develop strategies for academic success.

© Shutterstock

TEST YOUR LEARNING:

Now that you have reviewed the main points of this chapter, reread Allen's story. Pretend that you are Allen's adviser. Using the R.E.D. Model for critical thinking, help Allen critically review his concerns.

(R)

Recognize Assumptions

Facts: What are the facts in Allen's situation? List them.

Opinions: What opinions do you find in this situation? List them here.

Assumptions: Are Allen's assumptions accurate?

(E)

Evaluate Information

Help Allen compile a list of questions that will help him make the most appropriate decision.

What emotions seem to be motivating Allen?

What, if anything, is missing from his thought process?

Do you see any confirmation bias?

(D)

Draw Conclusions

Based on the facts and the questions you have presented, what conclusions can you draw?

What advice do you have for Allen? What solutions do you propose?

Based on your suggestions, do you see any assumptions?

Finally, based on what you learned about using critical thinking and learning styles, what plan of action do you suggest for Allen?

Class-Time Listening
and NOTE
TAKING

We are what we repeatedly do.
Excellence then is not an act,
but a habit.

—Aristotle, Greek philosopher

CHAPTER LEARNING OUTCOMES

■ By the time you finish reading this chapter and completing its activities, you will be able to do the following:

■ Explain the teaching style and classroom expectations of each of your instructors.

■ Identify common classroom distractions and strategies to deal with each.

■ Provide at least two tips to help you pay attention in class.

■ Describe a strategy to help develop respectful working relationships with your instructors.

■ Use and evaluate one note-taking style for at least one week.

The Case *of* CONSUELA

Consuela enjoys college life. She likes her professors, her courses, and her classmates. Generally speaking, she is positive and excited about being on campus. However, she just received the grades from her first round of exams for the term. They were not what she had hoped for. Each grade was a full letter grade lower than she expected to receive.

"I don't understand," she said to herself. "I write everything that comes out of the professor's mouth. How come I am not performing well on the exams?" Consuela knew she had difficulty identifying the important things from her professors' lessons. And

© Shutterstock

Key Terms

Active learning
Attention
Civility
Classroom success
Distractions
Instructor styles
Note-taking styles
Online classes

Chapter INTRODUCTION

Students are expected to listen, remember, comprehend, and apply a great deal of information. In some cases, the information is quite complex. Each day brings new concepts, skills, and strategies. This can be both energizing and overwhelming: energizing because of the new insights gained but overwhelming because of the sheer volume of material.

This chapter describes strategies for **active learning** that will help you manage and learn course information while becoming an active participant in the classroom. While it is the responsibility of the instructor to plan that is why she diligently worked to get every word in her notes that she needed to remember.

Consuela had found that although she liked the course material, she was having a difficult time paying attention in class. When she pulled her crumpled notes from the bottom of her book bag (where she had placed them after class last week), she noticed large gaps in what she had written—and there was a good bit of doodling in the margins. "Perhaps there is a problem with my notes," she said to herself. "I thought I knew how to take notes, but obviously not!"

Consuela has come to you for assistance.

CRITICALLY THINKING
about *Consuela's* situation

How would you advise Consuela?

well thought out lessons, active learning places a lot of responsibility on the student. Students must do what they can to be engaged—involved—in the lesson.

This chapter describes strategies that will help you become more active and effective *inside* the classroom. For instance, you will read about and practice ways to determine your purpose in the classroom. That is, beyond showing up for attendance, why are you in class each day? Do you understand your instructor's teaching style and what that means for you?

MyStudentSuccessLab

MyStudentSuccessLab (www .mystudentsuccesslab.com) is an online solution designed to help you 'Start strong, Finish stronger' by building skills for ongoing personal and professional development.

Being a successful student results from what you do inside and outside the classroom. This chapter will examine what you can do to get the most from the hours spent inside your classrooms, and it will propose strategies to help you focus your attention, find the main points of a lesson, and then record those ideas in an organized and usable format. Developing mastery (competence) in what you do in your classes will help you gain confidence. And that will help you remain calm and in control of your life.

Activity 7.1

Reflecting on Your Current Level of Classroom Performance Skills

Before you answer the items that follow, reflect on your current level of classroom success skills. Think of how well (or poorly) you have performed in past classes—and classes so far this term.

As you do in completing all of the reflective activities in this book, you should write from your heart. This exercise is not meant for you to answer just like your classmates or to match what you may think the instructor wants to see. Take your time and give a respectful, responsible general accounting of your experiences with classroom success. Making a truthful self-assessment now will help you build on skills you have while developing those you lack.

For each of the following items, circle the number that best describes your *typical* experience with classroom success skills. Here is the key for the numbers:

0 = never, 1 = almost never, 2 = occasionally, 3 = frequently, 4 = almost always, 5 = always

When considering your past successes and challenges in the classroom, how often:

1.	Were you able to figure out what most of your instructors expected you to do to earn the highest grades possible?	0	1	2	3	4	5
2.	Did you adjust successfully to your instructors' teaching styles?	0	1	2	3	4	5
3.	Did you develop respectful and civil relationships with your instructors?	0	1	2	3	4	5
4.	Were you able to fight off distractions and pay attention during class?	0	1	2	3	4	5
5.	Did you take notes of lessons during class time?	0	1	2	3	4	5
6.	Were you able to pick out the most important ideas from your instructor's lectures?	0	1	2	3	4	5
7.	Did you use a consistent note-taking format during class?	0	1	2	3	4	5
8.	Did you maintain an organized notebook of your classroom notes and papers?	0	1	2	3	4	5

Add up your scores for items 1, 2, 3, and 4. Divide by 4. Write your answer here: _____.

Using the key provided to explain each number (0, 1, 2, 3, 4, 5), complete this sentence: When it comes to class, I _____ am able to develop positive and focused working relationships with my instructors.

Add up your scores for items 5, 6, 7, and 8. Divide by 4. Write your answer here: _____.

Using the key provided to explain each number (0, 1, 2, 3, 4, 5), complete this sentence: When it comes to note-taking skills, I _____ take and organize my notes effectively.

Based on your answers, what insights have you gained about your experiences with successful classroom strategies?

DO YOU KNOW WHAT THE INSTRUCTOR IS DOING IN THE FRONT OF THE ROOM?

An expert is someone who has succeeded in making decisions and judgments simpler through knowing what to pay attention to and what to ignore.

—*Edward de Bono, author and creativity expert*

This section will look at the front of the room: what the teacher is doing and what his or her expectations are. The next section will look at the back of the room: what you are doing in class.

INSTRUCTOR STYLE AND EXPECTATIONS

Just as you have a particular learning style to process information, so, too, do instructors have their own teaching styles. These **instructor styles** may range from lecture, to question and answer, to group work, to lab work, to discussion, to seat work.

Regardless of the method of presentation, each instructor also has a set of expectations for student performance. Some emphasize minute details; others seek broad generalizations for application to new situations. One may require you to be actively involved, while another wants you to sit and diligently copy his or her words of wisdom.

You will be able to determine instructor style and emphasis from class attendance and the course syllabus. If you are aware of your instructors' styles, expectations, and emphases, your preparation for each class can be more focused and your anxiety will lessen.

There is an added benefit, as well. Knowledge of teacher methodology can be very useful in determining what courses you want to take next term. If you learn best from *lecturing* instructors, then you might want to avoid instructors who rely heavily on interactive work. Obviously, the reverse also holds true. Knowing about instructors' styles will allow you to be more proactive in determining your class schedule.

Activity 7.2 will help you to determine what expectations your instructors have. Being aware of these expectations will help you prepare for and participate in class. You may wish to make a copy of the chart provided in the activity and complete it for each instructor you have this term. Check all the items that apply. Then place the completed chart where you will see it and be reminded of these important expectations.

Activity 7.2

Do You Know Your Instructors' Expectations for Success?

This activity consists of two parts. Part I asks you to consider all of your instructors this term. Part II gives you an opportunity to focus specifically on one instructor.

PART I: Write your instructors' names across the top-right part of the chart. Down the left side of the chart, you will find descriptions of styles and methods. Check the ones that apply to each instructor.

Write an Instructor's Name On Each Line →					
Instructor style ↓					
Primarily lectures the entire class					
Uses lots of question-and-answer discussions					
Uses lots of group activities					
Uses lots of in-class seatwork					
Concentrates on details such as dates, formulas, and classifications					
Pays close attention to grammar and writing skills					
Seldom assigns a writing assignment					
Is very serious and does not allow for any joking in class					
Is very serious but allows some lighthearted moments					
Never accepts an assignment late					
Accepts assignments late but with a penalty					
Accepts assignments late with no penalty					
Takes attendance each class					
Expects punctual attendance in class					
Seems to often go off on a tangent (stray from the topic)					
Stays on target, seldom straying from the topic at hand					

How can you use this information to help you be successful in each of your classes?

PART II: Focus on *only one* of your instructors for this part of the activity (based on Piscitelli [2011], pp. 107–108). It may be helpful to do this for a class in which you are having some challenges. Once you have completed the form, place it in your notebook or at your study area. Refer to it to remind yourself of these important expectations.

Course title: _____ Instructor's name: _____

My instructor requires me to:	**My instructor grades me with:**
○ Maintain a notebook	○ Reading quizzes
○ Complete mostly reading homework	○ Homework assignments
○ Complete mostly writing homework	○ Class participation
○ Complete reading and writing homework	○ Exams
○ Participate in class	○ Projects and/or research papers
○ Do group work	○ Group work
○ Attend class	○ Service-learning activities
○ Other	○ Other

My instructor uses a lot of:

○ Group work

○ Lecture

○ Class discussion

○ Worksheets

○ In-class problems or writing assignments

○ Material from the textbook

○ Field trips/real-world experiences

○ Other

My instructor's tests are:

○ Multiple choice

○ Matching

○ Completion/Fill in the blank

○ True/False

○ Short answer

○ Essay

○ Some combination of the above

○ Other

In this class, my biggest challenges will be:

○ Taking notes

○ Understanding the teacher

○ Dealing with distractions

○ Staying focused

○ Completing my homework on time

○ Following instructions

○ Answering questions orally

○ Working with groups

○ Getting ready for tests

○ Dealing with the volume of homework

○ Being a procrastinator

○ Managing my priorities

○ Getting to class on time

○ Having excessive absences

○ Having a negative attitude

○ Feeling sleepy

○ Other

Steps I can take to do well in this class:

○ Seek tutoring from the teacher

○ Seek tutoring from a classmate

○ Follow through on my assignments

○ Reevaluate how I prioritize my time

○ Ask for a seat change

○ Review my notes more regularly than I already do

○ Prepare earlier for exams

○ Break big projects into smaller, easier-to-manage steps

○ Be on time for class

○ Come to class each day

○ Ask the teacher for assistance

○ Seek computer-assisted instruction where available

○ Read the textbook more carefully

○ Review class notes regularly

○ Devote more time to high-quality studying

○ Find/Form a study group

○ Other

Based on what you know about this instructor, what will be your biggest challenges in this course?

....

....

....

....

DO YOU KNOW WHAT YOU ARE DOING IN THE BACK OF THE ROOM?

> *Do more than belong;*
> *participate.*
> *Do more than care: help.*
> *Do more than believe: practice.*
> *Do more than be fair: be kind.*
> *Do more than forgive: forget.*
> *Do more than dream: work.*
> —*William Arthur Ward,*
> *author and teacher*

WHAT CAN YOU DO TO MAXIMIZE YOUR CLASSROOM SUCCESS?

The key to **classroom success** is participation: engagement and involvement. If you can discuss a concept, you will have a much better chance of understanding it. If your instructor's style does not lend itself to class discussion, you can still be actively involved by anticipating the content of the lecture (based on reading assignments outside the classroom and past class sessions), asking questions of yourself, and so forth. Do what you can to maintain focus.

If you understand your instructor's style and expectations (Activity 7.2), you will be better able to identify the important class material. Understanding the major points of a lesson makes note taking easier. You do not need to write down every word spoken by the instructor.

YOU REALLY WANT TO PAY ATTENTION IN CLASS—BUT IT'S NOT EASY

The class has just started. You're in your seat, the teacher starts the lesson, and you start to "drift away." You really want to pay attention, but you find it difficult. And if you are representative of students in research studies, you may very well start "drifting" within 10 to 15 minutes of the beginning of class (Medina, 2008, p. 74).

Distractions—all the things that interrupt your thoughts and actions—are all around us. We live in a 24/7 world that is littered with short-term distractions that hinder concentration and affect our long-term goals.

Activity 7.3

What Can Consuela Do to Fight Distractions?

R E D The R.E.D. Model (**R**ecognize Assumptions, **E**valuate Information, **D**raw Conclusions) provides a systematic way to approach critical thinking through the use of an easy-to-remember acronym.

Consuela, from the chapter-opening situation, said she has difficulty paying attention in class. Before finding a solution to help her, it will be helpful to understand why she and other people have attention problems. From the list that follows, identify what you consider to be the top-three reasons that you, Consuela, or other students might start to daydream, become restless, or otherwise lose attention in class.

○   The student next to you is making noise.

○   You find the teacher or the lesson boring.

○   There is noise outside the classroom.

○   The material is too advanced/too complicated.

○   You like the teacher and the course, but the pace is too slow for you.

○   You like the teacher and the course, but the pace is too fast for you.

○   You are hungry.

○   You stayed up late last night.

○   You are reading text messages from your friends.

○   You are sending text messages to your friends.

○   You do not understand the lesson.

○   You have left your class material (pencils, pens, paper, or book) at home or in the car.

○   You are thinking about the argument you had with a friend.

○   You do not know the answers to any of the questions the teacher is asking the class.

○   You are attracted to another student in the room.

○   A great sporting event is scheduled later this week.

○   It is your last class of the day.

○   List any other distractions you have encountered in class.

Now that you have identified the distractions, brainstorm with a classmate to identify methods for overcoming these distractions.

HOW DOES ONE "PAY ATTENTION"?

As a college student, you will receive and be expected to process a great deal of information. For our purposes here, let's examine the first step toward improving memory.

Before you can remember a name, a process, a date, or a telephone number, you must first notice it. This requires attention. But how does one "pay attention"?

Attention requires listening to and observing your surroundings. But more specifically, it requires you to sort through the vast amount of information that comes your way. You have to make sense of what is before you.

One researcher has described paying attention as "processing a limited amount of information from the enormous amount of information available" (Zadina, 2007). In other words, when you pay attention, you have to sift through all the stimuli bombarding you—and then decide to focus on a particular pertinent piece of that information.

TIPS FOR PAYING ATTENTION IN AND OUT OF CLASS

Follow these tips to help improve your ability to pay attention (Hallowell, 2007, pp. 178–185):

In Class

- Listen for verbal clues from the teacher.
- Stay involved in the class discussion.
- Move your seat away from distractions (such as noise and disruptive people).
- Listen to what classmates say and ask.
- Take notes and review them.
- Come to class prepared; read your assignments.

Outside Class

- Get appropriate sleep each night.
- Eat well, and avoid foods that make you sleepy.
- Exercise regularly.
- Eliminate distractions as best you can.
- Enjoy what you do.
- Avoid monotony.
- Avoid substance abuse.
- Laugh.
- Recognize that your attention has to be renewed; it is not an unending resource.

You can also allow yourself the luxury of "accepting" a distraction. Distracting thoughts can be merciless, continually nagging and interrupting you. Do this: Once the distracting thought intrudes, welcome it in. If possible, jot it down on a piece of paper: perhaps "Call Joe tonight" or "What time is the party on Friday?" Then, let it go. You have mentally told yourself that you will address the issue later.

A FRIENDLY REMINDER OF WHAT YOU ALREADY KNOW: Seven Steps to Classroom Success

You probably have heard instructors explain the importance of attendance. "You need to be here," they will say, "to learn and understand the material." The reality is that your physical presence, while important, is only part of the success equation.

Not only do you need to be there in class, but you also need to be there in class. That is, your attention and your thoughts need to be focused on the class lesson. Your physical presence is important, as it allows you to hear explanations, ask questions, and add to the class discussions. You know the importance of being in class—that is not new information.

But every so often, we can all find wisdom in reminders of past lessons. Think of the following checklist as providing basic strategies that will move you toward having a more active and successful term:*

*I would like to thank Professor Joseph B. Cuseo for helping me focus these thoughts. He facilitated a session at the 2004 Conference on the First Year Experience (Dallas, Texas) that addressed many of these issues.

1. **Do you come to class?** Be serious about your education. It is difficult to meet instructor expectations if you are sitting in the student lounge or asleep in your bed during class time.

2. **Do you bring everything you need for class?** This is not the time to be without paper, pen, or textbook. A baseball player would not take the field without a glove. You, too, need to have your proper tools of the trade.

3. **Do you arrive on time?** Punctuality is important. Many instructors orchestrate each moment of class. A review of the last class might be provided at the very beginning of the current class. Or perhaps the instructor will announce a new test date. You most definitely do not want to miss that important nugget of information. And remember that latecomers are almost always a distraction to the instructor and the rest of the students. If you do arrive late, enter quietly (hold the door) and quickly find a seat. And turn off your cell phone, please.

4. **Do you sit where you will benefit the most?** To minimize distractions, you may wish to sit close to where the instructor is standing. To see the PowerPoint presentation well, jockey for a good seat close to the screen. Remember basic civility. This is not the time to text message, and for goodness sake, don't put your head down for a quick nap. (Your snoring will annoy the student next to you.)

5. **Do you carry your passion with you?** Be excited! Developing passion can be difficult for some classes, but it is something that will pay dividends. Practice your active-listening skills. Listen intently. Ask questions. Be involved.

6. **Do you remain actively engaged?** The class period has a recognized starting and ending time. Just as it is important for you to be punctual, you should plan on remaining for the entire period. Think of a movie. If you come late or leave early, you will miss critical scenes that will hinder your understanding of the entire film. Avoid the temptation to pack up your books before the end of class.

7. **Do you review your class notes as soon as possible?** If you have the time, complete this review before you leave the room. Remain in your seat for a few moments, and quickly determine whether you have any questions or misunderstandings about the day's material. If the instructor has already left the room, this may be a perfect opportunity to visit his or her office. Of course, many times, you will need to leave the room quickly for another class or appointment. In those cases, find a quiet place to complete your review as soon as possible.

DEVELOPING RESPECTFUL RELATIONSHIPS WITH YOUR INSTRUCTORS

The relationships you have with your instructors should be positive, not distracting. Perhaps you have heard the expression "Do unto others as you would have them do unto you." When dealing with your professors, treat them as you want to be treated yourself.

Paying tuition does not entitle a student to treat *any* college employee or classmate in a rude, disrespectful, or demanding manner. Nor does college enrollment usually entitle students to immediate and around-the-clock access to their instructors. If you are in the classroom, visiting your instructor during office hours, or corresponding by e-mail, remember two things:

1. You are interacting with a fellow human being. Be courteous and respectful. You can expect top-notch teaching and appropriate feedback. However,

your instructors are not there to respond to your every demand, whenever you want.

2. Your professors have the professional obligation to require you to do meaningful and appropriate work and to turn it in by a certain time. Completing these assignments and exercises will help you master the course material.

USE OFFICE TIME FOR YOUR BENEFIT

It is not uncommon for some students to be intimidated by the idea of visiting a professor's office—and that is understandable. But if you can concentrate on behaving in a way that will build a strong foundation of support, encouragement, and respect, you will find the instructor/student relationship one of the most important you will develop in college. Take advantage of the opportunity to talk with and learn from your instructors.

CIVILITY IN THE CLASSROOM*

Civility—acting appropriately and with respect—should be a basic component of any working relationship. While it deserves its own chapter, let's review a couple basic rules of behavior that will go far in developing a respectful relationship with your professor and classmates:

- **Class participation.** Students who respectfully respond to instructors with on-task comments and questions help create a positive classroom atmosphere. When a student responds to an instructor's request with a grunt, shrug of the shoulders, or rude and inappropriate comment, he or she is being disrespectful of the instructor and the classmates (whether that is the intention or not).

- **Entering and leaving the room.** At times (and they should be very few), you may need to enter class after it starts or leave before it is over. Basic courtesy dictates that you make your way through the room quietly and with limited distraction to other students and the instructor. Always hold the door so it does not slam. Remember, any disturbance you create is not only being rude to the instructor, but it also shows a lack of respect for your classmates—who are attending to the instructor.

- **Communicating with other students.** Unless talking with classmates is part of the lesson, once class has started, do not hold conversations (written or verbal).

- **Texting.** Technology is wonderful. It allows us to easily reach out to the world around us. But one area of increasing concern in the classroom is the use of cell phones for texting. One source estimates that 94 percent of students send and receive text messages ("Texting Etiquette," 2009). Another states that in the year 2010, more than 2.3 trillion text messages were sent and received worldwide (Nadler, n.d.). While that many messages are not likely bouncing around U.S. campuses, there is increasing concern about the number of students checking and sending messages during class time. The classroom is not the place for texting, for a number of reasons:

  ☐ It takes your attention away from the class.
  ☐ It is distracting to those around you.

*This section based on Piscitelli (2011), pp. 109–110.

□ It is rude to the person speaking.

□ It is a bad habit that can inevitably lead to less than adequate progress or class failure. That is nothing to LOL ("laugh out loud") about.

On a related note, review your e-mails to professors for appropriateness. Do not treat a professor like your best friend or a personal assistant, expecting him or her to be available at every moment to serve your every need. And again, be civil! (See Glater [2006] for a look at how e-mail has affected the professor/student relationship.)

Students whose behavior is uncivil place themselves in a terrible position with instructors. Instructors are individuals with feelings, emotions, and expectations, just like students. If you disrupt the class with inappropriate behavior, you will have a difficult time building a positive relationship with the key person who is in the classroom to assist you and evaluate your performance.

Activity 7.4

Critically Thinking about Classroom Challenges

Let's apply the R.E.D. Model to examine one of the challenges you identified for yourself in Activity 7.2. Write one of those challenges here. Then complete the chart that follows.

R **E** **D**

Critical-Thinking Step	Application to Your Study Skills	Your Explanation (here or on a separate piece of paper)
RECOGNIZE ASSUMPTIONS	How do you know the challenge you listed earlier is actually a problem? What assumptions do you make about why you have this challenge?	
EVALUATE INFORMATION	Examine your identified classroom challenge beyond a superficial (simplistic) explanation. How do you know this assessment of your challenge is correct? What evidence supports your assumption? Be specific (give examples) in explaining this classroom challenge. Examine the challenge from more than one perspective (point of view).	
DRAW CONCLUSIONS	Based on your evidence, how does your conclusion about your classroom challenge make sense?	

Based on your answers, what insights have you gained about your classroom challenge?

What is the next step you will take to eliminate this challenge?

....

....

....

WHEN PROBLEMS OCCUR

Rarely does a problem fall totally in the lap of one person. For example, if you have a personality clash with a particular instructor, sit back and evaluate the situation. How have you contributed to the problem? What can you do to change the predicament? Is the instructor a difficult grader, or is it simply that you lack some basic process skills?

Use your critical-thinking skills to examine all assumptions. Some students assume that because they received high grades in previous classes, they will (or should) get high grades in subsequent classes. Please question that assumption. While getting good grades last term may establish a great foundation for this term, it does not guarantee anything. Just because you got an A in a previous course does not mean you are destined to get A's in all succeeding classes.

As you move through your course of study, each course will (generally speaking) provide a little more challenge. If you are prepared and apply excellent study and learning strategies, you will have an excellent chance of meeting the challenges effectively. The following sections will provide the strategies needed to help you succeed now and in the future.

Activity 7.5

What Has Surprised You?

Take a moment and reflect on a few of the major surprises you have encountered with your classes this term. For instance, were you surprised by the amount of work required, the sizes of your classes, or the ways instructors interacted with students? Perhaps using a syllabus was a new experience for you. Or maybe the first test result was not what you expected, or your study group did not prove to be very productive. You may not have known that your instructors held office hours; you might not even have known where their offices are located.

Write your response here. Be as specific as you can.

1. What has surprised you about your courses this term?

   ....

   ....

2. After reflection, you may find that you need to make a few changes to enhance your potential for success. Whether the adjustments involve your relationships with instructors or the way you take notes, this is a good time to build on the skills you have and accept the responsibility to make corrections that will benefit you. What changes have you made or do you plan to make to act on these reflections?

   ....

   ....

NOTE-TAKING AS AN ACTIVE LEARNING STRATEGY

> *Tell me and I forget.*
> *Teach me and I*
> *remember. Involve me*
> *and I learn.*
> —*Benjamin Franklin,*
> *colonial statesman and*
> *inventor*

Note taking is a very personal activity. Do not feel that you must copy any of the following **note-taking styles** exactly as shown. If the style you currently use works for you, great! If what you currently do is not working or if you do not have a consistent note-taking style, find one that works for you and use it consistently.

The styles described in this section are very basic approaches. If you are not satisfied with your current note-taking system, consider using one of these. You might also consider using parts of each style to develop your own. However you decide to take class notes, keep the following points in mind about your style:

Figure 7.1

Traditional Outline Note-Taking Style

NOTE-TAKING: THE TRADITIONAL OUTLINE

I. Main topic 1
    A. Subtopic
        1. important detail
        2. important detail
    B. Subtopic
        1. important detail
        2. important detail
II. Main topic 2
    A. Subtopic
        1. important detail
        2. important detail
    B. Subtopic
        1. important detail
        2. important detail
III. Main topic 3
    A. Subtopic
        1. important detail
        2. important detail
    B. Subtopic
        1. important detail
        2. important detail

- Be consistent.
- Practice daily.
- Periodically review your style to make sure it is working for you.

Having organized class notes will help you focus on teacher expectations and emphasis—and minimize distractions.

If you learn best by using a highly structured and orderly model, then the format in Figure 7.1 may be for you. Note that this outline is organized with roman numerals, letters, and arabic numerals. Each indentation represents a level of subordination—a subcategory, or information of less importance.

Perhaps you cannot easily use this note-taking strategy. You are not too sure where the instructor is moving with the lecture, and it is extremely difficult to determine the subcategory of a larger category. In other words, you need a model that allows more flexibility.

The model in Figure 7.2 has the same basic information as the traditional outline. If visuals help you learn, why not record your notes in a picturelike or chartlike structure? It is also very easy to add information when using this model by using a simple arrow or line.

The format in Figure 7.3 is an adaptation of the Cornell note-taking system (Pauk, 1993, pp. 110–114). Note the expanded margin on the left side of the page, which is for student questions and other organizing comments to use as a study guide. This model is more linear in fashion than the flowchart model (Figure 7.2) but not quite as structured as the traditional outline (Figure 7.1).

Figure 7.4 offers one more model for you to consider. This format allows you to arrange details around the body of an issue. Some people refer to this type of overview as a *spidergram*, while others call it *clustering* (see Matte & Henderson, 1995, p. 84). Using this format allows quick organization. It can be helpful in reorganizing your notes prior to a test, as well as in putting your thoughts together for an essay. This type of model might be what you need to jog your memory. The idea is to generate ideas, relationships, and analysis.

Figure 7.2

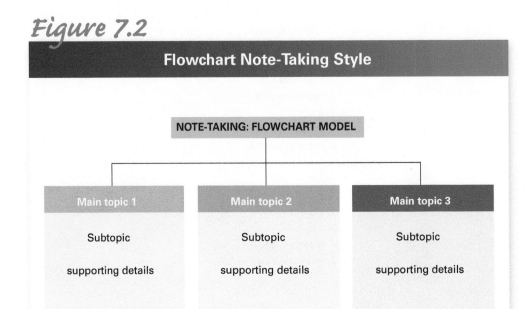

Figure 7.3

Notes with a Study Guide (Modified Cornell Note-Taking Style)

Personal	Date

Study Guide	Class Notes
Write a question you might have about topic 1 or any of its subtopics. Comment on an important detail the instructor emphasized.	I. Main topic 1
	A. Subtopic
	1. important detail
	2. important detail
	B. Subtopic
	1. important detail
	2. important detail
Write a question you might have about topic 2 or any of its subtopics. Comment on an important detail the instructor emphasized.	II. Main topic 2
	A. Subtopic
	1. important detail
	2. important detail
	B. Subtopic
	1. important detail
	2. important detail
Write a question you might have about topic 3 or any of its subtopics. Comment on an important detail the instructor emphasized.	III. Main topic 3
	A. Subtopic
	1. important detail
	2. important detail
	B. Subtopic
	1. important detail
	2. important detail

Figure 7.4

Spidergram or Concept Map Note-Taking Style

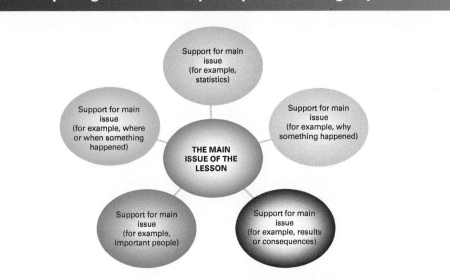

Table 7.1 **Comparing and contrasting note-taking styles**

Note-Taking Style	Potential Benefit(s)	Potential Drawback(s)
Traditional outline	Very organized and structured; items follow directly from one another	Instructors jump around in lessons
	Provides a neat presentation of main points and supporting points	May be difficult to distinguish main versus minor points *during* the lecture
Flowchart/Spidergram/ Clustering	Easy to insert information if the instructor skips around in the lecture	As the notes move to a second or third page, it may be difficult to see connections to previous pages
	The chartlike/picturelike structure may help visual learners	The loose structure may appear chaotic and hinder organization
Notes with a study guide (modified Cornell)	The note-taking section can be in any style	More paper is required as the note-taking section is reduced in size
	Provides space for an ongoing study guide, review, and questions	Requires a little extra time to complete the review questions

COMPARING AND CONTRASTING NOTE-TAKING STYLES*

Table 7.1 provides a quick comparison and contrast of potential benefits and drawbacks of all the note-taking styles explained. (This table is an example of a *data retrieval chart* (DRC)—another tool you can use to organize information.) You can easily adapt these individual note-taking styles to create your own.

Examine the notes you take in class now. Do they resemble one of the styles discussed? Is there *any* organization to your notes? If not, make some adjustments; maybe your study partner or tutor can help.

Even if a class is easy and you feel notes are not needed, consider taking them anyway. Taking notes will help in three ways:

1. Practicing note-taking will help make the habit permanent.
2. Writing notes helps you stay focused on the class and the material.
3. Writing helps you translate oral information to visual information (words and graphics on your paper), thereby using three learning preferences (visual, auditory, read-write) to help you remember the material. You could make an argument that the mere action of writing fits the fourth preference: kinesthetic.

USING SIMPLE ABBREVIATIONS TO INCREASE NOTE-TAKING SPEED

Regardless of your note-taking technique, consider writing or typing short phrases, rather than full sentences. By using this type of shorthand, you will have less chance of getting lost while recording the points presented by the instructor. Be sure to write down any key phrases or words the instructor emphasizes. And write legibly. Eventually, you will need to review this material for a quiz or exam.

Avoid taking notes word for word. That is, do not write every word the instructor says or every word that is on a PowerPoint slide. Look for key terms—words that have been emphasized and repeated by the instructor or those that are underlined or written in italic or boldface type.

*This section based on Piscitelli (2011), p. 116.

Table 7.2 **Abbreviations to use in your notes**

If the Word(s) Is (Are):	Consider Using:	If the Word(s) Is (Are):	Consider Using:
as a consequence	→	less than	<
because	b/c	number	#
decrease	↓	percentage	%
equals	=	plus	+
Florida	FL	question	Q or ?
greater than	>	therefore	∴
important	*	United States of America	US
increase	↑	with	w/
information	info	without	w/o

If you are not sure how to abbreviate, you can find examples on one of the many sites online. Start with English-Zone.com. To conduct a search, type in "note-taking abbreviations and symbols."

Once you have determined what to write, abbreviate words to increase your speed. If you know how to text message, you already use this strategy. Table 7.2 provides some very basic suggestions. Can you add to the list?

Activity 7.6

Practice Your Note-Taking Skills

Read the paragraphs that follow about effective teaching, and then, on a separate piece of paper, take notes on the selection using one of the note-taking formats described earlier. Once you have completed note taking, compare your notes with those of a classmate.

What Do Effective Teachers Do?*

With the beginning of a new semester, I took the opportunity to ask some students the question "What are the characteristics of an effective teacher?" Some students listed two or three characteristics; others six or more. The most a student listed was eleven. The total number of responses came in at 334. (That is why the percentages add to more than 100%.) Here are their top-five responses:

Top Five Student-Identified Characteristics of Effective Teachers

I. **Understanding/Patient/Compassionate.** 57.5% students listed one of these.

II. **Willing to help/explain clearly.** 50.0% want a teacher who is willing to lend a helping hand in explaining material—especially when it is difficult to comprehend.

III. **Interactive/Interesting/Energetic/Enjoys teaching/Enthusiastic/Likes to teach.** 39.4% students want their teachers to show some passion for what they are doing in the classroom. If we throw in "humorous/entertaining/makes light moments," the number rises dramatically to nearly 58% of the students—which would move this to #1 on our list.

IV. **Listens.** 24% of the respondents said they want a classroom instructor who listens to their questions and concerns.

*From Steve Piscitelli's blog, January 16, 2011.

V. Intelligent/Smart. 19.6% of student responses said knowledge of the subject matter is important to be an effective teacher.

There were a number of other characteristics that popped up a few times: "respectful," "organized," "firm," "encouraging," "well-spoken," "uses a variety of methods," and "approachable," to name a few.

What is interesting—but not surprising—in this anecdotal overview is that students (at least these students) place a lot of emphasis on the human side of teaching. They want a connection with another human being. Like so many things in life, we know it when we see it—but it is so difficult to quantify. While I might be able to place a number on how much a teacher knows about her subject area (say, with a test), it is much more difficult to measure her energy, enthusiasm, and humor. As one of the students said, "Everyone can be a teacher, but some teachers have the talent to really teach."

MANAGING YOUR STUDIES WITH A NOTEBOOK

Having well-organized notes will help you prepare for final course tests, national certification exams, and future courses. Having great notes is useless, however, if you cannot find them once you get *outside* the classroom.

Consider using a class notebook to organize and store your notes. A notebook will allow you to quickly find past notes and handouts that may prove helpful during a class discussion or group activity.

Students have found the notebook hints in Figure 7.5 helpful.

PRACTICE

Practice is extremely important. The strategies you examine here and in other chapters will not do any good if you do not use them. Moreover, not every strategy is for everyone. Select what works for you, and then practice, practice, practice. Practice may not make perfect, but it can help to make a skill permanent.

WHAT HAPPENS IF YOU DON'T FOLLOW ALL OF THE BASICS?

If some of the active-learning basics pass you by, consider the suggestions in Table 7.3.

CAN YOU THINK LIKE THE INSTRUCTOR?

In the movie *Caddyshack*, Bill Murray's advice for playing great golf is to "be the ball." Another way to actively engage your course material is to "be the instructor."

If you are sitting in a history class, don't just learn about history—*be the historian*. Don't just complete your science lab experiment—*be the mad scientist* (with all safety precautions, of course!). The point is to think like the course—and to *think like your instructor*. Ask the types of questions someone in this subject asks.

This may be hard to do while you are keeping up with the professor's lecture. But do it later, when reviewing your notes or reading your textbook. Formulate some questions. You can also practice this approach when reading your assignments. Consider the following:

Figure 7.5

Notebook Hints

HINT: Nothing can be more frustrating than finding English class notes buried in the middle of information on the lives of the Roman emperors or tips on how to solve a quadratic equation. Avoid this by having a separate three-ring binder for each class. Also, think twice about using those "stuff-it-in-the-pocket" folders. They may be useful every so often, but they tend to be agents of chaos, more times than not.

HINT: Place the course name, professor's name, and your name on the front cover of each notebook.

HINT: Keep all general yet important handouts in the first section of the notebook. They may include the syllabus, a listing of term assignments, and the instructor's office hours.

HINT: File all papers appropriately. Do not simply stick them in your notebook or textbook. Always follow an established order.

HINT: Have a separate section for each unit of the class. It may be helpful to identify the units with tab dividers, so it will be easy to find material. Each unit may include the following items:

- A summary outline or study guide for the entire unit
- Daily notes, with the date of each class noted clearly at the top of the page
- Handouts that pertain specifically to that unit
- Quizzes and other graded assignments
- The unit exam

HINT: Keep a grade sheet. Create one following this simple three-column format:

Assignment	Points Earned	Points Possible

Using this grade sheet, you will always know your grade. This is important for two reasons:

1. There will be no surprises about your final grade. You know all along how well (or poorly) you are doing. Just because you turn in all the assignments does not mean you will pass the course. Understand your instructor's grading scale, your grades, and what your average is throughout the entire term.
2. Sometimes, an instructor may make an error in grade calculation. If you have retained all your graded assignments and have kept an ongoing record, you will have a credible way to politely challenge an error. (This is similar to holding on to the receipt from a store purchase, on the chance you need to return or exchange it later.)

- In a history class, think about cause and effect, turning points, and how political and economic decisions affect the people of a nation.
- In a science class, think about how items are classified or grouped.
- In a literature class, examine tone, character development, and plot.

Actively use the course material, preferably while you are sitting in the classroom and hearing the material. At the very least, apply the concepts of the subject matter while you are reviewing your notes.

Table 7.3   **Follow-up strategies for when you miss the basics**

The Basics	Oops! I Missed the Basics. What Can I Do Now?
Take notes diligently each class session.	If you miss class, leave space in your notebook as a reminder to get notes for that class from a classmate or to visit the instructor as soon as possible.
Be punctual for each class.	Car trouble, a cantankerous alarm, a family emergency, or a late night out can make even the best student tardy. If you arrive late to class, enter the room quietly. Hold the door so it does not slam, and quickly find a seat. And have your cell phone in the "Off" position. Also, remember that your lateness is not the fault of your instructor. His or her expectations for punctuality and attendance still stand.
Come to class each day with your notebook and a fresh supply of writing paper (or a fully charged laptop battery).	Maybe you dashed out to class and left your class notes behind. As soon as you discover this, borrow some paper, quickly and quietly. You can transfer these notes to your class notebook later in the day. You might tuck an extra pad of paper and a few extra pens into one of the pockets of your book bag for such emergencies. If you are using a laptop, it may be beneficial to arrive early to get a seat next to a wall outlet, in case your laptop requires recharging.
Be ready—each day—to actively engage in class discussion and group activities.	Students often complain of boredom. Yes, the instructor might be a challenge to follow or the material might be dry and complicated. But *you* still need to focus. Doing so will require more effort on your part, but it is something you need to monitor and discipline yourself to do. Find a way to actively engage yourself.
Focus on the important points in each class. Write them down in your notebook.	Sometimes, you may not know what is important. Maybe a study partner can help by comparing notes. You may wish to visit your instructor during office hours and ask if your notes are capturing the main points of the lessons. Does the instructor have any suggestions for you?
If the class is one-hour long, "keep your head in the class" for the entire hour. If it is a longer class (perhaps one that meets only once a week), you still need to stay focused. Do not stop listening and participating before the class has ended. And remember that you enrolled in the section knowing the starting and ending times.	The classroom clock may seem to move backward, and the last 10 minutes of each class may seem like a whole semester. But fight the urge to pack up. Shoving your books and papers into your backpack early is distracting. Remember, the instructor assigns final grades. Impressions can be important—and perceptions can become realities.
Review your day's notes immediately after class—before you leave the classroom, if possible.	Sometimes, you need to get to another class or an appointment immediately and thus have to leave the classroom hurriedly at the conclusion of the lesson. In that case, make a commitment to review your notes as soon as possible later that day. Contact your study partner, if you have one. Working with someone else is a great way to review notes.

STAYING ACTIVELY ENGAGED AS AN ONLINE STUDENT

The availability of **online classes** has increased tremendously within the last few years. Technology has extended the classroom beyond the campus. Students today can complete coursework from locations beyond campus grounds and classroom walls.

The obvious advantage is flexibility: You can complete a course from (virtually) anyplace in the world. Even so, online education is not for all students. It requires a great deal of responsibility and self-discipline.

Here are a few tips to help you successfully complete an online class:

- Know how to use a computer. This sounds obvious, but again, sometimes what is obvious is missed. Know how to create, save, and send different kinds of files.

- You need computer access. Having your own computer—with unlimited access to it—will make life as an online student much easier. You can use a computer in a campus lab or library, but sometimes, those computers will not allow you to download files or programs you may need for your course. Also, you may find that a computer is not available when you need to use it.

- You will need an Internet service provider (ISP) so that you can send and receive communications.

- If there is an orientation for the course, find a way to attend (or read or view it online). This is when you will receive hands-on instruction about where to view assignments and how to submit work. Practice navigating the course site. Click on buttons and links, and know where everything is on the site. Be proactive and learn as much about the site as you can—as soon as you can.

- Back up all of your computer work—and back it up regularly. (This tip will be helpful for students taking traditional in-the-classroom courses, as well.)

    As you would for an on-campus class, turn in assignments for an online class according to the class schedule. Find an effective way to remind yourself of these dates. Probably the simplest advice from experienced online students has been to "stay current with all work."

- Remember to practice good "netiquette" (online etiquette). Some people use the anonymity of a computer to insult or incite others. Keep your discourse civil.

- Once you send an e-mail or post a message on a discussion board, it is out there for the class to see.

- Online courses may be flexible, but they still require a large quantity of time.

- Also, don't confuse flexibility with rigor. An effective online course will require as much—if not more—time to complete as an on-campus course. You may wish to talk with (or e-mail or text) the instructor prior to registering for the course. Make sure you understand the time commitment the course will require.

- Ask for help as soon as you recognize you may have a problem with content, timing, or technological glitches.

- Ask a current online student for advice. Or perhaps you have already completed an online class. If so, you may be able to act as a mentor for someone new to this form of course delivery.

Chapter SUMMARY

To be successful, students need to engage in active learning inside the classroom. Before leaving this chapter, keep the following points in mind:

■ Improve your classroom performance by being aware of your instructors' styles and expectations.

■ Paying attention requires listening and observing, eliminating or controlling distractions, and sorting through the vast amount of information presented to you.

■ Concentrate on behavior that will build a strong foundation of support, encouragement, and respect.

■ Being present in the classroom allows you to hear explanations, ask questions, and add to class discussions.

■ Choose a note-taking style you feel comfortable with and will use consistently.

■ Make your notebook work for you. Keep it current, and review it every night.

CRITICALLY THINKING
What Have You Learned in This Chapter?

Let's apply what you learned in this chapter to help Consuela, from the chapter-opening situation. However, before you examine Consuela's problem and propose a solution, take a moment to think about the main points of the chapter.

Review your notes from this chapter and also the key terms, chapter learning outcomes, boldface chapter headings, and figures and tables. For instance, consider how the chapter learning outcomes may be used to help Consuela:

■ Explain the teaching style and classroom expectations of each of your instructors.

■ Identify common classroom distractions and strategies to deal with each.

■ Provide at least two tips to help you pay attention in class.

■ Describe a strategy to help develop respectful working relationships with your instructors.

■ Use and evaluate one note-taking style for at least one week.

TEST YOUR LEARNING

Now that you have reviewed the main points of this chapter and reread Consuela's story, pretend that you are her adviser. Using the R.E.D. Model for critical thinking, help Consuela review her concerns:

R

Recognize Assumptions

Facts: What are the facts in Consuela's situation? List them.

....

Opinions: What opinions do you find in this situation? List them here.

....

Assumptions: Are Consuela's assumptions accurate?

....

E

Evaluate Information

Help Consuela compile a list of questions that will help her make the most appropriate decision.

....

What emotions seem to be motivating Consuela?

....

What, if anything, is missing from her thought process?

....

Do you see any confirmation bias?

....

D

Draw Conclusions

Based on the facts and the questions you have presented, what conclusions can you draw?

....

What advice do you have for Consuela? What solutions do you propose?

....

Based on your suggestions, do you see any assumptions?

....

Finally, based on what you learned about using critical thinking and classroom success strategies, what plan of action do you suggest for Consuela?

....

Reviewing and Using Your Notes OUTSIDE THE CLASSROOM

It always seems impossible until it's done.
—Nelson Mandela, South African statesman

CHAPTER LEARNING OUTCOMES

By the time you finish reading this chapter and completing its activities, you will be able to do the following:

- Establish a schedule to immediately review each day's class notes.

- Establish a goal that will help you turn your major note-taking challenge into a note-taking strength.

- Develop and write at least one T.S.D. for your class notes from the past week.

- Develop and write at least one "exit slip" for your class notes from the past week.

- Visit each of your professors at least once to discuss material from class.

- Understand why you should (or should not) consider working with a study partner.

The Case of MYRON

Myron is a quiet student. Although he seldom misses a class, he very seldom participates from his seat in the last row of the classroom. He is doing mostly C work in his classes—except biology, which he is not passing. Science has never been his strongest subject area, but in the past, he has been able to read his textbook and do well. He has found that his biology professor's exams rely heavily on classroom lectures, group discussions, and demonstrations.

Myron listens to everything his professor says. He copies all of the PowerPoint presentations word for word. His notebook is complete with classroom notes and handouts—all filed in precise order. The professor actually posts class notes on her websites. Myron prints them out and then puts

© Shutterstock

Key Terms

Connections
"Exit slip" strategy
Office hours
R.O.I.
Review-Relate-Reorganize
    strategy
Study partner
T.S.D. strategy

Chapter INTRODUCTION

While building relationships with classmates and instructors will help you persist and succeed in your studies, another type of relationship building is every bit as vital to your school success.

Research has shown that learning is more likely to occur when students establish **connections**—build relationships—between what they know

172

them in his notebook. This gives him a record of virtually every word the professor has used.

Myron recently told a study group member, "My thought has always been if the professor believes it's important enough to put on the screen, a website, or on the board, then it should go into my notebook." His classmates are in awe about how thick his class notebook has become.

Still, Myron struggles to pass his biology exams. The night before each test, he sits at his desk elbow deep in papers, notes, and PowerPoint copies, doing the best he can to understand it all. With all of these notes and handouts, though, he has so much material to study that he ends up getting lost in the details. He is tired of pulling all-night cram sessions prior to exams—and he is tired of getting less-than-satisfactory grades.

CRITICALLY THINKING
about *Myron's* situation

As a member of Myron's study group, what suggestions do you have for him?

from their experiences and what they read in textbooks and hear from their instructors and classmates. Note taking provides the chance to build these connections. In fact, opportunities for learning will occur at two levels: while writing or typing notes and while reviewing notes (Armbruster, 2000, p. 176).

MyStudentSuccessLab

MyStudentSuccessLab (www .mystudentsuccesslab.com) is an online solution designed to help you 'Start strong, Finish stronger' by building skills for ongoing personal and professional development.

LEARNING WHILE TAKING NOTES

You can learn while taking notes in class, attending a guest lecture in the campus auditorium, or reading your textbook. At this point in note taking, however, you will not have much time to build connections. You will more than likely be concentrating on following the speaker and writing or typing the main points in your notebook or on your laptop. Even if you have a well-honed note-taking style, the chance of creating a lasting connection with this new information *while* recording it will be difficult. You will be focused on determining what is important and what you need to write, not on how the new information supports or refutes what you already know.

But just having the notes is not enough. The next step is knowing what to do with the notes—and when to do it. Your learning will deepen when you take the time to review your notes (Armbruster, 2000, p. 178).

LEARNING AFTER YOU HAVE TAKEN NOTES: R.O.I.

Businesspeople invest their money and time when presented with an opportunity to earn a profit. The concept of **return on investment (R.O.I.)** many times drives business decisions. Why invest resources if no return, or benefit, seems likely?

The same concept can be applied to your investment in class. Beyond tuition and the cost of books, every day that you enter class, you invest your time and attention in what is being taught. Let's assume you take picture-perfect notes. You have recorded every piece of important information in an organized, legible form—much like Myron in the chapter-opening scenario. So far, so good.

But at this point, what is your R.O.I.? Perhaps you were able to see connections between the classroom discussions and your textbook. Possibly, as you wrote down the instructor's remarks, you had an insight about the material. But you might not know the true return on your investment of time until you take the unit exam. Then, you will have an idea of how much of the material you have retained and learned.

The second part of note taking—reviewing and storing—allows you to make deeper connections between what you know and what you are learning. This chapter will focus on these strategies.

Activity 8.1

Reflecting on How Your Notes Help You Understand Class Material

Before you answer the items that follow, reflect on your current skill level of using your notes to help you study for quizzes and exams and for other practical applications. Think of how well (or poorly) you have been able to use your notes from past classes.

As you do in completing all of the reflective activities in this book, you should write from your heart. This exercise is not meant for you to answer just like your classmates—or to match what you may think the instructor wants to see. Take the time to give a respectful and responsible general accounting of your experiences with your notes. Making a truthful self-assessment now will help you build on skills you have while developing those you lack.

For each of the following items, circle the number that best describes your typical experience when it comes to using your notes to study. Here is the key for the numbers:

0 = never, 1 = almost never, 2 = occasionally, 3 = frequently, 4 = almost always, 5 = always

When considering your past successes and challenges when using your notes, how often:

1.	Did you review your notes within the first 24 hours of taking them in class?	**0**	**1**	**2**	**3**	**4**	**5**
2.	Did you review your notes at any time before the next class?	**0**	**1**	**2**	**3**	**4**	**5**
3.	Did the notes (the words, sentences, phrases) you wrote during class make sense to you when you reviewed them after class?	**0**	**1**	**2**	**3**	**4**	**5**
4.	Were your notes legible and easy to read?	**0**	**1**	**2**	**3**	**4**	**5**
5.	Did your notes capture the main points from the instructor's lesson?	**0**	**1**	**2**	**3**	**4**	**5**
6.	Did your notes put the instructor's words into your words, rather than copy the instructor's PowerPoint slides or lecture notes almost word for word?	**0**	**1**	**2**	**3**	**4**	**5**
7.	Did you develop study guides from your notes?	**0**	**1**	**2**	**3**	**4**	**5**
8.	Did you review your notes and relate them to your textbook reading or the previous lesson's notes?	**0**	**1**	**2**	**3**	**4**	**5**

Add up your scores for items 3, 4, 5, and 6. Divide by 4. Write your answer here: _____.

Using the key provided to explain each number (0, 1, 2, 3, 4, 5), complete this sentence: When it comes to the quality of my notes, I _____ write legible notes that are in my words and that reflect the main points of the lesson.

Add up your scores for items 1, 2, 7, and 8. Divide by 4. Write your answer here: _____.

Using the key provided to explain each number (0, 1, 2, 3, 4, 5), complete this sentence: When it comes to actively using my notes after class, I _____ review and reorganize my notes to prepare for quizzes and exams regularly prior to exams and quizzes.

Based on your answers, what insights have you gained about your experiences with note-taking skills?

....

....

....

....

USING YOUR NOTES TO UNDERSTAND THE "BIG PICTURE"

I like a teacher who gives you something to take home to think about besides homework.

—Lily Tomlin, Comedienne

NOW THAT YOU HAVE YOUR NOTES, IT'S TIME FOR REFLECTION

Taking clear notes in class moves you another step closer to mastering your course content. But even more needs to be done. In fact, your studying begins the next time you look at those notes.

A common study skill recommendation is to review your notes as soon as possible after class. Here are the findings of one study:

> Controlled experiments show that students who take notes and review them out perform those who do not. . . . Evidence from several decades of research emphasizes the importance of taking complete lecture notes and of reviewing them. . . . In particular, note-taking strategies that promote rehearsal and review of lecture material enhance learning. (Pardini et al., 2005, p. 39)

For this review to be active and engaging, you need to do more than passively read the notes. A simple three-step strategy—Review-Relate-Reorganize—will help you understand the class material, cut down on last-minute test preparation (cramming), and be ready for your next test-day performance.

Review. As soon as possible after class, look at the day's notes. Read them and highlight what you consider important information. Make sure all the words have been legibly written, and neatly correct any words that are difficult to read. Is anything unclear? Do you understand all the principles, generalizations, and theories?

If you have a question about an item, put an asterisk or question mark next to it in the margin of your notes. This should be the first question you ask at the beginning of the next class meeting or when you visit the instructor during office hours. If you wait to ask the question until the night before the unit exam, it will probably be difficult to get clarification from the instructor.

In addition, by asking the question in the next class, you are actively participating—which is, coincidentally, another success strategy. Doing a nightly review of your class notes will help focus your attention on what you know and what you need to clarify.

Relate. Avoid the temptation to memorize isolated pieces of information. Memorizing long lists of dates, names, spellings, and formulas can be a daunting and boring task. As an alternative, look at the previous day's notes and reading assignments and ask yourself these questions:

- What connections exist between my new notes and the previous material?
- What patterns, or repetitions, are developing? How can I use them to help me remember?

- Does the new material help me, or am I confused and in need of clarification?
- What textbook information could help me fill in my notes?

Once you start seeing this big picture, the material will make more sense and be easier to remember.

Reorganize. As you look over your notes, see if there is a clearer way to understand the message of the lesson. Maybe all you need to do is reorder your notes. Sometimes, an instructor will present material out of order or go off on a tangent. Organize the information in your notes so it makes sense to you. You may wish to write a brief outline in the margin of the notes. Perhaps highlighting important concepts and facts with different-colored pens will help you focus on key points.

Activity 8.2

Helping Myron to Review, Relate, and Reorganize

The chapter-opening story revealed that Myron takes a lot of notes and that using this study method alone is not helping him. As a member of his study group, demonstrate how he can translate the instructor's words into his.

For this activity, choose the notes from one of your classes this term. They could come from this class or your history class, psychology class, math class, science class, computer class, or foreign language class. It might be best to pick the class in which you are having the most difficulty. In your notebook (or in a computer document file), practice the **Review-Relate-Reorganize strategy** for note review.

 The R.E.D. Model (**R**ecognize Assumptions, **E**valuate Information, **D**raw Conclusions) provides a systematic way to approach critical thinking through the use of an easy-to-remember acronym.

- **Review.** Read your notes. Highlight important words. Make sure everything is written legibly.
- **Relate.** As best you can, make connections between the class notes and what you talked about in earlier classes. Use the textbook to help you clarify your notes. Write your thoughts here.

  ....

  ....

- **Reorganize.** Do you need to reorganize your notes in any way? This can be as simple as writing some clarifying comments in the margins or as involved as rewriting or typing your notes. One last time, ask yourself whether any part of the notes is confusing to you. Perhaps you need to ask the instructor about this for further clarification.

  ....

  ....

CONNECTIONS, GROUPS, AND CHUNKS

Sometimes, in the flurry of a classroom lecture or the excitement of a group discussion, you take bad notes. Despite your best efforts, your notes may sometimes look like a long list of confusing and disjointed words, names, details, or dates. Making sense of these kinds of notes is where a nightly review can prove most beneficial.

As stated in this chapter's introduction, you have a better chance to understand a classroom lesson if you can connect new material with a textbook reading or your own knowledge. As you review your notes, look for logical groupings and connections. Attempt to establish categories of information. For instance, if you are given a list of 25 items to remember, "chunk" the terms into three or four major categories. In a history class, it might be helpful to group philosophers, scientists, and political leaders. From a literature discussion, you may have notes about setting, plot, characters, or theme.

This chunking strategy can even work for vocabulary lists. Take, for example, the following list of French vocabulary words. Note that the part of speech is provided as an abbreviation in parentheses after each word:

aimer mieux (v)　　　　lorsque (adv)

l'anorak (n)　　　　　　le peuple (n)

le bateau (n)　　　　　porter (v)

bientôt (adv)　　　　　prochain (adj)

célébrer (v)　　　　　　puissant (adj)

le danger (n)　　　　　le roi (n)

la devise (n)　　　　　tricolore (adj)

entouré (adj)

Rearranging these words according to parts of speech might help you remember them. Arranged into categories, the list of 15 words looks like this:

Nouns	Verbs	Adjectives	Adverbs
l'anorak	aimer mieux	entouré	bientôt
le bateau	célébrer	prochain	lorsque
le danger	porter	puissant	
la devise		tricolore	
le peuple			
le roi			

Now, instead of learning 15 isolated items, you can learn them in groups. Chunking the material creates four bite-sized categories, each containing no more than 6 words.

TALK TO YOURSELF—AND THEN TO SOMEONE ELSE

"I've tried all this stuff, but I still don't understand the new math formula," you say. In this case, "talk" your math problem through, step by step. Fully explain each step as best you can. Go as far in the process as possible. You may make it through four or five steps—or you might not be able to get past the first step.

Once you have done this, ask a classmate to listen to your explanation. Perhaps he or she can help you get past the spot where you stumble.

If you are still confused, it might be a good time to visit your professor. You will be able to explain exactly what you know and exactly where you get stuck. Doing so will help the professor understand where he or she needs to start working with you. This will make for a more effective and efficient office visit.

WHAT SHOULD YOU DO IF YOU STILL DON'T GET THE BIG PICTURE?

Even the best note taker can be overwhelmed by a mountain of information and miss the overall meaning of a lesson. Two complementary strategies you can use in conjunction with the Review-Relate-Reorganize strategy are the T.S.D. and "exit slip" strategies.

Title/Summary/Details (T.S.D.). You will have a better chance of understanding class notes if you record the material in your own words. Copying your instructor's lesson word for word (or nearly word for word) will not be useful if you cannot explain the material in language that makes sense to you. The **T.S.D. strategy** is an active review strategy that consists of three simple steps:

- **T**: Start by giving the notes a *title*. What is the big picture? Come up with your own brief title that effectively captures the day's notes.

- **S**: Write a brief *summary*. In a sentence or two, summarize the notes in your words. What was the central theme or main point? If you can do this, you understand the overall thrust of the instructor's lesson. Again, do not quote the instructor's words. *Use your own words.*

- **D**: List three *details* that support your summary. What do you see as the major details in the lecture? What questions might the instructor pose on the exam?

When you have written your review (or typed and saved it in a computer file), it may be no longer than one-quarter of a page in length. Thus, the T.S.D. strategy is quick, easy, and efficient.

Continue to review, relate, and reorganize each night in this manner. Keep your T.S.D.s at the beginning of your unit material (or in a computer document file). Add to them each day. By test time, you will have a full set of concise notes to serve as a practical study guide. You will have developed an ongoing study guide based on your class notes. No more cramming for exams!

T.S.D. in Reverse. The T.S.D. strategy asks you first to see the big picture (topic and summary) and then to look at the details that support that larger view.

Perhaps you are the type of student who has to focus on the details first before you can see the big picture. If so, you can still use the T.S.D. strategy, but do it in reverse. Work backward.

First, list the main details. Then, based on the details you have listed, write a summary that shows the connections among the details. Finally, write the topic that captures the idea of the entire class or reading assignment.

Activity 8.3

Developing a T.S.D.

The following information on maintaining a healthy weight comes from the Centers for Disease Control and Prevention website (www.eric.ed.gov/PDFS/EJ689655.pdf). As you read the article, circle, underline, or highlight the key details. After you complete the reading, write the three key details the article stressed. Then, write a statement that effectively summarizes the connection of the details you identified. Finally, create your own brief title that describes the topic of the piece.

HEALTHY WEIGHT

Whether you want to lose weight or maintain a healthy weight, it's important to understand the connection between the energy your body takes in (through the foods you eat and the beverages you drink) and the energy your body uses (through the activities you do). To lose weight, you need to use more calories than you take in. To maintain a healthy weight, you need to balance the calories you use with those you take in. . . .

There is a right number of calories for you to eat each day. This number depends on your age, activity level, and whether you are trying to gain, maintain, or lose weight. You could use up the entire amount on a few high-calorie foods, but chances are, you won't get the full range of vitamins and nutrients your body needs to be healthy. Choose the most nutritionally rich foods you can from each food group each day—those packed with vitamins, minerals, fiber, and other nutrients, but lower in calories. Pick foods like fruits, vegetables, whole grains, and fat-free or low-fat milk and milk products more often. . . .

Becoming a healthier you isn't just about eating healthy—it's also about physical activity. Regular physical activity is important for your overall health and fitness. It also helps you control body weight by balancing the calories you take in as food with the calories you expend each day. . . .

Whether you want to lose weight or maintain a healthy weight, it's important to understand the connection between the energy your body takes in (through the foods you eat and the beverages you drink) and the energy your body uses (through the activities you do).

Details: Write the key details of this lesson here:

1. ....

....

2. ....

....

3. ....

....

Summary: Based on the details you identified, write a statement that summarizes this piece accurately.

....

....

Title: In a couple of words, state the topic of the piece you just read.

....

....

Exit Slips: As Easy as 3-2-1. Another review strategy is the **"exit slip" strategy** used by some classroom instructors. Before students exit at the end of the class period, they write a sentence or two about what they learned from the lesson. A variation asks students to list the most confusing point in the lesson.

You can do the same thing to determine your level of understanding of the day's notes:

- After reviewing your notes, write (or highlight) three new things you learned in the lesson.
- Then write the two items from the lesson that you found the most interesting.
- Finally, note the one thing you found the most confusing.

You can adjust these steps to fit a particular class. For instance, in a computer class, you may find it helpful to list two new strategies you can apply immediately to help organize your computer files.

Activity 8.4

Critically Thinking about How to Use Your Notes

Let's apply the R.E.D. Model for critical thinking to examine one of the challenges you identified for yourself in Activity 8.1.

List your major note-taking challenge here:

R
E
D

Critical-Thinking Step	Application to Your Study Skills	Your Explanation (here or on a separate piece of paper)
Recognizing Assumptions	Clearly state this particular note-taking challenge. How do you know this assessment of your challenge is correct?	
Evaluating Information	Provide a specific explanation (give examples) of this note-taking challenge. How is your assessment of your note-taking challenge connected to your academic progress? Examine your note-taking challenge from more than one perspective (point of view).	
Drawing Conclusions	Based on your evidence, how does your conclusion about your note-taking challenge make sense?	

Based on your answers, what insights have you gained about your note-taking challenge?

What is the next step you will take to eliminate this challenge?

ADDITIONAL OUT-OF-CLASS STRATEGIES TO IMPROVE YOUR NOTES

HAVE YOU CREATED WORKING RELATIONSHIPS WITH YOUR INSTRUCTORS?

What if you are still confused, even after a careful review of your notes and use of the strategies provided? Then consider a visit to your instructor's office.

Instructors typically post the **office hours** they are available to students. You can find this information in the syllabus, on the instructor's office door or website, and/ or in the department office. If you still cannot locate an instructor's office hours, send him or her a quick e-mail or leave a voicemail.

Make it a goal to visit each of your instructors this term. Take a few moments to find each instructor's office and find out what office hours he or she keeps.

Use these hours as the valuable resource they are. When you enter an instructor's office, you can do any or all of the following:

- Obtain clarification on class notes.
- Obtain clarification on future assignments.
- Seek assistance on a particularly troubling lesson.
- Ask to review the last exam or quiz to learn from any mistakes you may have made.
- Develop a face-name relationship, as your instructor will likely remember you as a student who has taken the time to seek help and get clarification of course material.
- Discuss challenges you are experiencing in the class.
- Seek advice about future courses.

Activity 8.5

Finding Your Instructors

On the chart that follows, write the names of all the instructors you have this term down the left side. Next to each name, write the instructor's office hours and where his or her office is located. Make a note of the last time you visited this instructor (if ever) and when you will visit him or her next. Finally, jot down what course issues or questions you will bring to the office visit. If you know what you need to discuss before you walk in the door, chances for a positive meeting (and relationship) will increase dramatically.

Hint: When you visit an instructor, be as specific as you can about any challenges you are experiencing. Starting your visit with "I'm lost" or "I don't understand this book" or "I don't do math" does not give the instructor much to work with. You may, in fact, be lost—so start your conversation by telling the instructor what *you do know*. For instance, you may start a visit to your math instructor with something like this: "I can get up to the point where I try to find a reciprocal fraction—and then I'm totally lost." That way, you have provided the instructor with a place to start. (Also review the previous section, Talk to Yourself—and Then to Someone Else.)

Instructor's Name	Office Hours	Office Location	Last Visited	When Will You Visit Next?	What Topic or Question Will You Bring to the Office Visit? What Will Be the Purpose of Your Visit?
1.					
2.					
3.					
4.					
5.					

DO YOU NEED A STUDY PARTNER OR GROUP?

There is an old saying that "Misery loves company." A more positive approach holds that "Success loves good company!"

The importance of having a strong support network to help you develop your intellectual and collaborative skills cannot be overemphasized. Students who feel connected to their classes and their campus have a better chance to experience success. This support system can be as simple as a compatible roommate, as effective as a good mentor, or as socially dynamic as a study group.

A **study partner** (or a study group) can help you do all these things:

■ Make sense of the crazy scribbles you call "notes."
■ Understand lengthy and confusing reading assignments.
■ See different perspectives (interpretations) of the course material.
■ Choose a topic for the term research paper.
■ Prepare for an upcoming exam.
■ Understand a difficult concept.
■ Cope with classroom failures.
■ Celebrate classroom successes.

Your study partner may be one of the most important people you will meet. He or she can be the first member of a larger support group.

A major reason students leave college (especially within their first year) is because they do not feel part of the college community. As one professor noted, "Support is a condition for student learning. . . . Least [sic] we forget the first year is a period of becoming, a period of transition. . . . Without academic and social support some students are unable to make that transition" (Tinto, 2002). Getting a study partner is a small step toward building a much larger network of support.

Sometimes, however, working with a study partner or study group can seem like a nightmare that never ends. Differences in schedules, personalities, and work ethics can make for very challenging circumstances. If you function better without a group, then pursue another option.

This is where knowing your learning style will be helpful. Your campus may have peer tutors or other types of academic support services that can provide you with the resources you need.

USE TECHNOLOGY TO SHARPEN NOTE-TAKING SKILLS

Examine the following ideas, and then commit time to practice each one during the next week:

- Tune in to a TV channel or an online video presentation, and take notes on the content. You might look at an educational presentation, like the programs on the History Channel or a public television station. Or you might watch a program about solving crimes. Maybe you can find a podcast of interest to you. Have a friend do the same thing, and then compare notes.

- If you would rather work alone, record the presentation and take notes at the same time. Then, replay the presentation and compare your notes to the recorded material. Did you miss anything?

- You might choose to record a teacher lecture, take notes, and replay the tape later. But use this strategy with caution. Students can end up recording a lesson but fail to take notes at the same time. This strategy ignores the real issue: improving note taking. Practice is necessary. If you record a lesson, ask yourself "When will I have the time to listen to this and take notes?" Perhaps a more direct question is this one: "After sitting in class for an hour, do I want to listen to the same information for an additional hour of my own time?" Consider recording as a temporary measure until you are more comfortable with your note-taking skills. (And make sure you speak to your instructor before recording a presentation.)

After using one of these strategies, look at the notes you wrote and critically evaluate them. Are they clear, accurate, precise, and logical? Are they of sufficient depth to be useful at a later time—for instance, in studying for an exam?

Chapter SUMMARY

To be successful, students need to become involved and engaged in active learning outside the classroom. Before leaving this chapter, keep the following points in mind:

- As soon as possible after class, review your class notes.

- Learning is more likely to occur when students establish connections between class material and what they already know.

- Once you start seeing the "big picture" (that is, how the little pieces fit together), the material will make sense and be easier to remember.

- You will have a better chance of understanding class notes if you record material in your own words.

- Whatever it takes, find your instructors' offices, know their office hours, and make it a goal to visit all of them this term.

- A study partner (or a study group) can help you understand class material and review your notes.

CRITICALLY THINKING
What Have You Learned in This Chapter?

Let's apply what you learned in this chapter to help Myron from the chapter-opening scenario. However, before you consider Myron's problem and propose your solution, take a moment to think about the main points of the chapter.

Review your notes from this chapter and also the key terms, chapter learning outcomes, boldface chapter headings, and figures and tables. For instance, consider how the chapter learning outcomes may be used to help Myron:

© Shutterstock

- Establish a schedule to immediately review each day's class notes.

- Establish a goal that will help you turn your major note-taking challenge into a note-taking strength.

- Develop and write at least one T.S.D. for your class notes from the past week.

- Develop and write at least one "exit slip" for your class notes from the past week.

- Visit each of your professors at least once to discuss material from class.

- Understand why you should (or should not) consider working with a study partner.

TEST YOUR LEARNING

Now that you have reviewed the main points of this chapter and reread Myron's story, what advice do you have for him? Using the R.E.D. Model for critical thinking, help Myron critically review his concerns:

R

Recognize Assumptions

Facts: What are the facts in Myron's situation? List them.

....

....

Opinions: What opinions do you find in this situation? List them here.

....

....

Assumptions: Are Myron's assumptions accurate?

....

....

E

Evaluate Information

Help Myron compile a list of questions that will help him make the most appropriate decision.

....

....

What emotions seem to be motivating Myron?

....

....

What, if anything, is missing from his thought process?

....

....

Do you see any confirmation bias?

....

....

D

Draw Conclusions

Based on the facts and the questions you have presented, what conclusions can you draw?

....

....

What advice do you have for Myron? What solutions do you propose?

....

....

Based on your suggestions, do you see any assumptions?

....

....

Finally, based on what you learned about using critical thinking and note-review strategies, what plan of action do you suggest for Myron?

....

....

9 READING

The man who does not read good books has no advantage over the man who can't read them.

—Mark Twain, author

CHAPTER LEARNING OUTCOMES

By the time you finish reading this chapter and completing its activities, you will know how to do the following:

- Identify the purpose of a reading assignment.

- Identify the main idea of a paragraph.

- Demonstrate how to use the SQ4R reading process.

- Use highlighting to identify key information and improve understanding.

- Determine the meanings of vocabulary words by using the context of the reading assignment.

- Use graphics to help you understand a reading assignment.

The Case of LENA

Lena is a second-semester college student. She works hard, completes all of her assignments, and comes to class punctually every day. Her biggest challenge has been her history reading quizzes.

Actually, using the word *challenge* is putting things mildly. Lena has not passed one reading quiz this term. She uses the instructor-provided study guides but still scores poorly on the weekly quizzes. Lena says she has always been a "slow" reader.

Recently, Lena told her professor, "I don't have a lot of free time, so any spare moment I have, I open the book and begin reading." She proudly showed her professor her textbook, pointing to the pages as she flipped through the assigned chapter. "See, I highlight a lot. You can tell I read this stuff. I don't

© Shutterstock

Key Terms

Active reading
Brain-based learning
Comprehension
Context
Graphics
Highlighting
Main idea
Passion
Purpose
Scan
SQ4R
Strategic reading
Vocabulary

Chapter
INTRODUCTION

In today's society of instant Internet, on-demand videos, and music downloading, one may wonder whether reading has become a lost art. Some people wonder, "Why read a book when I can *listen* to a book or *see* a movie on my own personal hand-held portable digital device?"

The medium may have changed—becoming more digitized—but reading remains a crucial skill. In fact, being able to read well is perhaps even more important today than in the past.

As you progress through your college program of study, the required reading will increase in volume, difficulty, and complexity. Besides

have time to take notes, so I make sure to mark all the important things. And I was very lucky to have bought a used book, where all of the important words were already marked." Sure enough, anywhere from 50 percent to 75 percent of every page had been highlighted with a yellow marker.

Lena also told the professor she has prioritized her reading time extremely well by skipping over the chapter introductions and summaries. "I get right to the business of reading the meat of the chapter," she said.

Tomorrow is the last day to withdraw from classes—an option Lena has strongly considered. In one last effort to save her history class, Lena has come to you for advice.

CRITICALLY THINKING
about *Lena's* situation

Identify three strategies you would suggest to Lena. Tell her how using each strategy will help improve her reading quiz scores.

traditional textbooks, you will use library databases, indexes, and e-books for research purposes. Whether you read electronic material (Internet articles and blogs), a novel for English class, or your chemistry textbook, you will want to find effective and efficient ways to complete the reading and prepare you for discussions, applications, quizzes, and exams.

To do these things, you need to take an active part in the reading process. **Active reading**, like active learning, requires you to *do* something, not just passively look at the words on the page. Regardless of your current

MyStudentSuccessLab

MyStudentSuccessLab (www .mystudentsuccesslab.com) is an online solution designed to help you 'Start strong, Finish stronger' by building skills for ongoing personal and professional development.

comprehension level, you and your fellow students have at least one thing in common: You have read books before. This is not new territory for you.

Respect the reading skills you currently have and build on them. Activity 9.1 will give you the chance to reflect on your current reading skills—and think about how you can make immediate improvements.

Reading involves more than your eyes seeing words on a page. Effective and skilled readers know that reading is a strategic process. That is, if you follow a few basic steps, you can tackle your assignments more effectively and effortlessly. Once you master the techniques in this chapter you, too, can be an effective reader.

Activity 9.1

Reflecting on Your Current Level of Reading Skills

Before you answer the items that follow, reflect on your current level of reading skills. Think of how well (or poorly) you have performed in past classes.

As you do in completing all of the reflective activities in this book, you should write from your heart. This exercise is not meant for you to answer just like your classmates—or to match what you may think the instructor wants to see. Take the time to give a respectful, responsible general accounting of your experiences with reading. Conducting a truthful self-assessment now will help you build on skills you have while developing those you lack.

For each of the following items, circle the number that best describes your *typical* experience with reading skills. Here is the key for the numbers:

0 = never, 1 = almost never, 2 = occasionally, 3 = frequently, 4 = almost always, 5 = always

When considering your past successes and challenges with reading, how often . . .

1.	Did you scan your reading assignment for main points before jumping right into the reading?	0	1	2	3	4	5
2.	Did you take effective notes from your reading?	0	1	2	3	4	5
3.	Did you use your reading notes to help you with class discussions?	0	1	2	3	4	5
4.	Were you able to read an assignment and understand its main idea?	0	1	2	3	4	5
5.	Could you figure out the meaning of a word from the words surrounding it?	0	1	2	3	4	5
6.	Were you able to remember what you read?	0	1	2	3	4	5
7.	Did you review your reading notes immediately after completing your reading assignment?	0	1	2	3	4	5
8.	Was your vocabulary strong enough so that you could understand the meaning of a textbook assignment?	0	1	2	3	4	5

Add up your scores for items 1, 4, and 6. Divide by 3. Write your answer here: _____.

Using the key provided to explain each number (0, 1, 2, 3, 4, 5), complete this sentence: When it comes to identifying the main points of a reading, I _____ do this effectively.

Add up your scores for items 2, 3, and 7. Divide by 3. Write your answer here: _____.

Using the key provided to explain each number (0, 1, 2, 3, 4, 5), complete this sentence: When it comes to reading notes, I _____ take and use reading notes effectively.

Add up your scores for items 5 and 8. Divide by 2. Write your answer here: _____.

Using the key provided to explain each number (0, 1, 2, 3, 4, 5), complete this sentence: When it comes to vocabulary, I _____ understand the vocabulary in my reading assignments.

Based on your answers, what insights have you gained about your reading skills?

....

....

DO YOU KNOW WHY YOU READ AN ASSIGNMENT?

I find television to be very educating. Every time somebody turns on the set, I go in the other room and read a book.
—Groucho Marx, comedian and vaudeville star

At first glance, the question "Do you know why you read an assignment?" appears simplistic and obvious. You would likely reply, "Of course I know why I read my assignment: because the instructor said it would be on the test."

OK. That might identify the motivation that gets you to open the book. But once you have the assigned chapter in front of you, why do you read it? Or even more to the point, *do you know what you are looking for in the chapter?*

YOU READ YOUR ASSIGNMENT. SO, WHY DON'T YOU KNOW WHAT YOU READ?

If you were asked to clean the garage (or the student government office, or your room, or the athletic workout room), would you start working just anyplace, moving anything? Probably not. You would likely want to know exactly what should be moved, thrown away, put away, or cleaned. In other words, you would want to know the intended *purpose* or *result* of your work. Knowing that would help you avoid wasting time. You would be able to finish the job as effectively and efficiently as possible.

IDENTIFYING THE PURPOSE

The same holds true for reading. The key to increased reading **comprehension** is to know what the result should be. When you comprehend material you can describe it in your own words. You understand it.

There are various **purposes**, or reasons, for reading (Fry, 1991, p. 18; see also "Critical Reading Strategies," 2008). Common purposes for reading include the following:

- To answer specific questions (like those at the end of a chapter)
- To apply (use in new situations) the reading material (to solve a problem)
- To find details (to support an argument or to answer questions)
- To get a message (such as from a political candidate's statement)
- To evaluate (judge) the reading material (to help you make a decision)
- To entertain (as when you read a novel, a blog, or song lyrics)

If you can identify the purpose of a reading assignment before you start reading, you will have less chance of slamming the book closed in frustration.

© Shutterstock

But how do you determine the purpose of a reading assignment? The following list provides some quick tips to help you determine what to look for in the material:

- Pay attention in class. The teacher almost always gives clues about purpose.
- Review your class notes. Perhaps you will find a clue as to what has been emphasized over the past few lessons.
- Ask a classmate or study group partner for advice.
- Ask your instructor for advice.
- Learn to scan.
- Use the features of the textbook that give clues as to what is important. Look for key terms, a chapter introduction, and a chapter summary.

BRAIN-BASED LEARNING: Making Sense of What May Seem to Be Chaos

Research indicates that the brain seeks out meaning. It looks for connections as it establishes patterns that help it make sense of the world. These **brain-based learning** studies suggest we can take raw facts and make them mean something. And after all, isn't that what you want to do with all of the details thrown at you during the course of a college term? You want to make sense out of what, at times, can seem like chaos.

For learning to take place, you have to take three steps (Shapiro, 2006):

1. Sense or notice the material.
2. Integrate or combine it with what you already know.
3. Act on or use the information.

The same steps are involved in reading. If you want to understand and remember more of what you read, you have to do these three things:

1. *Notice* what you read—the words, the headings, the boldface type, the graphics, the questions, and the key terms.
2. *Connect* what you already know to the topic you are reading about.
3. *Use* the information as soon as possible to strengthen your learning and retention.

Activity 9.2

Why Do You Forget What You Read?

Have you ever completed an assigned reading but been unable to remember what you just read? Or have you found that while reading, you could not identify what material was most important to remember? So, you struggled to remember everything, got overwhelmed, and felt like you wasted your time. In a word, these experiences are *frustrating*.

For this exercise, think of your general experiences with school reading assignments. Whether it was this term or a previous one, do any of the following sound familiar? Check as many of the following reasons for forgetting what you have read as apply to you:

- ■ You did not understand the material.
- ■ You did not learn earlier background material.
- ■ You did not know what to remember.
- ■ You did not want to read the assignment.

- ■ You got bored.
- ■ You could not establish relationships.
- ■ You got distracted.
- ■ You did not understand the vocabulary.

- ■ Other:..

....

Briefly, what strategies have you used to address any of these issues?

....

....

Activity 9.3

Critically Thinking about How You Read Your Assignments

Let's apply the R.E.D. Model for critical thinking to examine one of the reading challenges you identified for yourself in Activity 9.2.

Write one of those challenges here: _____

 The R.E.D. Model (**R**ecognize Assumptions, **E**valuate Information, **D**raw Conclusions) provides a systematic way to approach critical thinking through the use of an easy-to-remember acronym.

Critical-Thinking Step	Application to Your Reading Skills	Your Explanation (here or on a separate piece of paper)
Recognize Assumptions	Clearly state this particular reading challenge. How do you know your assessment of your reading challenge is correct?	

Critical-Thinking Step	Application to Your Reading Skills	Your Explanation (here or on a separate piece of paper)
Evaluate Information	Provide a specific explanation (give examples) of this reading challenge. Examine your identified reading challenge beyond a superficial (simplistic) explanation, and look at all of the complexities involved. Examine your reading challenge from more than one perspective (point of view).	
Draw Conclusions	Based on your evidence, does your conclusion about your reading challenge make sense?	

Based on your answers, what insights have you gained about your reading challenge?

....

What is the next step you will take to eliminate this challenge?

....

....

HOW TO COMPLETE A TEXTBOOK READING ASSIGNMENT

We rate ability in men by what they finish, not by what they attempt
—Author unkown

HOW DOES THE INSTRUCTOR EXPECT YOU TO GET THROUGH THIS BORING TEXTBOOK?

You may have asked this question during your school years. Unfortunately, students find most textbooks dry and sleep inducing. But like it or not, your instructors *will* expect you to read the assignments.

Using the following plan will not only help you get through the dullest of textbooks, but it will also ensure that you retain more than you ever thought possible. Moreover, if this plan works for boring books, think of the results you might enjoy with exciting books you want to read.

YOUR CURRENT PLAN FOR TEXTBOOK READING

First, let's review what you currently do to complete a reading assignment.

Activity 9.4

My Plan for Completing a Reading Assignment

Select one of your textbooks from which you currently have a reading assignment. Write down the steps you normally take to complete a reading assignment.

Class: _____ Assigned pages: _____

To complete this reading assignment, I will follow these steps:

Step 1: ....

....

Step 2: ....

....

Step 3: ....

....

Step 4: ....

....

Step 5: ....

....

Once you have finished this assignment, compare your response with the SQ4R model that follows.

A PROVEN PROCESS FOR EFFECTIVE READING: SQ4R

Probably the most common approach to tackling a reading assignment is the **SQ4R** method. It is based on the famous SQ3R method developed by Franklin Pleasant Robinson during World War II. The first edition of Franklin's book *Effective Study* was published in 1946. Development of the SQ4R method has extended Robinson's pioneering work. Today, numerous sources reference the SQ4R method (see, for example, "SQ4R: A Classic Method for Studying Texts," 2007), and variations of the model have been developed (see "SQ4R Reading Model," n.d.).

Activity 9.5 provides a quick overview of this strategy. It also gives you the chance to identify how often you do each step.

Activity 9.5

SQ4R: What You Need to Know Right Now to Improve Your Reading

This introduction to SQ4R will allow you to rate how you currently use each of the six steps. A more detailed description of this process follows later in this chapter.

1. **Survey.** Quickly look over (**scan**) the reading assignment for clues as to what you will be reading. Look at the headings, captions, and boldface terms, and any other features the assigned pages might include. Engage your curiosity.

    ■ Circle the number that best corresponds to your answer to this question: *How often do you survey a reading assignment?*

    0 = never, 1 = almost never, 2 = occasionally, 3 = frequently, 4 = almost always, 5 = always

2. **Question.** Ask yourself questions about what you think the assignment will address. Also, while reading, continue to ask yourself questions about what you have just read.

    ■ Circle the number that best corresponds to your answer to this question: *How often do you ask yourself questions about a reading assignment?*

    0 = never, 1 = almost never, 2 = occasionally, 3 = frequently, 4 = almost always, 5 = always

3. **Read.** In this step, you actually read your assignment.

    ■ Circle the number that best corresponds to your answer to this question: *How often do you actually read a reading assignment?*

    0 = never, 1 = almost never, 2 = occasionally, 3 = frequently, 4 = almost always, 5 = always

4. **Recite.** Periodically, stop reading and put what you have just read into your own words. Consider this a self-quiz on your comprehension of the material.

    ■ Circle the number that best corresponds to your answer to this question: *While you are reading an assignment, how often do you summarize in your own words what you have read?*

    0 = never, 1 = almost never, 2 = occasionally, 3 = frequently, 4 = almost always, 5 = always

5. **Record.** Physically mark your book or write notes about the important words you are reading. You could highlight, underline, write in the book, or jot down notes on a separate piece of paper.

    ■ Circle the number that best corresponds to your answer to this question: *How often do you highlight or take notes on a reading assignment?*

    0 = never, 1 = almost never, 2 = occasionally, 3 = frequently, 4 = almost always, 5 = always

6. **Review.** Once you have completed your assignment but before closing the book, review what you have read to make sure you understand the material. If you find the material confusing, make a note of the troubling passages and ask a classmate or the instructor for assistance.

    ■ Circle the number that best corresponds to your answer to this question: *How often do you review a reading assignment as soon as you complete the assignment?*

    0 = never, 1 = almost never, 2 = occasionally, 3 = frequently, 4 = almost always, 5 = always

    Based on your answers, what insights have you gained about how you approach a reading assignment?

    ....

    ....

The SQ4R method is graphically portrayed in Figure 9.1.

Most study skills books have some variation of SQ4R. Call it what you will, but the plan has three stages, essentially: preread, read, and postread.

Preread. This part of the process involves the survey and question steps introduced earlier. Consider it the warm-up phase of reading. Before beginning practice or entering an actual game situation, athletes perform stretching exercises to limber up

Figure 9.1

Steps in SQ4R

WARM-UP!
Survey the material you are about to read. Stretch your reading muscles and move to the starting line.

GET SET!
Ask yourself *questions* about the reading assignment. Before you start reading, give yourself a purpose for reading.

GO!
Read the assignment. Quiz yourself along the way by *reciting* what you have read to that point. *Record* important information.

FINISH!
Before you close your book, *review* your notes.

their muscles. Reading should be no different, in terms of preparation. If you just open your book to the assigned page and start reading, you will have started "running" without warming up. For a reading assignment, anticipate (guess) what is to come.

Two simple questions will help you focus during this warm-up stage: "What do I already know about this material?" and "What would I like to know about this material?"

- **Warm up your intellectual muscles and establish a purpose.** Actively prepare to read. If you don't know what to look for, your reading may seem like torture. Refer to the purposes for reading listed earlier. Ask these basic questions:
  - ☐ What is this instructor concentrating on in class?
  - ☐ What kinds of test questions might come from this reading?
  - ☐ What past knowledge do I have about the reading assignment?

- **Scan the material.** If you were asked to find the phone number for Dominic Jones, would you pick up the phone book and start reading from the A's? Probably not. That would be a waste of your time. You would search for the J's and then scan for the last name and finally for the full name until you found it.

Make your reading as efficient as possible. While still warming up, quickly flip through the pages of the assignment. When you scan your reading assignment, you get a quick feel for what the "big picture" is. What you want is to get a general sense of the assignment. Read the introduction and the summary of the chapter. If you have to accomplish a certain outcome by the end of your reading—say, answer teacher-provided questions—then scan the material with that particular purpose in mind.

Although using this strategy adds a little time to the front end of your reading, it will aid your comprehension and actually trim time from the overall reading assignment. Once you finish this prereading activity, you will have a better idea of what you need to read.

Activity 9.6

Practice Scanning

Before you move to the next section, practice your scanning skill. Complete this activity using the textbook chapter you are reading right now. Do the following:

- Read the chapter introduction and the chapter summary.
- Based on the introduction and the summary, write a couple of sentences that explain what you will learn in this chapter. Hint: Be more specific than "This chapter will teach me how to read better."

....

....

....

- Look at the key terms listed at the beginning of the chapter. As you scan the chapter, ask yourself, "Why have these words been labeled key terms?"

....

....

....

- Read the chapter's headings/subheadings, and form questions based on them. These questions will give you a purpose for reading. As you read, you will be actively looking for information (answers to your questions). For instance, one section is titled Identifying the Purpose. The question you form might be "Why do I need to identify the purpose?" or "Can there be more than one purpose?"
- Write a couple of the questions you formed:

....

....

....

■ Look at all pictures, graphics, and captions in the chapter. They have a purpose for being in the text. What types of graphics are in this chapter? Why do you think they have been included?

....

....

....

■ Look at the boldface, italicized, and underlined words and phrases. Why do you think these particular words and phrases have been highlighted?

....

....

Your reading comprehension should increase with more effective practice. Take a few reflective moments now to complete Activity 9.7.

Practice for Lena: Developing Your Own Questions from Chapter Headings

In the chapter-opening situation, Lena mentioned that she typically jumped right in to complete her reading assignment. Let's demonstrate for Lena how a little prethought can help improve her reading interest and comprehension.

Some of the headings from this chapter are shown in the following list. For each heading, develop a question that will help you find the purpose of the section. Be an investigative reporter and ask the *Who? What? When? Why? Where?* and *How?* questions. The first one has been completed as an example.

■ Do You Know Why You Read an Assignment? *My question about the heading: Why is it important that I know why I am reading an assignment? OR How can I find out why I am reading an assignment?*

■ Brain-Based Learning: Making Sense of What May Seem to Be Chaos

....

....

■ Identifying the Purpose

....

....

■ A Proven Process for Effective Reading: SQ4R

....

....

■ Using Context Clues to Build Your Vocabulary

....

....

Read. Once you have warmed up, you are ready to read, recite, and record.

■ This is the time to satisfy your curiosity and look for answers to the questions you posed in Activity 9.7. As you read, ask more questions.

■ Look for the **main idea** of the reading selection. What is the main reason the author wrote the paragraph, chapter, or book you are reading? Remember your English training. Whether you find paragraphs in a textbook or on a website, they (usually) have a topic sentence—a sentence that explains the main idea of the paragraph. Many times, the topic sentence is the first sentence, but sometimes, it appears later in the paragraph. As you develop stronger reading skills, you will find the topic more easily and have a better understanding of the passages you read.

■ Pay particular attention to words that give you trouble. The author may be using these words for a specific reason (Adler & Van Doren, 1972, p. 102). In other words, if a word appears awkward, unusual, or strange within the context it appears in, there is a good chance that it's an important term. If you pay attention to the context of the paragraph, you will have a better chance of determining the main point. (See the following section titled Vocabulary.)

■ Textbooks of different disciplines are not meant to be read in the same manner (Adler & Van Doren, 1972, chapters 13 and 19). A science book, which contains lots of facts and a complex vocabulary, should not be read like a history text or a novel. Recognize the differences and make adjustments:

☐ When reading a *history* text, look for cause and effect, names of important people, impacts of events on people, turning points, and hints of bias or prejudice by the author.
☐ When reading a *science* book, focus on classifications, experimental steps, hypotheses, and unexplained phenomena.
☐ When reading a novel for *English*, look for symbolism, character thresholds, a hero, tragic flaws, and a developing message.
☐ Even when reading a *math* book, look for its particular characteristics. Determine which variables, functions, theorems, and axioms are the "building blocks" of the chapter.

Strategic Reading

Highlighting is a **strategic reading** behavior. That is, when used properly, it is part of a planned and thoughtful action to achieve a desired result. In this case, reading comprehension is the goal. If highlighting is done without thought—that is, just "painting the page yellow" by marking everything—then it is neither strategic nor effective. Apply your skills of surveying, questioning, and using context clues in highlighting. Consider highlighting just one more form of active learning. As summed up in one study, "Students need to be dynamic, active learners, actively participating with their encoding process of material being read" (Gier et al., 2011, p. 40).

Activity 9.8

Read the following passage, and then write a sentence stating what you think is the main idea. Then, share your answer with a classmate.

> One 2004 study found that 3.8 million Americans weighed more than 300 pounds; more than 400,000 people weighed in excess of 400 pounds ("Obesity," 2011); and nearly 64% of the population is overweight. How can a wealthy nation like the United States end up with such a weight problem—including a 31% obesity rate? Some say it is precisely because of the lifestyle we lead (Hellmich, 2002). "Junk food" is readily available (and widely marketed). Cars and elevators replace bicycles and walking. Video games and big-screen televisions substitute for participation in physical activity. And although genetics and medications may have an impact on weight gain, other controllable factors such as method of food preparation (frying), size of portions (all-you-can-eat), and lack of self-discipline can contribute to obesity. (Piscitelli, 2011, pp. 246–247)

What is the main idea of this passage? Write a sentence stating it.

....

....

Record. The importance of this step is to make the words you read your own. The better able you are to put the author's words into your own words, the more likely you will remember the material.

There are a couple of ways to handle the recording part of SQ4R:

- **Highlighting.** Use a pen, pencil, or brightly colored marker to underline, circle, or box important information. But remember this word of caution about **highlighting**: Identify only the *major* points. Too many students highlight almost every word, which is useless. Look for key words and phrases.

- **Making margin notes.** As you read, make notes in the margins of your book. Maybe you have a question about the paragraph you just completed reading. If so, jot it down in the margin. Or as you highlight part of a sentence or passage, write the main point—in your words—in the margin. Learn to use your book: Read it, write in it, and consume it! And consider keeping your textbooks for future reference—especially those in your major area of study.

- **Note taking.** Using the strategies you have already practiced, actually record notes in your notebook. You may find note taking more effective than highlighting, because it forces you to encode the material—putting it into your own words. If you can do this, you *understand* the material. Concentrate on main points, themes, and questions you might have.

Used Books, Highlighting, and Effective Reading

Buying used textbooks gives students an opportunity to save money. But as with buying anything that has been previously owned, the buyer has to be a wise consumer. Carefully review any used book to see how it was used by the previous owner(s). One group of researchers advises used-book buyers to examine the highlighting, in particular. Consider these findings: "Students who buy used textbooks may find that the previous owner(s) highlighted the passages in the textbook inappropriately . . . [and that] relevant material was not highlighted, and non-relevant material was highlighted" (Gier et al., 2011, p. 39). Assuming the previous owner has already "done all the work" by picking out the important material could be costly for the student who buys a used book. Because unfortunately, "all the work" may be totally wrong.

Activity 9.9

Practice: Recording in Your Own Words

Read the passage that follows. Highlight, underline, and/or circle the important words, details, and points that are raised. Based on what you noted, write a summary in your own words. Once you have completed the activity, share your answer with a classmate.

Have you ever believed in something or someone with such intensity that you would gladly sacrifice for the benefit of that thing, issue, or person? Have you ever been in a class that was so exciting you literally lost track of time—the class ended, but you wanted it to continue? Do you have a class this term that is so energizing that you cannot wait to attend the next session? If the answer is yes for any of these, then it can be said you have a passion for that particular person, place, or thing.

Identifying your **passion**—what you are committed to and what you love to do with your days—can help you understand why you get up in the morning. This "why" provides the purpose for your day. Sometimes, though, people pursue goals that do not connect to their passions, talents, and desires.

Because you complete a goal does not mean it furthers your life or otherwise has a positive impact on you or those around you. The same for your major. Once you have declared a major, how do you know it is the correct choice for you? Will it contribute to your overall balance and wellness? (Piscitelli, 2011, p. 287)

Write your summary of the passage here.

....

....

....

Postread. Once you have completed your reading assignment, do not immediately close the book. It's time to review! Even if your review is brief, the repetition will help you strengthen connections and deepen your learning. According to one researcher, "The brain strengthens learning through repetition. Repetition is bad only when it becomes boring" (Jensen, 2000, p. 78). The question to ask yourself at this point is "What did I just read?"

Immediately after reading, take 5 or 10 minutes to study the notes you just wrote or the words you highlighted. Organize and reorganize your notes according to categories, theories, trends, or other qualities. It may help to ask yourself these questions:

- What is the "big picture"?
- How can I connect this new knowledge to previously learned material?
- What relationships do I see emerging?

Performing this step keeps you focused while preparing for the next class and the upcoming exam. If you are confused about the reading, bring your question(s) to the next class.

Activity 9.10

Practice: What Have You Just Read?

Before you move on to the next section, briefly ask yourself—and answer this question: What have you read thus far in *this chapter*? Write your answers here:

- ....
- ....
- ....
- ....
- ....

Well, there you have it. SQ4R provides an achievable plan with many benefits. The notes you develop while reading, for instance, will serve as an excellent complement for your classroom notes. With your reading complete and organized, you will be ready for the instructor's presentation. You can participate, actively learn, and get better grades, and you will be able to use your precious time more effectively.

ADDITIONAL STRATEGIES FOR READING SUCCESS

> *Once you learn to read, you will be forever free.*
> —Frederick Douglass, abolitionist

USE SUPPLEMENTAL SOURCES

If you have a difficult time understanding your textbooks, look for other sources. For instance, most bookstores sell short versions of American history. Such books concentrate on the major points of historical periods. The same holds true for books in other disciplines. A *supplemental* book provides an outline of major points.

Do not use these sources as *substitute* for your textbooks. Rather, use them to help you understand the main points.

VOCABULARY

Your **vocabulary** is your "bank" of words. It contains the words that allow you to communicate your feelings and views. And the richness of your vocabulary will have an impact on how well you understand the people—and the world—around you.

One author has estimated that the average 18-year-old student has a 60,000-word vocabulary. By the end of college, the typical student will add another 20,000 words to his or her vocabulary (Henry, 2004, p. 46). The broader your vocabulary, the better you will read.

Here are two strategies to help you continue to add to your word bank:

1. Use a dictionary to clarify meanings of words you don't understand. Look up new words, correct misspellings on exams and homework, and learn synonyms and antonyms. You can buy a small (pocket) dictionary and thesaurus, or you can use online tools.
2. Play word games, such as Scrabble, or work with crossword puzzles. (You may even be able to download "apps" for these games to your cell phone.) This strategy has two benefits: (a) it builds your vocabulary, and (b) it limbers up your "mental muscles" for the coming academic day.

USING CONTEXT CLUES TO BUILD YOUR VOCABULARY

The reality is that few students stop, reach for a dictionary, leaf through the pages (or, if online, type in a word), and read the definition of a troublesome word. And in some situations, such as taking an exam, using a dictionary may not be practical or possible.

In such instances, you will want to rely on context clues. In this usage, **context** refers to the words that surround the word you want to understand. Using the words you do understand, you make an educated guess about the meaning of the unknown word.

Activity 9.11

Practice: Using Context Clues

For each sentence, write the meaning of the underlined word *and* briefly explain how the context (surrounding words) helps define it.

- *Rather than <u>accelerate</u>, Jeremy tapped his brakes as he entered the intersection.*

  ☐ The meaning of <u>accelerate</u>: ....
  ☐ How does the context help you understand the underlined word?

  ....

- *Successful leaders know when to <u>delegate</u>, or assign, work to other people.*

  ☐ The meaning of <u>delegate</u>: ....
  ☐ How does the context help you understand the underlined word?

  ....

- *The customer showed his <u>integrity</u> when he came back to the store to return the extra money the cashier had given him in error.*

  ☐ The meaning of <u>integrity</u>: ....

☐ How does the context help you understand the underlined word?

....

■ *Joe <u>overhauled</u> his old car with new tires, a sparkling paint job, and an engine tune-up.*

☐ The meaning of <u>overhauled:</u> ....

☐ How does the context help you understand the underlined word?

....

HAVING TROUBLE FINDING THE MAIN IDEA? USE MINI-SQ4RS

According to one author, "The most important reading skill you can develop as a college student is the ability to determine the author's main idea. The main idea of a paragraph is the most important point the author makes about the topic" (Henry, 2004, p. 108).

If you have difficulty determining the main idea, then break your reading task into smaller pieces. Read one paragraph at a time, and use the SQ4R strategy: Scan the paragraph, ask yourself a question or two about it, jot down a few notes, and then review what you have read.

Once you find that you can understand a single paragraph, expand your reading to two, three, or more paragraphs at a time. If you get to a point where you do not comprehend the main idea, back up and read fewer paragraphs. While using this approach will take more time at first, think of the time you will have wasted if you read an entire chapter and do not understand most or all of the content.

UNDERSTANDING AND USING GRAPHICS

Authors use **graphics** to simplify their messages. Using fewer words than sentences or paragraphs, they can help readers make the connection between concepts, understand the main point of a paragraph, and show support for a particular opinion. Graphics also are important guides to help you survey your reading—the first step of SQ4R.

Authors use many different kinds of graphics. (For a review, see Smith [2008], pp. 534–547.) Some of the most common kinds are shown in Figure 9.2.

Activity 9.12

Using the Graphics in Your Textbooks

Using any of your textbooks, find an example of each of the following graphics. For each graphic, briefly explain the information that is provided.

■ Bar graph ....

....

■ Chart ....

....

Figure 9.2

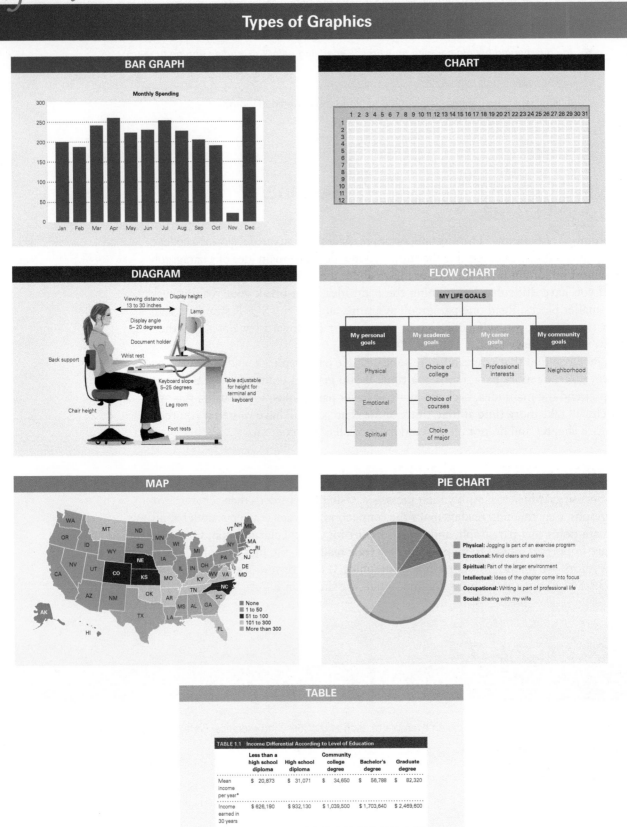

- Diagram ....

  ....

- Flowchart ....

  ....

- Map ....

  ....

- Pie graph ....

  ....

- Table ....

  ....

"NOW, WHAT DO I DO WITH MY READING NOTES?"

Completing your reading assignment is important, but as you study, you also need to review, reorganize, and find relationships in the information you read. Once you have mastered the reading assignment, bring any reading notes you write to class. Using reading notes in class serves a variety of purposes. These notes can do any or all of the following:

- Serve as a guide for discussion.
- Help you answer teacher-posed questions.
- Remind you to ask clarifying questions.
- Allow you to focus on the important points the teacher is making.

In short, you will be more prepared to listen and participate actively.

As a reflective self-assessment, ask yourself whether you can intelligently discuss the reading material in a class discussion. If you can, congratulate yourself. If you can't, review the assignment briefly before you get to class. Remember that practice makes permanent.

"MY INSTRUCTOR ALWAYS FALLS BEHIND SCHEDULE"

Instructors have great intentions. They meticulously plan a unit of study, neatly matching and spacing reading assignments to complement well-thought-out lectures and activities as they move toward the unit exam.

Unfortunately, great plans sometimes get lost in the realities of day-to-day classroom business. Have you ever had an instructor who painstakingly covered one chapter in three *weeks*, only to finish the unit with a "big push"—covering four chapters in three *days*? Picking up the pace like this can be stressful for everyone concerned, but you have to deal with it.

It's best to do homework reading that corresponds with classroom topics—for example, preparing for the lesson prior to coming to class. But don't wait to digest 90 pages of new material in a couple of nights. Put yourself on a schedule, read, and keep your notes handy for when the teacher finally reviews that material in class.

Table 9.1 An example of a character chart

Chapter 1		
"MY CREATIVE TITLE"		
Character 1	**Character 2**	**Character 3**
When introduced:	When introduced:	When introduced:
Connection to another:	Connection to another:	Connection to another:
Significant quote:	Significant quote:	Significant quote:
Symbolism:	Symbolism:	Symbolism:

Brief chapter summary:

....

....

....

Confusing points:

....

....

"THE READING PLAN IS FINE FOR TEXTBOOKS, BUT WHAT ABOUT NOVELS?"

Most novels do not provide readers with neat headings and subheadings. Chapters might be identified only by numbers, not by descriptive titles. For a novel, your reading strategy will be more difficult but not impossible. It will just take some creativity:

- Once you have completed reading a chapter, give it your own title. Whatever title you choose, it should answer the question "What is the main point of this chapter?" Be as creative and descriptive as you can.

- Why was the chapter written? Briefly summarize the purpose of the chapter and its connection to the rest of the book. Also write a brief summary of what happened and why. Even if you can't identify the plot at this point, summarizing what happened will help point you in the general direction.

- Identify the characters, their relationships with other characters, their significance, and their connection to the plot. Did anyone utter a particularly meaningful statement? Some students have found character charts beneficial for listing characters' traits and importance to the story. Table 9.1 shows one way to do this.

- Be sensitive to literary symbols. Is water being used to depict rebirth? Is an old animal synonymous with dying? Is autumn representative of old age? Add these symbols to your character chart, as appropriate.

- Finally, make note of what you do *not* understand. Be as specific as possible.

Chapter SUMMARY

This chapter presented efficient reading strategies to improve comprehension. Before leaving this chapter, keep the following points in mind:

- Always know your purpose for reading.
- Use the SQ4R method to organize your reading.
- Be sure to warm up first by scanning the material.
- Make connections between what you read and what you already know.
- When taking notes on your reading, use *your* own words.
- Use context clues to help you understand unknown vocabulary.
- Find the "big picture"—the main idea.
- Immediately after finishing your reading assignment, evaluate your reading comprehension.

CRITICALLY THINKING

What Have You Learned in This Chapter?

Let's apply what you learned in this chapter to help Lena from the chapter-opening scenario. However, before you address Lena's problem and propose your solution, take a moment to think about the main points of the chapter.

Review your notes from this chapter and also the key terms, chapter learning outcomes, boldface chapter headings, and figures and tables. For instance, consider how the chapter learning outcomes may be used to help Lena:

- Identify the purpose of a reading assignment.
- Identify the main idea of a paragraph.
- Demonstrate how to use the SQ4R reading process.
- Use highlighting to identify key information and improve understanding.
- Determine the meanings of vocabulary words by using the context.
- Use graphics to help you understand a reading assignment.

TEST YOUR LEARNING

Now that you have reviewed the main points of this chapter and reread Lena's story, what advice do you have for her? Using the R.E.D. Model for critical thinking, help Lena critically review her concerns:

(R)

Recognize Assumptions:

Facts: What are the facts in Lena's situation? List them.

Opinions: What opinions do you find in this situation? List them.

Assumptions: Are Lena's assumptions accurate?

(E)

Evaluate Information:

Help Lena compile a list of questions that will help her make the most appropriate decision.

What emotions seem to be motivating Lena?

What, if anything, is missing from her thought process?

Do you see any confirmation bias?

(D)

Draw Conclusions:

Based on the facts and the questions you have presented, what conclusions can you draw?

What advice do you have for Lena? What solutions do you propose?

Based on your suggestions, do you see any assumptions?

Finally, based on what you have learned about using critical thinking and reading strategies, what plan of action do you suggest for Lena?

10 MEMORY

I'm always fascinated by the way memory diffuses fact.
—Diane Sawyer, television journalist

CHAPTER LEARNING OUTCOMES

By the time you finish reading this chapter and completing its activities, you will be able to do the following:

- Identify and use at least two strategies to improve your skill of noticing what you need to remember.

- Identify and use at least two strategies to help you improve how you store information.

- Demonstrate active-listening skills.

- Identify and use at least two organizational models to help you reclaim information.

The Case of BILLY

Situation: Billy's biology professor told him today that he was in serious danger of failing for the semester. Billy knows he can do better. He told his professor that his biggest problem is with memory. "I take notes. I study the notes. But I still do poorly on the exams."

Billy reads his textbook, although it is not easy. Not only is the book filled with a lot of terms and complicated explanations, but Billy is not particularly interested in the subject. He wants to major in business and does not see the

© Shutterstock

Key terms

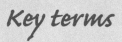

Acronym
Active listening
Data retrieval chart (D.R.C.)
Extinction
Forgetting
Long-term memory
Memory
Memory block
Notice
Reclaiming
Response competition
Short-term memory
Situational variation
Storing information
Working memory

Chapter
INTRODUCTION

In the late 1800s, psychologist Hermann Ebbinghaus described the "forgetting curve." He found that if you do not immediately use what you have learned during, for instance, a class lecture or demonstration, you will lose it—forget it. According to Ebbinghaus's findings, most of what you will forget will happen within a few hours of your leaving the classroom or lecture hall. And if you don't work with the material within 30 days of receiving it, you will forget 90 percent of it (Medina, 2008, p. 100).

connection between that and his science and math courses.

Billy studies for each exam by setting aside three hours the night before to review notes and textbook readings and to quiz himself on the major concepts. Since he does not really understand the material, Billy does his best to memorize everything he can. By time he gets to class, he is exhausted— and he remembers very little of what he studied.

"I have a terrible memory. I can't remember a thing!" Billy said one day.

CRITICALLY THINKING
about *Billy's* situation

Help Billy figure out his memory problem. That is, what likely causes his memory lapses, and what can he do about them?

Now, apply this information to the context of a school term. You listen to and take notes on a class lecture during a 9:00 a.m. psychology class on Monday. You leave class and do not review your notes. Four weeks later, it's test time. Unless you have a remarkable and rare type of memory (like the character Ray in the movie *Rain Man*), you will have lost most of that information. (Recall that Ray was a savant with an amazing capacity for memorizing numbers.)

MyStudentSuccessLab

MyStudentSuccessLab (www .mystudentsuccesslab.com) is an online solution designed to help you 'Start strong, Finish stronger' by building skills for ongoing personal and professional development.

Figure 10.1

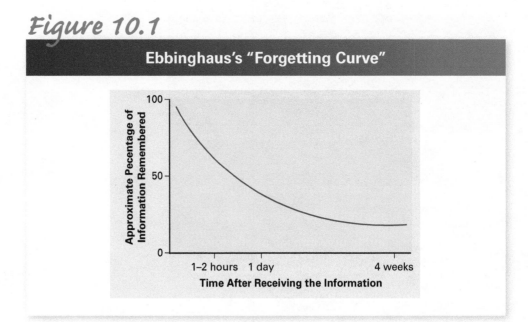

Ebbinghaus's "Forgetting Curve"

Besides reviewing and working with the information, other factors affect what you will remember, such as your interest in the topic and the complexity of the material. Nonetheless, spending time with the material is still *the* critical component. Figure 10.1 provides a visual approximation of the rapid loss of material that is not reviewed soon after receiving it.

Think about Ebbinghaus's finding. You can put in "face time" (actually show your face and sit through each class), take notes, and still fail if you do not *do* something with the information. That is what this chapter will focus on: how you can *do* something effective to retain information.

College requires students to read a lot of material and absorb a great deal of detail. In addition, it requires you to truly understand the readings and lectures, rather than simply memorize information and spit it back on a test.

Like Billy at the beginning of the chapter, you may have heard someone say (or you may even have said it yourself), "I have a terrible memory. I can't remember a thing!"

Typically, this is an overstatement. You can remember things. If you didn't, how would you have found your way to class today? When someone complains of having a poor memory, he or she needs to dig deeper and critically examine assumptions and broad generalities. This chapter will look at three basic components of memory and strategies to help you improve each one.

THREE SIMPLE STEPS TO IMPROVED MEMORY

The concept of **memory** simply refers to your ability to grab, hold, and recall information. If you want to improve your memory, you will need to do three things (Minninger & Dugan, 1994, pp. 27–41):

1. **Notice** the material. Before anyone can learn anything, he or she must notice the material. If you want to remember the date and time of a study group meeting, you must make note of it. Do you want to remember the formulas for the math test? You have to notice them. When learning a new route to school or the beach or to work, you first have to notice the landmarks—where to turn, where to stop, and where to park. So, step 1 in improving your memory requires you to take note of what is around you. In short, you must pay attention.

2. **Storing information** is the second step in improving your memory. When we want to protect a cell phone or a digital reader, we keep it in a safe and secure spot. Then, we want to remember where we put it so we can retrieve it for later use. The same holds true for what we want to remember. If we store the information in a secure place in our minds, we will be able to access it easily when we need it. So, if you want to return to the beach—using our example from earlier—you could continually ask for directions, or you could store the information for future use.

3. **Reclaiming** (or retrieving) the information you have stored is the third step. When we say, for example, someone has "a good memory for names," we typically mean he or she can meet someone and then later recall the person's name. A student with "a good memory for dates" may do very well on a history exam—or remember dates such as his or her spouse's birthday or their wedding anniversary. When you reclaim information, you are finding it and using it.

This chapter will suggest strategies to help you *notice*, *store*, and *reclaim* information. Figure 10.2 graphically depicts this relationship.

Figure 10.2

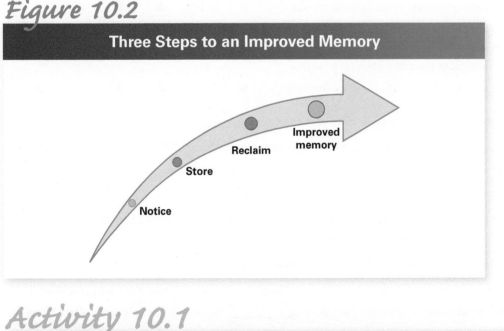

Three Steps to an Improved Memory

Improved memory

Reclaim

Store

Notice

Activity 10.1

Reflecting on Your Current Level of Memory and Recall Skills

Before you answer the items that follow, reflect on your current level of memory and recall skills. Think of how well (or poorly) you have performed in past classes.

As you do in completing all of the reflective activities in this book, you should write from your heart. This exercise is not meant for you to answer just like your classmates—or to match what you may think the instructor wants to see. Take the time to give a respectful, responsible general accounting of your experiences with memory and recall. Making a truthful self-assessment now will help you build on skills you have while developing those you lack.

For each of the following items, circle the number that best describes your *typical* experience with memory skills. Here is the key for the numbers:

0 = never, 1 = almost never, 2 = occasionally, 3 = frequently, 4 = almost always, 5 = always

When considering your past successes and challenges with remembering information, how often . . .

1. Were you able to remember the name of a person introduced to you just five minutes ago?	0	1	2	3	4	5
2. Could you describe what your roommate (or wife or husband) was wearing when he or she left the house in the morning?	0	1	2	3	4	5
3. Would you be able to remember the last three songs you heard on the radio or your personal hand-held device?	0	1	2	3	4	5
4. Did you attempt to make connections between what you read in a textbook assignment and what you heard in class from the instructor?	0	1	2	3	4	5
5. Did you participate in class by asking questions (or answering questions) about the day's lesson?	0	1	2	3	4	5
6. Did you visit the instructor's office to seek clarification or ask a question to make sure you understood the class material?	0	1	2	3	4	5
7. Did you take an exam and remember almost everything you had studied?	0	1	2	3	4	5
8. Did you use memory aids (such as charts, acronyms, and sayings) to help you remember the information for a test?	0	1	2	3	4	5
9. Did you "freeze up" or "blank out" on a test and perform poorly?	0	1	2	3	4	5

Add up your scores for items 1, 2, and 3. Divide by 3. Write your answer here: _____.

Using the key provided to explain each number (0, 1, 2, 3, 4, 5), complete this sentence: When it comes to noticing information, I _____ take effective note of things around me or materials in front of me.

Add up your scores for items 4, 5, and 6. Divide by 3. Write your answer here: _____.

Using the key provided to explain each number (0, 1, 2, 3, 4, 5), complete this sentence: When it comes to storing information I am learning, I _____ store this information effectively.

Add up your scores for items 7, 8, and 9. Divide by 3. Write your answer here: _____.

Using the key provided to explain each number (0, 1, 2, 3, 4, 5), complete this sentence: When it comes to reclaiming (or recalling or remembering or retrieving) information I am learning, I _____ am able effectively to reclaim information I need.

Based on your answers, what insights have you gained about your experiences with organization?

....

....

....

Activity 10.2

Critically Thinking about Your Memory Skills

Let's apply the R.E.D. Model for critical thinking to examine one of the memory challenges identified in Activity 10.1. (Choose one of the items on which you scored a 0, 1, or 2.)

Do you have more of a problem recognizing what to notice, or is your biggest challenge storing the information? Or perhaps you notice and store information fine but have difficulty recalling it when you need it.

Write your memory challenge here: _____

> **R E D** The R.E.D. Model (**R**ecognize Assumptions, **E**valuate Information, **D**raw Conclusions) provides a systematic way to approach critical thinking through the use of an easy-to-remember acronym.

Critical-Thinking Step	Application to Your Memory Skills	Your Explanation (here or on a separate piece of paper)
Recognize Assumptions	Clearly state this particular memory challenge. How do you know this assessment of your memory challenge is correct?	
Evaluate Information	Provide a specific explanation (give examples) of this memory challenge. How is your assessment of your memory challenge connected to your academic progress? Examine your identified memory challenge beyond a superficial (simplistic) explanation, and look at all of the complexities involved.	
Draw Conclusions	Examine your memory challenge from more than one perspective (point of view). Based on your evidence, does your conclusion about your memory challenge make sense?	

Based on your answers, what insights have you gained about your memory challenge?

....

....

....

....

What is the next step you will take to eliminate this challenge?

....

....

....

....

IMPROVING YOUR MEMORY: NOTICING THE INFORMATION

One must always be aware to notice even though the cost of noticing is to become responsible.

—*Thylias Moss, poet*

WHY DO YOU FORGET?

Forgetting is the failure of a previously *learned* behavior to reappear. Using the terminology you read in the introduction to this chapter, if you do not notice and effectively store information, it becomes much more difficult to recall it (as on a test, for example).

People forget for a variety of reasons:

- They fail to use what they have learned in a timely manner. (Refer to the so-called forgetting curve at the beginning of the chapter.)
- The reward they received for learning is no longer present.
- A previously learned behavior interferes with a newly learned behavior.
- A newly learned behavior interferes with a previously learned behavior.
- The situation in which the new behavior must occur is different from the one in which the behavior was learned.
- An emotion (fear, anger, anxiety) may interfere with reclaiming the information.
- Physical stress may interfere with reclaiming the information.

CHOOSING TO NOTICE

Let's do a little demonstration. Close your eyes and, without looking, picture the area to the left of where you are sitting. Describe what you see. Be specific. If there is a bookshelf, don't just say there are books on the shelf. In what order do they appear? What are their topics? What colors are they? Are they hardcover or paperback?

Now, mentally look to your right. What kind of furniture is there? Colors? Fabrics? Designs? Lengths and widths?

Who sits to your right? To your left? What are these people wearing? Colors? Styles? Leather, cotton, knit, suede? Socks? Flip-flops or no shoes?

If you are like most people, you probably couldn't answer many of these questions. More than likely, you had not taken the time to really notice the items.

Each of us encounters a dizzying amount of stimulation within a day. Most of it, we hold on to for a very brief period (milliseconds) and then let go. In other words, we do not pay attention to this information.

The information that we do give attention to moves into **short-term memory**, which is also known as **working memory**. Our short-term or working memory will allow us to work with (manipulate) anywhere from five to nine items for a short period of time. The average is seven and is sometimes referred to as "Miller's magic number"—named after George Miller, who studied short-term memory.

Think of remembering a phone number without writing it down or punching it into your cell phone. You may repeat the seven-digit number over and over until you can physically touch each number on the keypad. The information may or may not eventually be transferred to long-term memory. If it is not, we typically say it has been "forgotten" (Pastor, n.d.).

Sometimes, we forget because we *choose not to remember*—or at the very least, we choose not to *notice*. If we can train ourselves to notice—to use our senses—we will have a better chance of remembering those things we come into contact with. When we learn to heighten our senses of seeing, listening, touching, tasting, and smelling, we will find it easier to recall a particular situation or reading or physical experience.

Listening, for instance, is an activity that requires focus. It goes beyond *hearing*; you will do better if you choose to *listen*. That is, when you want to understand the words you are hearing, you will have a better chance of remembering the information by paying attention to the material.

The following activity provides practice to help you strengthen your awareness of your surroundings.

Activity 10.3

Practice: Improving Your Senses

Brainstorm with a classmate ways you might be able to sharpen each of the five senses. An example is provided for each sense to get you thinking.

1. **Seeing.** How can you sharpen this sense?
   - Example: Look—*really look*—at one of your classrooms. (If you are on an online student, do the same with a coffee shop or another place you frequent.) Describe it in detail. Go beyond saying "it has four white walls with desks in rows." Estimate its dimensions. Is the color off white, bright white, or some other color? What is the ceiling made of? What is on the walls? The more detail you describe, the better the chance you will have of remembering the room.
   - Your practice: Stretch your visual awareness by describing a person, a thing, an event, or a location.

   ....

   ....

   ....

2. **Listening.** How can you sharpen this sense?
   - Example: The next time you are in the student center or a restaurant, listen to the sounds around you: the voices, the noise, the games, and the music. Become aware of the volume and whether it is pleasing to your ears. Why is or isn't it pleasing to you?
   - Your practice: Stretch your listening skills by describing what a current celebrity's voice sounds like. Is it soothing, piercing, grating, sweet, or whiney?

   ....

   ....

3. **Touching.** How can you sharpen this sense?
   - Example: Describe how it feels to sit where you are sitting: hard, soft, cushy, relaxing, or pain inducing.
   - Your practice: Stretch your awareness by describing the touch of something very soft (such as a baby's skin) or something really rough (such as sandpaper).

   ....

   ....

4. **Tasting.** How can you sharpen this sense?

- Example: Think of the last meal you ate. Describe the tastes of your food: sweet, sour, fruity, scalding hot, icy cold, salty, or bland.
- Your practice: Stretch your awareness of taste by describing your favorite latte, espresso, cup of tea, or soft drink.

....

....

5. **Smelling.** How can you sharpen this sense?

- Example: Take a whiff of your favorite cologne or perfume. How would you describe it to a friend?
- Your practice: Stretch your awareness of smell by describing the smell of a damp room or old running shoes.

....

....

IMPROVING YOUR MEMORY: STORING THE INFORMATION YOU HAVE NOTICED

> *There are lots of people who mistake their imagination for their memory.*
>
> —Josh Billings, author

Once you notice the information, you need to file it away for future use. Remember, just because you have *heard* or *seen* or *touched* or *tasted* or *smelled* something does not mean you have paid attention to it.

To move information (a textbook reading, lecture, song lyrics, or statistics about a sports team) from your working memory to long-term memory, you have to learn how to encode it into something meaningful to you. This section will suggest strategies that, if practiced (rehearsed), can decrease the times you freeze or go blank when you want to recall something important.

ACTIVE LISTENING IMPROVES MEMORY

People who perform **active listening** are engaged in what they hear. They make meaning of what is said.

Following these tips will help you become a more active listener—and effectively store more information:

- **Focus.** Practice basic courtesy, and you will retain more. Pay attention to the speaker. Put aside other distractions. Focus on the words and meanings. Take notes, if need be.

- **Find relevance.** Not every speaker, instructor, or reading assignment will be exciting and engaging. Find something you connect with

in the presentation, and then focus on it. Perhaps you can find a relationship to something you already know or an explanation you have never heard of before.

- **Listen rather than hear.** Do this with your ears—not your mouth. If you mentally begin phrasing your response while the speaker is still talking, you may very well miss an important point. It can be difficult to understand the speaker if you are just waiting to jump in and give your opinion. If you "listen" in this manner, you are creating your own distraction.

- **Participate.** Once the speaker has finished, rephrase what he or she said. If you can explain, in your own words, what has just been presented, you will have a better chance of retention. By paraphrasing, you are, in effect, rehearsing the new material, which leads to understanding.

- **Ask questions.** This is also part of the participation strategy. Ask for clarification, relationships, or the significance of the topic at hand. Not only are you repeating the information, but you are also doing it in the context of the "big picture" of the presentation. This will help in the development of so-called memory hooks (discussed later).

- **Offer another explanation or application.** This is a particularly effective strategy to use in classes that follow a discussion or seminar format. As you process the instructor's information, offer another side of the issue. This can be done in a tactful, noncombative manner as an attempt to understand other aspects of the topic. This allows for analysis and, consequently, better understanding.

By becoming actively involved, you will be more likely to retain the information.

Activity 10.4

Practice: Active Listening

Pick one of the strategies described, and practice it later today when you have a conversation with a classmate, friend, faculty member, or family member. After the conversation, write down your observations:

- Which strategy did you use?..
- What did you find easy about using the strategy?..
- What was difficult about using the strategy?

....

- How do you think using this strategy can increase your academic success?

....

USING CHARTS TO MAKE CONNECTIONS

Another helpful technique to organize information is the **data retrieval chart (D.R.C.).** Used for many years in education, this model allows for easy categorization, comparison, and contrast of information.

As shown in Figure 10.3, a D.R.C. can be used to show how one event leads to another. In this case, it allows students to see the connection between the actions and responses of two groups. This simplified view of cause and effect demonstrates how England found itself in a war with its colonies.

Figure 10.3

D.R.C. Showing Cause-and-Effect in American War for Independence		
Prime Minister	**Example of British Action**	**Example of Colonial Response**
Grenville	Stamp Act passed to collect taxes	Colonists upset with Stamp Act; Congress convened
Townshend (Pitt)	More taxes placed on the colonists	Colonists upset; boycott English goods
North	Tea Act passed	Colonists *REALLY* upset; Boston Tea Party dumps tea into Boston Harbor

Another example of a D.R.C. is shown in Figure 10.4 about sexually transmitted infections. In this case, a student can quickly understand the nature of the infection (or disease) and its consequences.

A D.R.C. can be used to compare authors, scientific findings, historical developments, artistic relationships, and the like. Each cell can be easily compared with another cell. Relationships and connections, which are vital to improving memory, can be easily established.

Don't wait for the instructor to provide a D.R.C. Make up your own when reviewing and reorganizing your notes. It will provide a great one-page study guide—efficient, effective, and practical.

Activity 10.5

Practice: Creating Your Own D.R.C.

R E D

Billy, from the chapter-opening scenario, has been attempting to memorize lists of terms and definitions. Demonstrate for him how a D.R.C. can help make the course material more memorable by creating connections and visualizations. To do this, complete the following D.R.C. using five strategies this chapter has introduced.

Chapter Concept	Brief Description of the Strategy	Specific Example of How to Use the Strategy
1.		
2.		
3.		
4.		
5.		

Figure 10.4

D.R.C. of Types of Sexually Transmitted Infections		
Name of the Infection or Disease	**Brief Description**	**Consequences**
Chlamydia		
Genital herpes		
Gonorrhea		
Human Papillomavirus (HPV)		
HIV/AIDS		
Syphilis		
Vaginitis		

USE YOUR IMAGINATION: Create Mental Pictures

Albert Einstein is reported to have said, "If I can't picture it, I can't understand it." This leads us to another suggested way to improve memory: think in pictures.

For instance, refer to the D.R.C. on the American war for independence in Figure 10.3. Visualize the British in their red coats. See the Boston Tea Party in your mind. Imagine the first shots fired at Lexington and Concord. This sort of creativity uses much more of the brain than if you just attempt to memorize facts, dates, and so on without having a clear conception of what actually transpired. By bringing together the creative brain and the orderly brain, you use the whole brain to help you make connections—and increase your chances of being able to recall information.

IMPROVING YOUR MEMORY: RECLAIMING THE INFORMATION YOU HAVE STORED

> *To know where you can find anything, that in short is the largest part of learning.*
> —Author unknown

The third step of memory, reclaiming (retrieving) the information you have stored, typically refers to what we have remembered or forgotten. In the storage process, you placed the information in "files." To reclaim it, you have to flip through the "file cabinet" and locate the "folder." In this step, you reach back into your brain's file drawers and pull out the information you need to use.

Whether it is a phone number, directions to a party, or information for a test, this step requires that you effectively noticed and stored the material.

RETRIEVAL: Start With What You Already Know

Before we examine some new strategies, pause for a moment and reflect on what you have read about so far in this book. Think about how you can use strategies from preceding chapters to improve your memory. For instance, if your retrieval problem (failure to remember something when you need to know it) stems from poor labeling, review the SQ4R reading strategies (surveying, questioning, read, recite, record, and review). Scanning, questioning, outlining, and anticipating make information processing more efficient. Also refer to the forgetting curve mentioned at the beginning of the chapter.

The more you review (study), the more likely you will be able to retain and retrieve. And the more timely your review is (soon after being exposed to the material), the more dramatic the increase in the chance for storing and reclaiming.

"What about my class notes?" you may ask. "I can't seem to make any lasting sense of these scribbles." You can practice a couple of strategies here. First, think of the links you can make with other study skills. You could ask yourself, "What are the connections between my homework readings and the instructor's presentations?"

For instance, perhaps your economics instructor has been describing how the economic concepts of supply and demand set the price of a product. Later that day in your textbook assignment, you read about rising gas prices in the United States. Looking at your notes from class, draw a connection (a relationship) between your instructor's lecture and what you just read: How do the concepts of supply and demand affect the price you pay to fill your car at the gas pump?

With a little practice, you will be able to determine these relationships easily. Once you establish them, you will have an increased ability to retain, understand, and retrieve. This moves beyond shear memorization. The material starts to take on a life of its own. It makes sense—you understand it.

MEMORY BLOCKS

It has happened to most students at one time or another. They have prepared for an exam, they know the material, but they "freeze" on test day because of a **memory block**—something that impedes their ability to notice, store, or reclaim information.

There are several types of memory blocks:

- **Emotional memory blocks.** Perhaps you have struggled in your math class. No matter what you seem to do, your grades are less than satisfactory. As you prepare for the next math exam, you do not expect to do any better. Whether it is a fear of failure, the memory of a distressing prior experience, or some other traumatic issue, some students fear the challenges that wait them inside the classroom door. The emotion effectively blocks any attempt to reclaim the information.

- **Physical memory blocks.** Our physical well-being can affect how clearly we think and remember. For instance, you stay up late studying for tomorrow's psychology exam. You gulp caffeine drinks and snack on donuts while you review all your readings, notes, and study guides. When you awaken the next morning, you are so tired you cannot think clearly—and what you studied just a few hours earlier is a jumbled mess. A physical memory block can result from lack of sleep, an inappropriate diet, or a lack of exercise.

■ **Mechanical blocks.** You put a lot of time into your studies, but you can't seem to recall the data during the exam. You feel at ease, and you are well rested. But you still can't pull the information you studied "out of your brain." This is usually an indication of some retrieval difficulty. It is typically due to a problem with the second step of the memory process: You did not store the information in a clear and recognizable location in your brain's "filing cabinet." If you just throw the information into the "drawers" without "labeling" it, so to speak, you will have difficulty retrieving it.

RETRIEVAL FAILURE: What Can You Do about It?

Failure to retrieve (or reclaim) is another way of saying "I forgot it!" For whatever reason, you cannot access—*find*—the information that you tucked away in your mind (Cherry, 2011).

As stated earlier in the chapter, you have a short-term and a long-term memory. The short-term (working) memory can last anywhere from 30 seconds to a couple of days. If the information is not used, though, it will be lost to you.

Long-term memory consists of those items that have not been "lost." For whatever reason—practice, concentration, or desire—you have retained this information.

"But," you reasonably may ask, "why do I still forget things when it comes to test time? I've practiced. I have desire. But my test grades sure don't reflect that!"

Let's examine a few reasons this may be. After each point in the following list, you will find a strategy or two to combat the retrieval challenge:

■ **Poor labeling.** Just as you would store valuable documents carefully, you should do the same with the facts, concepts, and generalizations you come into contact with.
   □ **Strategy.** Review your notes nightly. Reviewing, relating, and reorganizing will help you develop connections to previous lessons and readings, which is the best way to fight improper filing. Refer to the forgetting curve introduced earlier in this chapter.

■ **Disuse (or decay).** Your memory is like your muscles, in a sense. If you don't use information you have filed away, you will more than likely lose it. Do you ever have difficulty remembering course material after a prolonged vacation or absence from school? Because you have not used the information in some time, it is more difficult to "find" in your mind. Once you start using the information again, your memory usually returns (assuming you labeled the information correctly).
   □ **Strategy.** Once you have stored the material, find ways to use it as soon and as often as possible. Consider this practice or rehearsal for when you will need to use the information for real. For instance, once you learn a vocabulary word in class, use it soon after. Doing so will increase your chances of remembering the word.
   □ **Strategy.** Research tells us the best way to remember is to review information at "fixed, spaced intervals." That is, if you have seven days to review for an exam and you know you want to review at least five times before test day, the best strategy is space out the five study times. Do not squeeze all your study time into the end of the week. The more repetitions, the better (Medina, 2008, p. 133).

- ☐ **Strategy.** If you find practicing information tedious and boring, reframe the way you view the information (or course) that does not hold interest for you. Make a short-term commitment to yourself to find in the instructor's lesson at least two items of interest each day you go to class. Perhaps you can go a step further and search for a connection between the course and your passion (or eventual major). If that proves difficult or impossible to do, use that as a reason to visit your instructor's office—for instance, "I love science and do very well in those courses. Could you help me find a connection between your U.S. history course and science? Do they have anything in common?" Such questions let the instructor know of your passion and your interest to do well in the course. Asking questions also helps build or maintain an important relationship.

- ☐ **Strategy for class notes.** Set aside time each day to review your class notes. Memory is all about prioritization. If you *choose* to make the time for accurate storage and reclamation of your knowledge, that will increase your chances of improving your memory (Medina, 2008, p. 143).

- ☐ **Strategy for reading material.** Use the SQ4R process. The final R asks you to review what you have read immediately after you have finished reading. Additionally, as soon as possible *before* class, review your reading notes or your highlighting. This will prepare you for the day's class.

- ■ **Extinction.** Education or school is based, in part, on providing a series of rewards. These incentives vary, ranging from grades to awards for having a high grade-point average (GPA)—like making the dean's list. Many students have been conditioned by these *extrinsic* rewards—that is, awards given by someone else. Getting a good grade, for instance, becomes the overriding reason for performance. Once the reward (grade) is removed, the incentive to continue to work with the material is removed. It has been extinguished, or at the very least, it has been greatly diminished. No reward, no effort, no retention.

  - ☐ **Strategy.** Can you find an intrinsic (internal) reward to help motivate you? If the reading is related to your major, you might be motivated because you have a passion for the content. Maybe success with the material will satisfy a personal goal. However, the reality remains that your required courses may hold little interest for you. Someone with a deep passion for literature may find it difficult to stay focused in a history course. Perhaps the best advice is to remember that these prerequisites serve as "gatekeepers." You must pass through them to move into the course work that really interests you. Once you navigate these early courses, you will be able to concentrate on the subject areas that hold intrinsic motivation for you.

- ■ **Response competition** *(interference)*. Visualize this scenario: You have studied for a science unit exam. Your science class, however, comes right after your math class, in which the instructor has introduced a new process complete with formulas and equations. Your brain feels like it is going to burst! Or perhaps earlier that morning, you had an argument with a friend. In your mind, you are still running through what he or she said. By the time you get to science class, your mind is moving in three or four directions—and none of them seems related to the exam in front of you. The new information interferes with what you studied for the exam.

  - ☐ **Strategy.** This is where having an efficient filing system in your brain really will pay off. If you develop connections, rehearse (practice) the material, and develop a feeling of confidence, you have a better chance of the material becoming second nature to you—almost automatic. While you may not be able to stop the competing signals, you will have a better chance of finding and recalling the information needed.

☐ **Strategy.** This strategy looks to the future. When scheduling classes for your next term, leave an hour or two between classes, so that you will have time to sit somewhere quiet and refocus before going into a test situation. The same goes for work schedules. Leave yourself some breathing room, rather than rushing from work to the parking lot to the classroom.

■ **Situational variation.** Let's call this *stage fright*. Consider these scenarios: You practiced a guitar lead for months. You never missed a lick. But the first time you perform it in public, your fingers fumble with the strings. Or you are in a play. You never flubbed a line during rehearsals. But it is opening night, and you can't remember your name! Why? The situation—the setting—has changed. You practiced in one environment but had to perform in quite another environment.

☐ **Strategy.** Practice the material in various situations to help eliminate this distraction. Perhaps you can sit in the classroom where you will take the real exam. If you can, do practice exercises within the same time frame as you will have on test day. If your instructor will allow only 50 minutes for the test, practice in 50-minute blocks of time. Prepare for the content as well as for the timed situation. Maybe your study group (if you choose to be part of one) can meet one day in the actual classroom in which you will sit for the exam. Does your textbook have a website that provides practice questions? If it does, use it regularly. Maybe the instructor has an old exam for you to practice with. Do as many practice tests as you can in a testlike environment. Depending on how much of a concern this is for you, you might think about actually doing a practice test in the classroom for the specified time.

Activity 10.6

What Strategies Have You Used?

Pick at least one of the following challenges that you have encountered. What have you done to eliminate or minimize this memory challenge?

■ Memory blocks

■ Extinction

■ Poor labeling

■ Disuse

■ Response competition

■ Situational variation

....

....

....

NAMES

Remembering names does not have to be difficult. Applying a few simple techniques will avoid embarrassment and may even impress people:

- **Decide you want to remember the name.** Make a conscious effort. Say to yourself, "I want to remember this person's name."

- **Listen and repeat.** Carefully listen to the name of the individual. Repeat it. Ask for a spelling of the name. Use the name immediately. An exchange might go something like this:

  "Steve, I would like you to meet my friend Shannon."
  "Shannon, I'm pleased to meet you. Are you new to our community, Shannon? It was nice meeting you, Shannon. I look forward to talking with you later."

  In the course of a few seconds, the new name is used multiple times. Practice makes permanent.

- **Look at the face.** Lock the name to the face.

- **Notice physical features.** Does this person possess any unique features? Very short, very tall, long hair, big nose, beautiful eyes, or lots of jewelry? Exaggerate this feature. Have fun with this!

MNEMONICS

This strange-looking word (pronounced "nih-MON-icks") is used to refer to memory tricks that help you recall information. Mnemonics is a strategy that allows you to get creative. Let's look at four examples:

- **Acronyms.** An **acronym** is a word formed from the letters (usually the first letters) of other words. Do you wish to remember the names of the Great Lakes? Just remember HOMES: Huron, Ontario, Michigan, Erie, and Superior.

- **Acrostics.** An *acrostic* uses the first letter of each word in a sequence to create a message. Having trouble with the order of mathematical operations? Then remember *Please Excuse My Dear Aunt Sally*. Now you will forever remember to do the operation in parentheses first, followed by exponents, multiplication, division, addition, and subtraction. (But see Patin [n.d.] for exceptions to this often-cited rule.) Do you want to remember the notes (EGBDF) assigned to the lines of a musical staff? (*Every Good Boy Does Fine*). How about the taxonomic levels in biology? *King Philip Came Over For Green Spaghetti* (*Kingdom, Phylum, Class, Order, Family, Genus, Specie*).

- **The hook, number, linking, location, or peg system.** A peg is something you can hang an item on. Using a mental peg (or mental hook) allows you to attach a concept, word, or item to one or more known objects. You "locate" what you want to remember by calling up the object. For instance, you may tend to forget where you put your keys after using them. The next time you toss them onto the table, think of the table spinning or maybe even lighting up. By creating a vivid and outrageous picture of the peg (movement, light), you engage your brain with this concept. Doing so makes it more likely you will be able to reclaim what you want to remember—where you put your keys.

  Here's another example: If you have to remember the steps of a mathematical formula, visualize the rooms in your house. Have each room of the house hold one of the steps of the formula. As you move from one room to another, you find the next step until you finally complete the formula. The associations do not have to be logical. All you are doing is creating a picture of the item or items you need to remember. This system works well with lists, such as vocabulary words, bones of the body, and parts of speech.

> The more elaborately we encode information at the moment of learning, the stronger the memory.
>
> —**John Medina, molecular biologist and author**

PRACTICE, PRACTICE, AND MORE PRACTICE

When learning new material, it helps to do three things: practice, practice, and practice some more. To learn a new skill, perform activities that stretch your mind. Just like an athlete does stretches, calisthenics, and wind sprints to get in shape, you will improve your ability to learn if you do "mental gymnastics." Consider your mental warm-ups as mind exercises. Use them and you will expand your capabilities.

Activity 10.7

Practice: Acronyms, Acrostics, and Peg Systems

With a classmate, provide an example of each of the following memory strategies. You can either provide one you have learned in another class or make one up on your own.

■ Acronym.

....

■ Acrostic.

....

■ Peg system.

....

MEMORY DOES NOT EQUAL UNDERSTANDING

Having an effective memory may seem impressive, and it may even help you get by on tests. But it does not indicate that you understand the material. In fact, a good memory might end up being one of your (unknown) weaknesses.

For instance, some students spend many hours in school *memorizing* lists of vocabulary words and spelling words. Their exams and quizzes reflect high scores. But in reality, these students could be missing out on understanding the important rules that guide spelling exceptions.

True learning usually causes some frustration. After all, learning indicates a change in behavior. Learning anything new can be challenging to some of us. The same thing is true of memory strategies.

As you look back on the ideas from this chapter, keep two points in mind:

1. If you are not accustomed to using memory strategies, they may seem awkward. But don't give up on them for that reason alone.
2. Not every technique is for everyone. Pick and choose, but find something that works for you—and then use it regularly. Remember, practice makes permanent.

Chapter SUMMARY

To cope with the vast quantity of information vying for your attention, develop observational and listening skills. Doing this requires discipline and concentration. If you have followed the organizational and active-learning strategies provided in these chapters, you are well on your way to establishing effective recall strategies.

Before leaving this chapter, keep the following points in mind:

- Remembering information involves three steps: noticing, storing, and reclaiming. You must see something, put it someplace, and then go find it.

- There is a difference between *memory* and *understanding*. Memory requires retention *and* retrieval of material. Understanding takes you to a higher level of comprehension.

- The key to comprehension is to create relationships.

- Understand why your memory might be blocked—and then apply a strategy to remove that block.

- Develop an efficient and effective "filing system" in your brain.

- Use organizational strategies and models (D.R.C., mnemonics, mental imaging).

- Practice active listening every day.

- Whatever you learn, use the new knowledge as soon and as often as possible.

CRITICALLY THINKING

What Have You Learned in This Chapter?

Let's apply what you learned in this chapter to help Billy from the chapter-opening scenario. However, before you analyze Billy's problem and propose your solution, take a moment to think about the main points of the chapter.

Review your notes from this chapter and also the key terms, chapter learning outcomes, boldface chapter headings, and figures and tables. For instance, consider how the chapter learning outcomes may be used to help Billy:

- Identify and use at least two strategies to improve your skill of noticing what you need to remember.

- Identify and use at least two strategies to help you improve how you store information.

- Demonstrate active-listening skills.

- Identify and use at least two organizational models to help you reclaim information.

© Shutterstock

TEST YOUR LEARNING

Now that you have reviewed the main points of this chapter and reread Billy's story, what advice do you have for him? Using the R.E.D. Model for critical thinking, help Billy critically review his concerns:

Recognize Assumptions:

Facts: What are the facts in Billy's situation? List them.

Opinions: What opinions do you find in this situation? List them here.

Assumptions: Are Billy's assumptions accurate?

Evaluate Information:

Help Billy compile a list of questions that will help him make the most appropriate decision.

What emotions seem to be motivating Billy?

What, if anything, is missing from his thought process?

Do you see any confirmation bias?

Draw Conclusions:

Based on the facts and the questions you have presented, what conclusions can you draw?

What advice do you have for Billy? What solutions do you propose?

Based on your suggestions, do you see any assumptions?

Finally, based on what you learned about using critical thinking and memory strategies, what plan of action do you suggest for Billy?

Test Preparation *11*
and **TEST**
PERFORMANCE

The difference between school and life?
In school, you're taught a lesson and
then given a test. In life, you're given a
test that teaches you a lesson.

— *Tom Bodett, author*

CHAPTER LEARNING OUTCOMES

By the time you finish reading this chapter and completing its activities, you will be able to do the following:

- Identify at least two successful test-preparation strategies you have used in the past, and evaluate their benefit to you now.

- Identify at least one unsuccessful test-preparation strategy you have used in the past.

- Apply one strategy to address your unsuccessful test-preparation strategy.

- Identify and use at least one strategy to combat test anxiety.

- Apply at least one study skill strategy to improve your test-performance skills.

- Use the postexam analysis strategy to review at least one of your most recent exams.

The Case of AMANI

It seems to be the same tired story. Even though Amani has taken hundreds of tests over the years, she still gets nervous every time an exam is placed in front of her. She will admit there have been times when she has gone into a test situation unprepared, but usually, Amani has at least done a little studying to get ready. Still, whether she is prepared or not, as soon as the test starts, she gets jittery, her mind goes blank, and eventually, she runs out of time.

A couple of weeks ago, the campus testing center offered a workshop on test-taking skills, so Amani went. When she was asked about her testing

© Shutterstock

Key Terms

Academic integrity
Anxiety
Distracters
Emergency studying
Postexam analysis
Reframe
Test anxiety
Test-performance skills
Test-preparation skills
Trigger words
Types of exams

Chapter
INTRODUCTION

Tests may strike fear into the hearts of many students, but in fact, they are nothing new. Whether you are a student right out of high school or one returning after a 20-year break, you have confronted—and mastered—tests all your life.

Tests provide opportunities for you to demonstrate that you understand course materials and can perform required skills. Because your classroom success depends in part on the grades you receive on tests, you should begin to prepare for tests the day you enter a class. That preparation includes strategies, she told the workshop leader that she does all of the following:

- Attends class regularly
- Studies everything from class two days prior to the exam to keep it fresh for the test
- Depends on her study group for additional information, since she did not buy the Internet access code that came with her textbook (She said she didn't see the need to have this code.)
- Is using the same study methods that have brought her some success in the past
- Feels like she is about to faint every time she walks into a testing situation

CRITICALLY THINKING
about *Amani's* situation

Pretend you are the workshop leader. What advice would you give Amani?

participating in class discussions, completing course assignments, and reviewing course materials on a regular basis. In other words, if you apply basic study skill strategies before test day, you will improve your chances for success.

You probably visualize walking into class on test day, completing the test, and earning the highest grade possible. All students want that result. But before you can *perform*, first you must *prepare*.

MyStudentSuccessLab

MyStudentSuccessLab (www .mystudentsuccesslab.com) is an online solution designed to help you 'Start strong, Finish stronger' by building skills for ongoing personal and professional development.

Too often, "test prep" is seen as an ending activity: how to successfully complete (or perform on) an exam. Therefore, this chapter will separate the two very distinct parts of testing.

First, you will examine effective strategies to prepare for a test. You will examine how to organize and prioritize your efforts from the beginning of a unit of material, so that you will be preparing long before the actual performance is required. If you use simple organizational tools early, both in class and outside class, you will not need to cram for tests. Also, you will be able to reduce your anxiety about tests, and you will enjoy successful test results (Piscitelli, 2011, p. 148).

Once you have mastered how to prepare for exams, you will turn your attention to the second part of testing: strategies for effective test performance. Just like test preparation, test performance is influenced by many factors. Those factors affect how successful you will be when you step into a testing situation. Draw on your past successes. Ask yourself this question: "What strategies have worked for me in the past—and how can I use them today?" Use your experiences for your benefit. Then build on them with the new strategies introduced in this chapter.

Activity 11.1

Reflection on Your Current Level of Test-Preparation and Test-Performance Skills

Before you answer the items that follow, reflect on your current level of test-preparation and test-performance skills. Think of how well (or poorly) you have performed on tests in past classes.

As you do in completing all of the reflective activities in this book, you should write from your heart. This exercise is not meant for you to answer just like your classmates—or to match what you may think the instructor wants to see. Take the time to give a respectful, responsible general accounting of your experiences with test preparation and test performance. Conducting a truthful self-assessment now will help you build on skills you have while developing those you lack.

For each of the following items, circle the number that best describes your typical experience with test-preparation and test-performance skills. Here is the key for the numbers:

0 = never, 1 = almost never, 2 = occasionally, 3 = frequently, 4 = almost always, 5 = always

When considering your experience with test-preparation and test-performance skills, how often . . .

1.	Did you prepare for an exam earlier than the night before it?	**0**	**1**	**2**	**3**	**4**	**5**
2.	Did you prepare for an exam a week or more before the exam date?	**0**	**1**	**2**	**3**	**4**	**5**
3.	Did you review your graded exam for more than your grade? That is, how often did you seek clarification about missed questions so that you could learn from your mistakes?	**0**	**1**	**2**	**3**	**4**	**5**

4.	Did you review your test-preparation strategies for effectiveness or ineffectiveness?	**0**	**1**	**2**	**3**	**4**	**5**
5.	Did you ask your instructor (or read the syllabus) about the test format before exam day?	**0**	**1**	**2**	**3**	**4**	**5**
6.	Could you complete a test without having your mind going blank or freezing up?	**0**	**1**	**2**	**3**	**4**	**5**
7.	Did you read all the directions and quickly survey the exam for its content and format before you started it?	**0**	**1**	**2**	**3**	**4**	**5**
8.	During an exam did you complete all of the easy items before you attempted the more difficult items?	**0**	**1**	**2**	**3**	**4**	**5**

Add up your scores for items 1, 2, 3, 4, and 5. Divide by 5. Write your answer here: _____ .

Using the key provided to explain each number (0, 1, 2, 3, 4, 5), complete this sentence: When it comes to test-preparation skills, I _____ prepare for tests effectively.

Add up your scores for items 6, 7, and 8. Divide by 3. Write your answer here: _____.

Using the key provided to explain each number (0, 1, 2, 3, 4, 5), complete this sentence: When it comes to test-performance skills, I _____ perform on tests effectively.

Based on your answers, what insights have you gained about your experiences with test taking?

....

....

TEST PREPARATION: WHAT SKILLS DO YOU HAVE?

> *One important key to success is self-confidence.*
> *An important key to self-confidence is preparation.*
> —*Arthur Ashe, tennis player*

If you added up all of the tests you have ever taken—in school, on jobs, for your driver's license, and so on—you would likely come up with a number in the hundreds. Does that surprise you? Whatever your background or age, you bring positive experiences and perhaps a few challenging experiences to your college exams.

Activity 11.2 gives you the opportunity to build on Activity 11.1. Take a moment to think about your testing experiences. Specifically, examine how you prepared and when you prepared, along with what worked and what did not work. Your goal is to identify practices you may want to continue in college—and practices it is time to eliminate.

Activity 11.2

What Test-Preparation Skills Do You Have Right Now?

(R) (E) (D) The R.E.D. Model (**R**ecognize Assumptions, **E**valuate Information, **D**raw Conclusions) provides a systematic way to approach critical thinking through the use of an easy-to-remember acronym.

Let's gather some information on your experiences. Reflect on your **test-preparation skills** experiences. Think about the "big picture." That is, don't just concentrate on an exam you completed last week. And don't concentrate on only the good experiences or only the poor grades. Rather, think about your testing experiences in general as you complete this activity.

1. **Preparation.** How have you prepared for exams? Check all of the following items that apply to you:

_____ I used instructor study guides when provided.

_____ I reviewed my notes nightly.

_____ I participated in a study group.

_____ I asked the instructor if there were old tests I might be able to use for practice.

_____ When available, I used the textbook publisher's website to review chapter objectives and take practice quizzes and tests.

_____ I used a tutor.

_____ I visited my instructor's office for content clarification.

_____ I seldom did any preparation for a test.

_____ Other methods of test preparation I used included these:

....

....

2. **Timing.** Generally speaking, when did you start preparing for an exam? Check all of the following items that apply to you:

_____ At the beginning of a new unit of material, I would study my class notes nightly.

_____ I would start reviewing my notes and readings at least three or four days prior to the examination.

_____ I waited until the night before the exam.

_____ I looked over my notes the morning of the exam.

_____ Generally speaking, I never studied for exams.

_____ Is there any other way to describe when you started to prepare for exams? If so, do so here:

....

....

3. **Good results.** What test-preparation strategies *have worked well* for you in the past? Describe them.

....

....

4. **Poor results.** What test-preparation strategies *have not worked well* for you in the past? Describe them.

....

....

5. **Best practices.** Based on your past successes, which strategies do you believe will continue to work for you in school? Explain how you know these are beneficial strategies.

....

....

6. **Questionable practices.** Based on your past challenges, which strategies do you need to discontinue? Explain how you know these are not beneficial test-preparation strategies.

....

....

TEST ANXIETY

Anxiety is a general feeling of unease, uncertainty, anticipation, and even fear about an event. The resulting stress may be positive, helping you stay on your toes and perform well, or it may be so debilitating that it causes you to freeze up.

There are two forms of stress: positive stress and negative stress. Both physically arouse the body. *Positive stress* helps you remain focused and move toward a goal. This may be similar to having "butterflies in your stomach," but your heightened sense of awareness allows you to perform at a higher level of competence. *Negative stress* goes beyond a few butterflies. You may actually feel as though a boulder is crushing your chest, because breathing becomes difficult. Your fight-or-flight response may be triggered.

The same kinds of feelings can occur on test day, resulting in **test anxiety**. Most students are likely to feel a reasonable amount of uncertainty. They wish to perform well, get a high score, maintain a respectable grade-point average (GPA), and feel good about their efforts. But even when well prepared, students may still have nagging doubts: "Did I study the correct material?" "Maybe I should have looked at my notes one more time." "I wonder if a study group or a visit to the professor's office would have been helpful." Whatever may cause their anxiety, these students make their way to class, complete the test successfully, and move on to the next unit of material.

Other students, though, become so paralyzed by thoughts of an examination that they make themselves sick with worry. One unsuccessful testing experience leads to another, which leads to another, and a self-fulfilling prophecy is born: "I never do well on tests!"

Once a student sits down and sees the test paper lying on the desk, his or her reaction might be anything from a mild case of the jitters to full-blown terror. This test-day anxiety, however, can be reduced considerably with effective test-preparation strategies (Piscitelli, 2011, pp. 150–151). But first, it's important to understand why test anxiety occurs.

WHY DOES TEST ANXIETY HAPPEN?

One organization maintains that 16 percent to 20 percent of students experience a high level of test anxiety and another 18 percent feel a moderate level (American Test Anxiety Association, n.d.). Among the reasons for this common response are fear, feelings of inadequacy, and lack of preparation.

- **Fear.** The consequences of the test or performance may be so great as to cause an unhealthy physical or emotional response. For instance, if one test result will determine whether you get into a particular program (say, nursing or engineering), your level of anxiety may increase from the fear of losing your dream. This form of so-called high-stakes testing heightens your physical and emotional arousal.
  - □ **Suggestion.** You may be catastrophizing. That is, you may be making too much of this one exam. One opportunity does not (very often) determine your life's direction. Stop, take a breath, and **reframe** the situation. Look at it from another perspective. If you have difficulty doing this, ask a friend, family member, or mentor for input. Failing, while not pleasant, is rarely the end. In many cases, it presents an opportunity to regroup and move forward (Piscitelli, 2011, p. 151).

- **Feelings of inadequacy.** You believe that no matter what you do, your lack of ability (perceived or real) will be the reason you cannot perform to an acceptable standard. This may be the case, for instance, when a student enrolls in a course he or she has struggled with in the past.
  - □ **Suggestion.** What would you tell a good friend if he or she admitted having the same feeling? It is doubtful you would say, "You are right! There is nothing you can do. You will fail!" You would look for something positive to say to help your friend through the anxiety. Do the same thing for yourself. As you prepare for the exam, make a list of all the strengths you have. Build on these positives, and minimize the negative self-talk (Piscitelli, 2011, p. 151).

- **Lack of preparation.** The final exam is in one hour—and you have not read the assigned readings, looked at your notes, or reviewed the instructor-provided study guide. No wonder your blood pressure is elevated, your hands are sweating, and your mouth is a little dry!
  - □ **Suggestion.** This is where priority management has a significant impact. At some point early in your weekly planning, preparing for your math exam has to move up on the list of "Things I Must Do This Week." The more time you spend with the course material before exam day, the more familiar you will be with it—and the more confident you will feel when you enter the testing situation. In this case, test-day anxiety can be eliminated (or at least greatly reduced) by organized preparation. Priority management does rule!

Take a moment to complete Activities 11.3 and 11.4.

Activity 11.3

What Is Your Level of Test Anxiety?

How often do you experience test anxiety? For each of the following items, rate yourself on a scale from 0 (not at all) to 5 (all the time). Circle the number that most closely applies to you.

1. When you look back on your test performance this term (or over a number of years, if you so desire), how often do you experience the following?

Symptom	Frequency (0 = not at all, 5 = all the time)					
Headaches	0	1	2	3	4	5
Nausea	0	1	2	3	4	5
Vomiting	0	1	2	3	4	5
Diarrhea	0	1	2	3	4	5
Sweating	0	1	2	3	4	5
Increased heartbeat	0	1	2	3	4	5
Shortness of breath	0	1	2	3	4	5
Dizziness	0	1	2	3	4	5
Crying	0	1	2	3	4	5
Your mind "going blank"	0	1	2	3	4	5

2. Add your ratings, and divide by 10. On a scale from 0 to 5, you have rated your level of test anxiety to be _____. (A score of 4 or higher indicates that testing situations create a high level of apprehension for you.)

3. Reflect on your score in item 2. Why do you think you have come to respond to tests in the manner you do? What insights can you draw from this exercise?

....

....

....

Activity 11.4

Identifying Your Sources of Test Anxiety

Identifying stressors is the first step in learning to overcome them. What are your sources of test anxiety?

1. Do you tend to be anxious about exams because of any of the following? Check all that apply to you.

_____ Lack of appropriate effort on my part

_____ Lack of ability (course material beyond my capabilities)

_____ Negative self-talk (convinced myself I would do poorly)

_____ Not studying

_____ Fear of how others may judge me

_____ Listening to classmates complain about the difficulty of exams

_____ Poor previous testing experiences

_____ Panic brought on by timed situations

_____ Focusing on the effect the test grade will have on my GPA

_____ Comparing my performance to the performances of other students

_____ Pressuring myself to get nothing but an A

_____ Other sources:

....

2. Share your answers with a close friend or mentor. Brainstorm ideas to lessen your test anxiety. Write your
answers here.

....

....

....

Activity 11.5

Critically Thinking about Your Test-Preparation Skills

R E D Let's apply the R.E.D. Model for critical thinking to examine either one of the best practices or one of the
questionable practices you identified in Activity 11.2, 11.3, or 11.4.

Write the best practice or questionable practice here: _____

Critical-Thinking STEP	Application to Your Testing Skills	Your Explanation (here or on a separate piece of paper)
Recognizing Assumptions	Clearly state this particular testing practice. How do you know this assessment of your testing practice is correct?	
Evaluating Information	Provide a specific explanation (give examples) of this testing practice. Examine your identified testing practice beyond a superficial (simplistic) explanation, and look at all of the complexities involved. Examine your testing practice from more than one perspective (point of view).	
Drawing Conclusions	Based on your evidence, does your conclusion about your testing practice make sense? How is your assessment of this testing practice connected to your academic progress?	

Based on your answers, what insights have you gained about your testing practice?

....

....

What is the next step you will take to improve your testing skills?

EVERYTHING IS CONNECTED

Let's pause and examine how the study skills strategies you already have mastered are related and connected to test preparation. If you can consciously tie the strategies together, you will see that test preparation is not a one-time event. Table 11.1 shows the interconnectedness of just a few selected study skill strategies to test preparation.

Figure 11.1 shows how one skill relates to others. The power of study skills lies in the fact that they all reinforce one another. As you master each skill, your academic foundation becomes stronger—and your academic future brighter!

Table 11.1 Test-performance strategies: Building on previous skills and strategies

Study Skill Strategy	Application to Successful Test-Peparation Strategies
Critical thinking	■ Take time to analyze any test-preparation difficulties you may have. Go beyond a superficial explanation (assumption); move into a deeper examination of the factors that affect your test performance. ■ Use critical thinking steps to solve your test-preparation problems.
Problem solving	■ Using your critical-thinking skills, propose a solution to improve your test preparation—for instance: □ Using the information received from your review of previous exams, your instructor's input, and a tutor's opinion, you may decide to begin a new studying program that will set aside time to visit your professor once a week with specific questions about new material covered in class. □ You may consider working with a study group. □ At the very least, you may decide to write a brief summary for each day's notes. This 10-minute exercise will be the beginning of a nightly review of your notes.
Creative thinking	■ Maybe you feel that you have done absolutely everything to turn around your testing practices—but nothing seems to work. The frustration mounts. It's time for creative, outside-the-box, outside-the-lines, novel thinking—for instance: □ You recognize that you have not been exercising as you once did. You feel sluggish most of the time. Combining physical activity with intellectual stimulation, you decide to engage in a yoga class once a week. You believe yoga's meditative emphasis will help calm and focus your mind.

(continued)

Table 11.1 **Test-performance strategies: Building on previous skills and strategies (continued)**

Study Skill Strategy	Application to Successful Test-Peparation Strategies
Attitude	■ When you examine why you have difficulty with tests (in general or in a particular course), do you use self-defeating words or positive words? ☐ Self-defeating: *What should I expect? I have never done well on math exams. There is no reason to expect that will change this term. I'll hope for the best.* ☐ Positive: *My experience with math has been troubled, at best. I might not earn an A in this course, but I do know that by using the campus resources available to me, I will do better this term than I have ever done before.*
Intrinsic and extrinsic motivators	■ Find a motivator that will help move you through the test challenge you have been experiencing. Whether intrinsic or extrinsic, look for incentives that will prove motivating enough for you to meet and defeat your challenge. ☐ Intrinsic: *I know what I need to do to achieve favorable test results. I've worked hard and owe it to myself to do the very best I can.* ☐ Extrinsic: *Regardless of what I have done in the past, my financial aid depends on passing all my courses. Doing well on tests will not only prepare me for other course work, but it will also allow me to continue receiving the funding I need for school.*
Review your notes	■ Every night, reflect on class work through a brief writing activity. Do the following: ☐ Maintain an ongoing file of your nightly summary review. Perhaps creating a computer folder labeled "Notes Review" will make it easier to organize and keep up with your daily reviews. Over the course of a unit's material, you will build a comprehensive study guide. Reviewing your review will help prepare you for each coming exam.
Reading	■ Use the SQ4R strategy (survey, question, read, recite, record, review) to make sense of your reading assignments and to remember more of what you read. Remember these points: ☐ Before reading, understand the purpose of the assignment—why you are reading. ☐ Take reading notes, review them, and use them with your class notes. ☐ Build your vocabulary.
Learning preferences	■ We all have unique ways to process information. Make sure you understand your learning preferences, and practice strategies to make your learning preferences work for you: ☐ Understand how you take in information effectively. ☐ As best as you can, create a study environment that complements your learning preference.
Memory	■ Remember the three components of an improved memory: Notice the material, store the material, and reclaim the material. Consider the following: ☐ Use review time and organizational charts to help you make connections. Schedule your study time in regular intervals. (Don't cram.) ☐ Understand why you forget, and then review strategies to help you more effectively retrieve information.

Figure 11.1

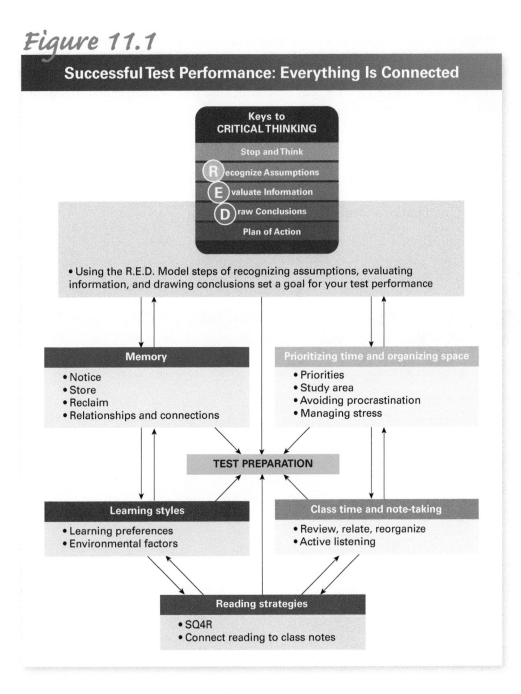

Successful Test Performance: Everything Is Connected

Keys to CRITICAL THINKING

Stop and Think

Recognize Assumptions

Evaluate Information

Draw Conclusions

Plan of Action

- Using the R.E.D. Model steps of recognizing assumptions, evaluating information, and drawing conclusions set a goal for your test performance

Memory
- Notice
- Store
- Reclaim
- Relationships and connections

Prioritizing time and organizing space
- Priorities
- Study area
- Avoiding procrastination
- Managing stress

TEST PREPARATION

Learning styles
- Learning preferences
- Environmental factors

Class time and note-taking
- Review, relate, reorganize
- Active listening

Reading strategies
- SQ4R
- Connect reading to class notes

PREVIOUS TEST RESULTS

Effective test preparation requires continual review and practice. Effective preparation for your exam next week should begin immediately after you complete your most recent exam.

A common reaction by many students following the completion of an exam is to forget it and concentrate on the next opportunity. Although this is an understandable reaction, you should pause and reflect on the exam. Consider this the first step in preparing for the next exam.

Completing Activity 11.6 will help you get ready for the upcoming exam. It requires you to anticipate the exam. But also notice that the last portion is a **postexam analysis**. This type of activity accomplishes a couple of things. While the material you were just tested on is still fresh in your mind, review the content. You may see some of this information again on a midterm or final examination (or in another course). Make sure you have it correct now. If you answered an item incorrectly on this exam, you do not want to get it wrong again. It is important to understand what worked and what did not work for you. Use this time to identify your challenges and strengths—and set a goal for the next exam.

If you are getting ready to take the first exam in a class, consider any quizzes you might have taken thus far. Or you can skip this step until you prepare for your second exam.

Completing the following checklist will help you prioritize your preparation activities, reduce your levels of anxiety, do well on your latest opportunity, and prepare for your next testing situation.

Activity 11.6

Test-Preparation Checklist (✓)

Select one of the courses you are taking this term, and complete the following checklist to help you prepare for the next exam. _____

Class: _____

Instructor: _____

Test date, location, and time: _____

1. Type of exam:

    ○ Multiple choice

    ○ True/False

    ○ Matching

    ○ Completion or short answer

    ○ Identification

    ○ Essay

    ○ Lab work

    ○ Problems

    ○ Other _____

2. What I need when I study:

    ○ Textbook

    ○ Notes

    ○ Teacher's study guide

    ○ Worksheets

    ○ Past exams (these can be very helpful)

    ○ Supplemental readings

    ○ Calculator

    ○ Pens, pencils, paper

    ○ Other _____

3. Will I study alone or with a study group?

○ Alone

○ Study group

(To get the most from a study group you may wish to set an agenda before the meeting.)

4. Will the teacher lead any study sessions?

○ Yes

○ No

If "yes," when and where? _____

5. When will I study? Make a specific plan—and stick to it. Write the steps and dates on your calendar.

6. Prioritization: What topics will the exam cover? Which topics are you most confident about, and which ones need a lot more of your time?

Topic	I Really Know This Stuff	I Am Not Too Sure about This Stuff	I Have No Clue about This Stuff	Topic Reviewed at Least Once
1.				
2.				
3.				
4.				

7. Predict some test questions.

8. Things I need for the test:

○ Pens, pencils, paper, "blue book"

○ Calculator

○ Notes (if I can use my notes during the test)

○ Textbook (if the test is open book)

○ Ruler

○ Other _____

Test preparation does not end when you hand in your test. Start preparing for your next exam by doing a postexam analysis:

....

....

9. I was most prepared for _____

Why? _____

10. I was not well prepared for _____

Why? _____

11. The biggest help:

○ My notes   ○ My study group

○ My homework   ○ My study environment

○ Tutoring sessions   ○ Meeting with my instructor outside class

○ My study schedule   ○ Other_____

12. My major weakness(es):

- ○ Ran out of time during the test
- ○ Did not expect this type of test
- ○ Studied the wrong material
- ○ Did not start studying early enough
- ○ Other_____

13. The grade I realistically expect to receive: _____

Grade I actually received: _____

14. My realistic plan to improve for the next exam:

....

....

....

BEFORE YOU WALK INTO THE CLASSROOM*

Let's assume it is the night before your exam. You have followed all (or at least most) of the strategies you have learned from reading this book, and there is no need to cram for your exam. In short, you feel confident about the exam you will take the next day. You have prepared. All is good! You have worked hard and are now ready to reap the rewards of your efforts. You would like to see a return (in the form a great grade!) on your investment of study time.

The following suggestions will help you maximize the hours of study time you have invested thus far. Even if you did not study as much as you would have liked to, still follow these tips.

- **Know your material**. Don't just memorize it—understand it. More than likely, the wording on the exam will be different from what you found in your book or what the teacher said in class. The more comfortable you become with the course content, the more confident you will be on the exam. Timely and organized studying will help you become comfortable, confident, and successful. Your strategies for reviewing class notes will help here. Competence leads to confidence and will help lessen your anxiety.

- **Consider tutoring.** If you have been diligent with your studies but still have difficulty with the subject matter, you may wish to seek help from the instructor or a student tutor. Your academic adviser should have information on peer tutors.

- **Be rested and ready.** Do not sabotage yourself and your good efforts. On exam day, you want to be rested and ready to go. Emotional and physical memory blocks can be minimized (if not eliminated) by getting a restful night's sleep. The night before your exam is not the time to party, watch late-night television, or work until the wee hours of the morning on other class assignments. You know the amount of sleep you need to wake up rested and alert. Get it on the eve of an examination.

*This section based on Piscitelli (2011), pp. 173–175.

- **Set your alarm.** Wake up early enough so you have plenty of time to arrive at the test site. In fact, for test day, plan on arriving anywhere from 15 to 30 minutes ahead of time. This will give you extra time in case traffic or some other unexpected event causes a delay. *Anticipate* the *unexpected* and be ready.

- **Feed your body appropriately.** After a wonderfully relaxing night's sleep, treat yourself to a nutritious meal prior to the exam. Depending on the time of the exam, eat a good breakfast or lunch. But don't overeat—that might leave you groggy. Again, use strategies that fit you. If your exam will be during a night class, consider having a small snack before entering the classroom.

- **Become familiar with format.** Ask the instructor if he or she has past versions of the exam you can review. Becoming familiar with the teacher's particular format will help you master the content, as well.

- **Find out if "props" are allowed.** If you have a math test requiring many formulas, can you write the formulas on an index card to use during the exam? How about your notes? Will the instructor allow you to use them during the exam?

- **Ask your instructor about an alternative testing environment.** If distractions are really a problem for you, perhaps the instructor will allow you to complete the exam in the campus testing and assessment center. If you have a documented disability, the student services office may be able to assist with specific accommodations.

- **Let your friends know your schedule.** This is particularly important if you travel to campus with someone else. On test day, your travel schedule will need a slight adjustment so you can arrive early.

- **Gather your materials.** The night before the exam, gather all the materials you will need for test day. These materials can include paper, pens, pencils, calculators, notebooks, textbooks, and/or take-home essays (or some other portion of the exam). Place them where you will find them in the morning: in your book bag, on a table, or by the door. Save time and emotional energy by knowing where everything is before you head out the door in the morning. If you will be using a laptop, be sure to charge the battery.

- **Bring extras.** In addition to the usual pen, pencil, and paper you may need for your exam, pack extras. A couple of sharpened pencils with good erasers, a few extra sheets of paper, a spare pen, or extra batteries may come in handy during the exam.

- **Keep accurate time.** It will be your responsibility to keep track of time during the exam, not the instructor's. Some students use a watch, and some use their cell phones to keep track of time. If you do this, be sure to get your instructor's permission to have your cell phone on your desk during the exam.

- **Arrive early.** This bears repetition: Get to the test site early. Doing so will give you a few moments to sit quietly and get ready, intellectually and emotionally. Athletes speak of "getting in a zone" or "putting on a game face." This is your time to "put on your test face"!

- **Avoid negative people.** You want to stay positive, obviously. Avoid classmates who dwell on how hard the test will be. Also avoid those students who have not prepared and come running in, all anxious and hyped up on caffeine. Because they have chosen not to prepare does not mean you have to be drawn into their drama and self-defeating game.

- **Talk positively to yourself.** Finally, as you prepare for the exam, be kind to yourself. Don't sit there saying "I am going to fail." Respect your skills, talents, and experiences.

EMERGENCY STUDYING

"OK," you say. "Organization is great, but what can I do if I have not kept up? What can I do to survive a test when I'm down to the night before, and I'm not ready?"

Here are some pointers for last-minute or **emergency studying**. This is not a desirable situation, but if it's all you have, then know how to get the most from it.

Do not . . .

- Be tempted to read quickly everything you have not read yet. If you read a large quantity of information too fast, you probably will have poor recall of the details.

- Panic. OK, so you didn't study as you wish you had. Test day is no time to panic.

Do . . .

- Accept the fact you will not be able to study everything.
- Relax as best you can.
- Start by anticipating your teacher. What type of questions will he or she ask? What types of content and/or skills will he or she test? Recall? Relationships?
- Go to your notes and text to find the most important material. Here are clues to guide you: chapter titles and subtitles, major emphasis in class discussions and lectures, relationships with past materials, chapter summaries. Use the SQ4R strategy.
- Follow these steps when you find important information:
  - ☐ Read it.
  - ☐ Create a question for which the information is the answer.
  - ☐ Say the information to yourself.
  - ☐ Check to see whether you are correct.
  - ☐ Do it until you get it correct twice.
  - ☐ Find and study some important information from every chapter that was assigned.

Next time, plan ahead and establish a study schedule!

Activity 11.7

Searching for Test Clues

Select one of your courses for this term, and complete this activity to help you determine potential exam questions.

Course title: _____

Instructor: _____

1. **What kind of tests will your instructor give during this term?** Your instructor may present you with multiple-choice questions, fill-in-the-blank items, matching exercises, true/false statements, short-answer definitions, or lengthy essay exams. Some teachers use a combination of these formats on their tests. What will your teacher use this term?

....

....

2. **What does the instructor do in class to emphasize key points?** Does he or she write on the board, provide PowerPoint slides, or emphasize points with his or her voice?

....

....

3. **Did the instructor provide a study guide?** Perhaps there is a study guide in your syllabus, or maybe one was distributed at a study session.

....

....

4. **Does your school provide supplemental instruction?*** If so, where and when is it held?

....

....

5. **Finally, work with a classmate to find other clues to help you prepare for exams.** Keep searching. The clues are there—and they will help you be successful on your exam.

*More and more colleges are providing some form of supplemental instruction (SI). It typically takes the form of an additional class session per week, in which participating students use their notes and class discussions to better understand the course content and prepare for exams. See your instructor or visit the learning resource center to find out whether such a program is available on your campus.

TEST PERFORMANCE: WHAT SKILLS DO YOU HAVE?

Don't go to the fishpond without a net.
—Japanese proverb

Test-performance skills can be organized into two categories: skills for efficient test taking and skills for handling different types of tests.

EFFICIENT TEST PERFORMANCE

You are prepared and sitting in the classroom, and the test is placed in front of you. It's time for all of your preparation efforts to pay dividends for you! But effective test preparation can be hampered by inefficient behaviors during the test. If this is your problem, consider the following test-taking strategies:

- **Review the entire exam.** Before you begin writing answers, review all of the items in the exam. Get a "feel" for the test. How long will you need to do page 1? Page 2? In other words, establish a pace for yourself. Use your SQ4R reading strategy here.
- **Do the easy items first.** If you do run out of time, you don't want to have missed the easy points. "Easy" in this case refers to content as well as item type. Obviously, make sure you answer all the questions you *know*. You may wish to do the types of questions you are most comfortable with before you tackle the more challenging ones. If matching is easy for you, do the matching items first.

- **Watch for so-called trigger words.** Don't get an item wrong because you failed to see a trigger (key or important) word. <u>Underline</u>, ⟨circle⟩, and/or [box] key words. (We will discuss trigger words again later in this chapter.)

- **Block your test paper.** If your eyes tend to drift from one item to another during an exam, use a so-called blocking technique to help you focus. Use two blank pieces of paper to cover the items immediately above and below the item you are working on. For example, if you are working on problem 3, block out problems 2 and 4. Use this technique to force your eyes to focus on only one item.

- **Remove yourself from distraction.** If possible, sit as far away from any distractions as you can. Get away from windows, open doors, noisy students, and the like. In a large lecture hall, this may be difficult, but your instructor may be able to suggest some alternatives.

SPECIFIC EXAMS REQUIRE SPECIFIC STRATEGIES

There are several **types of exams**: multiple choice, true/false, matching, completion, essay, and so forth. But no matter what type of test you are taking, you need to read all instructions carefully. And regardless of the type of test, you should not start until you know what you are expected to do. More than likely, the wording on the exam will be different from what you found in your book, what is on the website, or what the teacher said in class. (That is why it is important to know your material. Do not just memorize. Relate concepts to concepts.)

© Alex Stojanov/Alamy

Here are descriptions and examples of the common types of tests and strategies for taking them.

Multiple-Choice Tests. This kind of test provides a stem, distracters, and an answer. The *stem* is the beginning of the item. It may be in the form of a question or a statement. Following the stem, you will find four or five possible answers. Unless otherwise stated, one answer is correct and the others are incorrect. The incorrect items are known as **distracters**.

Here is an example of a multiple-choice item:*

The best way to prepare for a test is to: [Stem]

   a. depend on your study partner to give you her notes. [Distracter]
   b. review your notes nightly.   [Correct answer]
   c. pull an all-night study session and drink a lot of caffeine. [Distracter]
   d. pray the test will be cancelled.   [Distracter]

Follow these suggestions to help improve your performance on multiple-choice tests:

- Read carefully. Look for words such as *not, except, which is incorrect, best, all, always, never,* and *none.*

- <u>Underline</u> key words (if you are allowed to write on the exam) to help you focus.

*This and other examples of test items are from Piscitelli (2011), pp. 178–179.

- Treat each item like a fill-in-the-blank question. Cover all the answer choices before you look at them. Then come up with the answer on your own.

- If you are not sure of the correct answer, use the process of elimination to arrive at it or at least to narrow your options so you can make an educated guess.

- Answer the easy questions first. Save the tough ones for last.

- If you are using an answer sheet, make sure you mark your answers correctly. Match up each answer and question.

Matching Tests. Matching items usually are organized in two columns, as in Figure 11.2. The items in the first column are to be matched with the items in the second column. One column may have more items than the other. That is, one or more choices may not be used, or some choices may be used more than once. Read the test directions carefully.

Keep the following suggestions in mind when taking a matching test:

- Read all the answer choices first.

- Cross out the items as you use them (if you are allowed to write on the exam).

- Answer the easy items first. Save the tough ones for the end.

True/False Tests. True/false items can be tricky. Pay attention to "all or nothing" phrasing, which should give you a clue. Words such as *always* and *never* are clues that a statement is "false." Words such as *sometimes*, *maybe*, *occasionally*, and *frequently* usually accompany "true" statements.

Here are some examples of true/false items:

SQ4R is a reading strategy.
True
False

Never study the night before an exam.
True
False

Sometimes, a study partner will help you prepare for an exam.
True
False

If you can define the word priority, you will have no problem organizing yourself.
True
False

Figure 11.2 **Matching test items**

Directions: For each item in Column A, choose its best match from Column B. Write the letter from Column B in front of the item in Column A.

Column A	Column B
___ 1. This memory block may be caused by a lack of sleep.	a. Physical
___ 2. Feelings of inadequacy may bring about this memory block	b. Mental
___ 3. Not properly storing information will cause this memory block.	c. Emotional
	d. Lazy

Completion/Fill-in-the-Blank/Short-Answer Tests. A completion item will provide either an incomplete sentence or a brief question for you to answer. Look for key words or clues within the sentence. Unless the instructions say otherwise, the length of the blank does *not* indicate the length of the word or words needed to complete the item correctly.

Here are some examples:

1. Forming a word from the first letters of the words in a series is called a(n) _____.
2. When we establish an order of importance for doing a list of activities, we are said to be _____ our day.
3. Briefly explain one memory strategy to help you effectively store information.

Essay Tests. Taking essay tests requires both knowledge of the material and the ability to communicate that knowledge. Essay items can appear as questions or statements. The question or statement sometimes is called the *prompt*.

Here are examples of essay test questions:

1. Explain two ways that knowledge of learning preferences can help you be more successful in class. [This prompt is a statement and specifically asks for two items to be addressed.]
2. What did the colonists do between the years of 1763 and 1776 to show their displeasure with the British government? [This prompt is in the form of a question and restricts the answer to a particular period of time.]

Follow these suggestions for improving your answers to essay questions:

- Read the question carefully so you know exactly what you are being asked. Refer to the list of trigger words later in this section.
- Underline, circle, box, or in some way highlight important words in the prompt.
- Look for dates and other types of words that will direct or limit your topic.
- Develop a main idea (thesis).
- Support your thesis with substantial facts. Avoid writing "fluff."
- Pay attention to grammar and sentence structure. Yes, English does count!
- Organize your response clearly so that your instructor can identify your main points easily as he or she reads your paper. You may even consider underlining your main points to make them stand out.
- Never leave an essay item blank. Make an educated attempt at an answer. You might get some credit.
- Know what your task is. At the very least, know the following **trigger words** (or key words):

  analyze: to divide a topic or issue into its parts; to show the relation of one part to another
  apply: to use your knowledge in a new or different situation
  assess: to judge the merits of some issue; to evaluate
  classify: to put things into categories
  compare: to provide similarities, differences, consequences (see *analyze*)
  contrast: to provide differences
  criticize: to judge critically
  defend: to argue for a particular issue
  describe: to explain an event, issue, topic; to explain the main characteristics

discuss: to explain in detail; to go beyond mere description

evaluate: to judge, criticize, establish standards

identify: to show how something is unique or individual

illustrate: to provide examples

interpret: to describe the meaning of an issue

motivations: to suggest what caused something to happen

relative importance: to explain how two or more factors compare with one another

summarize: to restate briefly

trace: to provide an order or sequence of events

TEST PERFORMANCE AND ACADEMIC INTEGRITY

Having *integrity* means conducting oneself in an honest, responsible, and respectful manner. When it comes to testing, **academic integrity** means doing and submitting your own work without any unauthorized assistance. Any violation of academic integrity on an exam is broadly classified as cheating and will be punished according to specific guidelines established by your school.

The following examples are violations of academic integrity during an exam, unless the instructor has given permission prior to the exam:

- Copying from a classmate's paper
- Using "cheat sheets"
- Using class notes, the textbook, and/or any other supplemental source
- Receiving assistance from or giving assistance to another student
- Accessing a cell phone or other digital aid
- Listening to recorded material
- Using a laptop computer to access information
- Looking at or otherwise using old copies of the exam
- Removing any testing information from the exam room

Colleges and universities publish academic integrity policies and consequences for violations. They expect students to be responsible for completing their work in a manner that is honest and respectful of their classmates and instructors.

Activity 11.8

Helping Amani Connect Testing with Success Strategies

Review the chapter-opening scenario about Amani. For each of the following topics, identify one strategy and briefly explain how it could help Amani improve her test performance.

- Organization:

....

....

- Motivation and goal setting:

  ....

  ....

- Critical thinking and learning styles:

  ....

  ....

- Note taking and collaboration:

  ....

  ....

- Reading and review time:

  ....

  ....

  ....

Chapter SUMMARY

As you reflect on this chapter, remember that you have been confronted with tests, in one form or another, your entire life. While the types of tests described in this chapter are academic in nature, you have taken them often in your career as a student.

Whether your transcript reflects a test-savvy student or a person who freezes at the thought of an examination, don't lose sight of this fact: You have been down this road many times before. The content and courses may have changed, but you already have test-taking strategies. Remember them, learn from them, and then move to a higher level of competence and success.

Before leaving this chapter, keep the following points in mind:

- Whatever your background, you bring positive experiences and perhaps a few challenges to testing situations. Recognize and build on these experiences.

- Test anxiety is common. Even when you are well prepared, you may still have doubts. Recognize them, but don't let them paralyze you.

- The strategies introduced earlier in this book can be applied to address your test-performance challenges.

- Take time to analyze the reasons you have difficulty with tests. Go beyond a superficial explanation. Move into a deeper examination of the factors that affect your test performance. Use your critical-thinking skills.

- Effective test preparation can be hampered by inefficiency during test taking.

CRITICALLY THINKING

What Have You Learned in This Chapter?

Let's apply what you learned in this chapter to help Amani from the beginning of the chapter. However, before you address Amani's problem and propose your solution, take a moment to think about the main points of the chapter.

Review your notes from this chapter and also the key terms, chapter learning outcomes, boldface chapter headings, and figures and tables. For instance, consider how the chapter learning outcomes may be used to help Amani.

- Identify at least two successful test-preparation strategies you have used in the past, and evaluate their benefit to you now.

- Identify at least one unsuccessful test-preparation strategy you have used in the past.

- Apply one strategy to address your unsuccessful test-preparation strategy.

- Identify and use at least one strategy to combat test anxiety.

- Apply at least one study skill strategy to improve your test-performance skills.

- Use the postexam analysis strategy to review at least one of your most recent exams.

© Shutterstock

TEST YOUR LEARNING

Now that you have reviewed the main points of this chapter and reread Amani's story, what advice do you have for her? Using the R.E.D. Model for critical thinking, help Amani critically review her concerns:

R

Recognize Assumptions:

Facts: What are the facts in Amani's situation? List them.

....

....

Opinions: What opinions do you find in this situation? List them here.

....

....

Assumptions: Are her assumptions accurate?

....

....

E

Evaluate Information

Help Amani compile a list of questions that will help her make the most appropriate decision.

....

What emotions seem to be motivating Amani?

....

What, if anything, is missing from her thought process?

....

Do you see any confirmation bias?

....

....

D

Draw Conclusions

Based on the facts and the questions you have presented, what conclusions can you draw?

....

What advice do you have for Amani? What solutions do you propose?

....

Based on your suggestions, do you see any assumptions?

....

Finally, based on what you learned about using critical thinking and testing strategies, what plan of action do you suggest for Amani?

....

....

CIVILITY

*We never touch people
so lightly that we do not
leave a trace.*

—Peggy Tabor Millin, author

CHAPTER LEARNING OUTCOMES

By the time you finish reading this chapter and completing its activities you will be able to do the following:

◾ Identify the stage of group development that you have found most difficult, and practice a strategy to cope with that challenge.

◾ Explain at least two considerations for forming your own group.

◾ Identify at least one healthy way to minimize how negative people affect you.

◾ Use at least three active-listening techniques to improve your communication skills.

◾ Use at least one conflict management strategy.

The Case of THE GROUP

© Shutterstock

Situation. Hakeem and four other students have been assigned to a group by their psychology professor. The group's project is to choose one topic from their textbook and develop a 15-minute presentation (complete with PowerPoint slides) to explain the topic.

The group met for the first time today. After class, Hakeem told a friend what happened in the group.

"The instructor passed out one sheet of instructions for each group. No one grabbed for the instructions, so I picked up the paper and read them to the group. There are a number of tasks that our group will have to complete by the end of this four-week assignment. Each member will be responsible for taking on at least one of the tasks.

Key Terms

Active listening
Aggressive
Assertiveness
Boundaries
Bullies
Civility
Collective monologue
Communication
Conflict
"Elephant in the corner"
Emotional intelligence
"Energy vampires"
Interpersonal skills
Limits
"Nutritious people"
Passive
Trust

INTRODUCTION
Chapter

"Class, please form a group with three other people, and complete the assignment by the end of the hour."

How many times have you heard something similar from one or more of your instructors? Group work—or *collaborative learning*, as some call it—can be one of the most challenging experiences for students.

Instructors will tell you that real life—careers, relationships, and the like—requires that you learn how to interact with all types of people. That

"So, after I read the instructions and assignment descriptions, no one spoke. No one volunteered to do anything! This is why I hate groups!

"I then asked whether anyone wanted to be the group leader. Jamesha looked at the floor; Rhonda pointed at John; Tony had his head on the desk! Thank goodness, John reluctantly agreed to take charge.

"John quickly broke down the assignment into bite-sized tasks. And before we left class for the day, we all agreed to meet in the campus cafeteria 30 minutes before the next class to discuss the project further. Each person is to think about which part of the assignment he or she wants to tackle."

"Unfortunately," Hakeem sighed, "I did not notice anyone but John and me write down the time and place of the next meeting. I am not feeling good about this at all."

CRITICALLY THINKING
about *the group* situation

What is going on with this group? Does Hakeem have reason to worry, or is his group displaying typical group dynamics that will play themselves out?

may be true, but in the classroom, where your grade-point average (GPA) is at stake, you may prefer to be responsible for your own work and not have to depend on the guy in the back of the room, who is either late to class or sleeping through the lecture!

The reality is that unless you plan on living the life of a hermit, you will interact with people for the rest of your life. You will have intimate relationships, casual friendships, and important professional associations. Your ability

MyStudentSuccessLab

MyStudentSuccessLab (www .mystudentsuccesslab.com) is an online solution designed to help you 'Start strong, Finish stronger' by building skills for ongoing personal and professional development.

to communicate a message of confidence, competence, and civility will affect how people perceive you. Developing effective interpersonal relationships can be the difference between a group that maximizes its resources and one that squanders its opportunities.

Maximizing relationships does not equate to "using" people or "taking advantage" of their good graces. It refers to how you and the people you interact with can enjoy a rewarding experience. Whether the association is a short-term group project or one of enduring intimacy, showing respect for yourself and others will help you make meaningful connections.

Not all of your relationships will be harmonious. If you interact with people long enough, conflict will present itself. It is part of the human drama—but it can be a positive force in your life. The key to dealing with conflict successfully is first to recognize when and why it is happening and then to develop a healthy plan for managing and resolving it. Doing so requires practice, patience, and persistence.

More than likely, when you were a young child, you were told by parents, grandparents, aunts or uncles, or teachers to "play nice" with the other children. That simple piece of advice still holds true, now that you are an adult—probably even more so. For that reason, this chapter will address the concepts of civility, healthy interpersonal relationships, effective communication, and conflict management.

Students choose their classes, but for the most part, they do not decide who else will register for the same class and sit in the same classroom. Thus, all sorts of personalities converge each day in campus classrooms. This convergence creates challenges, as the quiet student deals with the loud student, the obnoxious student offends the contemplative student, a student's rude e-mail insults a professor, or a demanding instructor intimidates an anxious student.

Civility—polite and courteous behavior—will make the classroom and college experience more enjoyable for everyone. **Interpersonal skills**—your strengths and challenges when interacting with other people—are as important during your school years as your academic skills.

EMOTIONAL INTELLIGENCE

We have all heard stories of intelligent people who never seem to be able to "make it." While they may have scored well on an intelligence test and can boast a high IQ (intelligence quotient), they never realize their potential. How can that be?

Daniel Goleman, in his book *Emotional Intelligence*, states that "at best, IQ contributes about 20 percent to the factors that determine life success, which leaves 80 percent to other factors" (Goleman, 1997, p. 34). He and other psychologists believe a person needs more than a high score on an IQ test to be successful. For instance, Robert Sternberg (1997) suggests there are three types of intelligence: analytical, creative, and practical. And Howard Gardner's theory of multiple intelligences maintains that interpersonal intelligence allows someone to recognize what motivates others and how best to work with them.

Emotional intelligence, says Goleman, is a more accurate predictor of success in life. In particular, the emotionally intelligent person displays these qualities (Goleman, 1997, p. 43):

- Is aware of his or her emotions as they occur
- Can soothe himself or herself appropriately and "shake off rampant anxiety, gloom, or irritability"
- Delays gratification and controls impulses
- Has the ability to "tune in" to the emotions of others
- Is skilled at helping others manage their emotions

As you work with people, be mindful of how you manage your emotions and impulses, how you respond to disappointments, and how well you work with others. The emotionally intelligent person practices civility even when the circumstances are not what he or she would like them to be. To be successful, "book smarts" must be complemented with "people smarts."

Activity 12.1

Reflecting on Your Current Level of Collaborative Skills

Before you answer the following items, reflect on your current level of interpersonal skills. Think of how well (or poorly) you have related to classmates and instructors in past classes.

As you do in completing all of the reflective activities in this book, you should write from your heart. This exercise is not meant for you to answer just like your classmates—or to match what you may think the instructor wants to see. Take the time to give a respectful, responsible general accounting of your experiences with interpersonal relations. Conducting a truthful self-assessment now will help you build on skills you have while developing those you lack.

For each of the following items, circle the number that best describes your *typical* experience when relating to other people. Here is the key for the numbers:

0 = never, 1 = almost never, 2 = occasionally, 3 = frequently, 4 = almost always, 5 = always

When considering your past strengths and challenges with interpersonal skills, how often . . .

1.	Have you been able to identify and appropriately deal with the feelings of a group member?	0	1	2	3	4	5
2.	Have you been able to soothe and calm yourself when you have become angry?	0	1	2	3	4	5
3.	Were you able to work effectively with a group on a class project?	0	1	2	3	4	5
4.	Have you been able to distance yourself from people who continually drain your energy?	0	1	2	3	4	5
5.	Are you able to associate with people who energize and excite you?	0	1	2	3	4	5
6.	Have you let a speaker know, either by body language or verbal response, that you were truly listening?	0	1	2	3	4	5

| **7.** | Have you asked questions of the person speaking to you? | **0** | **1** | **2** | **3** | **4** | **5** |
| **8.** | Have you been an energizing force for another person? | **0** | **1** | **2** | **3** | **4** | **5** |

Add up your scores for items 1 through 8. Divide by 8. Write your answer here: _____.

Using the key provided to explain each number (0, 1, 2, 3, 4, 5), complete this sentence: When it comes to relating to other people, I _____ effectively relate to other people.

Based on your answers, what insights have you gained about your experiences with interpersonal skills?

CIVILITY AND COMMUNICATION

> *As a society we have done a good job of encouraging self-esteem, but not as good a job of teaching self-control.*
>
> —*P. M. Forni, author*

THE ART OF COMMUNICATION: Are You Really Listening or Just Talking?

Effective **communication** is an art form. One person constructs and passes along thoughts, information, and feelings about a particular subject to another person. This can occur one to one, as when a friend sends you an e-mail, tweets, posts a status update, engages you in a face-to-face discussion, or gives you a heartfelt hug.

Communication can take place on a larger scale, as well. The term *mass communication* refers to the transmission of information to large numbers (thousands and millions) of people. This occurs via Twitter, Facebook, blogs, newspapers, cable network news programs, and radio talk shows. When mass communication is done well, a connection develops between the sender and the receiver. One conveys a message, while the other listens (or reads).

DIALOGUES VERSUS COLLECTIVE MONOLOGUES

It has also been said that communication is a lost art. The thought here is that people have lost the ability to meaningfully exchange ideas with one another. When done poorly, there is no communication, no connection—just words passing in space.

Tune in to a television or radio talk show, and chances are great that you will hear *talking*—but *not conversation*. One person talks, and the other interrupts. The first person interrupts the second person by raising his or her voice. Inevitably, a shouting match results, leaving the listener with a headache. Just because two people are in the same room and talking *at* one another does not mean they are communicating or conversing *with* one another.

A dialogue presupposes that two people have engaged in a conversation, in which one person speaks and the other listens. The second person then appropriately responds to the first with comments relevant to the conversation. The conversation continues back and forth—one person listening and the other person speaking.

Unfortunately, what passes for conversation most times is not dialogue. Think of a recent time when you either observed a group of people talking or you were involved in a conversation with a few friends. Was there true communication? While one person was talking, were the other people quietly listening? When the person talking finished his or her thoughts, did the others respond to those ideas, or did they start talking about something else, not even recognizing what the other person had just said? Did people continually interrupt one another to get their own opinions into the conversation? Were many people talking but no one listening?

If so, what you experienced was a **collective monologue**. When one person speaks without any expectation of an answer from someone else, he or she is presenting a monologue. The air vibrates with words, but not much communication takes place. When two or more people do this together, it is a collective monologue.

It is probably safe to say that you have engaged in a collective monologue at one time or another. Most times, it just passes as typical conversation. But at other times, it can be frustrating and even border on being disrespectful.

Like any action that is repeated often enough, communicating in this way can become a habit—a bad habit. A person who continually engages in collective monologues will eventually be considered a bore, at the least. And while this may be irritating in a social setting, it can be disastrous in a group or professional setting.

ACTIVE LISTENING

An antidote to participating in a collective monologue is **active listening**. It requires the listener to pay attention to what the speaker is saying. Active listening cannot be done halfheartedly. It is work. Listening to the actual words, as well as paying attention to verbal clues (tone of voice) and nonverbal clues (posture, eye contact), requires a degree of focus you may not typically use in daily conversation. But practicing active listening is worth the effort. Active listening is one of the characteristics of "nutritious people," which will be discussed later in the chapter.

As you read the following characteristics of an active listener, conduct a mental review of how you measure up:

- **An active listener has to be quiet and focus on the speaker.** It becomes increasingly difficult to listen to another person if you are talking yourself. Quiet your mouth. An old saying reminds us that "We have two ears and one mouth," so we should listen twice as much as we talk.

- **The active listener needs to quiet his or her mind.** Attending to the chatter in your own mind will make you miss what the speaker is saying.

- **An active listener pays attention to what is said.** In a face-to-face conversation, maintain eye contact, do not interrupt, and work to understand what the speaker wants to convey.

- **The active listener lets the speaker know that he or she is listening.** Nod your head, say "I see," or in some other way indicate that you hear what is being said. The key is to be sincere. Nodding and saying "I understand" while really thinking about what you will be doing tonight is not actively listening. It is preparing for a collective monologue.

- **Active listeners not only hear the words but "listen" to the body language.** Look for clues in the speaker's body position that will help you understand the message being delivered.

- **The active listener often asks questions about what the speaker has just said.** The questioning is not meant to be confrontational; rather, it is an attempt to make sure the message has not been misunderstood. Asking questions indicates your interest in the other person's comments.

■ **Finally, the active listener attempts to repeat what he or she has just heard to ensure the message has been understood.** Paraphrasing the message makes the speaker feel affirmed. You do not have to agree with the speaker but only convey you have correctly understood what he or she said.

Activity 12.2

Critically Thinking about Your Interpersonal Skills

R
E
D

The R.E.D. Model (**R**ecognize Assumptions, **E**valuate Information, **D**raw Conclusions) provides a systematic way to approach critical thinking through the use of an easy-to-remember acronym.

Let's apply the R.E.D. Model for critical thinking to your ability to relate to and work with others in a civil manner. Activity 12.1, which you completed earlier, may be helpful for this activity.

Identify one of your interpersonal strengths or challenges here:

....

Critical-Thinking Step	Application to Your Interpersonal Skills	Your Explanation (here or on a separate piece of paper)
Recognize Assumptions	Clearly state your strength or challenge with relationship skills. How do you know this assessment of your interpersonal skills is correct?	
Evaluate Information	Provide a specific explanation (give examples) of your strength or challenge with relationship skills. Examine your strength or challenge with relationship skills beyond a superficial (simplistic) explanation, and look at all of the complexities involved. Examine your strength or challenge with relationship skills from more than one perspective (point of view).	
Draw Conclusions	Based on your evidence, do your conclusions above make sense? How is your assessment of your strength or challenge with relationship skills connected to your academic progress? What is the next step you will take to improve your interpersonal skills?	

CIVILITY AND GROUP DYNAMICS

"None of us is as smart as all of us."
—Ken Blanchard, author

By the time you find your way to college, you will have already been involved in group work on various levels. Whether collaborating on a community project or doing a school assignment, group work is a common experience for all students. Some groups last for a very brief time. For instance, teachers commonly assign students to groups for in-class activities. Other groups may last for an entire school term. Being involved in groups helps the participants develop communication, collaboration, and conflict resolution skills.

UNDERSTANDING GROUP DYNAMICS

Whether you work with a group on a short-term classroom assignment or become the member of, say, a sports team for a longer period, you will find that certain stages of group development are present. Merely knowing about these stages will not eliminate the potential for interpersonal problems, but being familiar with common group dynamics can help you anticipate what is to come and, consequently, be better prepared for what lies ahead.

Groups present an opportunity for two, three, or more people to share their talents and develop a better product than any of them could produce alone. But human behavior can be unpredictable and create some challenges along the way (Lencioni, 2002, p. vii).

A common model views group development as a predictable, step-by-step process. That model was created by Bruce W. Tuckman, who published "Developmental Sequence in Small Groups" in 1965. He described the stages groups progress through, from development to conclusion. His initial model included only four stages, but in a later article, Tuckman and a colleague added a fifth stage. Table 12.1 describes these five stages and provides examples. (For more on Tuckman's research, see Smith [2005]. Many other websites and books also contain descriptions of Tuckman's often-cited work.).

While there is a certain predictable unpredictability about groups, the five stages are common to all of them. Depending on the purpose of the group, the stages may take place over months or years. Or in the case of a short-term group, all five stages may be exhausted in less than an hour.

Table 12.1 **Stages of group development**

Stage of Group	Common Dynamics	Example from Hakeem's Group (beginning of chapter)
1. FORMING	▪ Group members introduce themselves to one another and learn about the task they are to address. Apprehension and anxiety may be present.	▪ The instructor distributes the guidelines sheet to group members.
2. STORMING	▪ Conflict (tension) typically arises as members struggle to find a leader, assign tasks, and agree on rules. Groups can end up splitting up at this early stage.	▪ Students are reluctant to commit to the tasks at hand.
3. NORMING	▪ Members become more comfortable and tackle their tasks. Trust may start to develop.	▪ John volunteers to lead the group.
4. PERFORMING	▪ This is the productive stage, as members work on their assignments.	▪ The group agrees on a time and place to meet.
5. ADJOURNING	▪ The group's task is finished, and the group ends.	▪ Not yet! This group is just beginning.

FORMING YOUR OWN GROUP

At times, you may be assigned to a group by the instructor, and you will have no choice in determining your group members. The instructor may group students randomly or according to some preset criterion, such as grades. On other occasions, you will be able to form your own groups. For instance, you may form a study group with a few classmates when you decide to study for a test together. In this situation, there is the desired way to choose members—and then there is the college reality.

In reality, study groups are made up of friends or, if not friends, acquaintances from the same class. The only criterion for group membership, in most cases, is that the students have the same test, essay, or project to prepare for. Perhaps a student who scores well on exams will be asked to join the group. Some members will look for friendly faces to provide comfort until the task is completed.

In fact, this informal method of selecting group members can produce the needed results on short-term assignments. The suggestions that follow, however, may maximize the productivity of a group—especially for a long-term group project. And if you are not part of a class or study group, you might find yourself a member of another group—perhaps the homecoming committee, the campus speakers bureau, or the student government issues committee.

Whatever the purpose of the group, when you have the option to choose your own members, consider the following points:

- Size matters. Keep the group at a small, workable number.
- Team members need to have complementary skills. If you have a four-member team, the ideal composition is to have a full-of-ideas creative person, a facts-based thinking person, an organizer who can pull together all the ideas and research, and a "people" person who has a talent for helping others work together.
- Know why you exist. Just as with a reading or writing assignment, everyone in the group needs to agree on your common purpose as soon as possible. Know your direction.
- Disagree. A passionate exchange, in which all speakers and views are respected, can energize a group.
- Accountability is a must. Ensure that all team members have specific tasks to perform and that they are held accountable to the group for completing their assigned tasks.
- Don't ignore the **"elephant in the corner."** The "elephant" is a metaphor for a problem so big that it is impossible to miss. The elephant's being in the "corner" indicates the problem is being pushed to the side, because no one wants to talk about it. If a problem is big enough that every group member knows it exists, do not ignore it. Address and deal with the problem before it sabotages your group.

Numerous books address the power of teams. You may find any of the following helpful: Lencioni (2002), *The Five Dysfunctions of a Team*; John R. Katzenbach and Douglas K. Smith (2003), *The Wisdom of Teams: Creating the High-Performance Organization*; and Jose Stevens (2002), *The Power Path: The Shaman's Way to Success in Business and Life*. Also see *Keys to Success* by Carol Carter, Joyce Bishop, and Sarah Lyman Kravits (2006, pp. 273–274).

TRUST: Building on a Shared Experience

All successful groups share at least one key quality: **trust**. Having meaningful, passionate, and respectful discussions—as opposed to shouting matches—will be fostered when members recognize that their main shared concern is arriving at a reasonable answer. This cannot happen when members are worrying whether someone in the group will attempt to undermine them with personal attacks and hidden agendas. You can disagree and argue about an issue, but do not launch a personal assault on another member. Attacking others in this way will undermine trust.

But many times, individuals are thrust together with little or no knowledge of one another. Or perhaps the pieces of information they *do* have do not give an accurate view of each person. How do you come to trust people you don't really know?

The simple answer to this complex question is that you must build trust over time. It cannot be built by giving money to people, it cannot be built with glitzy technology, and it cannot be built with motivational pep talks. Trust will be built when group members share an experience over a period of time. The experience can be positive, like winning a volleyball championship for the college. Or the experience can be harrowing, such as surviving a natural disaster with the help of a neighbor. The commonality in both situations is that the people involved came to rely on one another. They anticipated each other's needs—they supported one another.

Members of an effective study group or class project team will experience such trust building. When one student is having a difficult day, the others will come to his or her assistance. Each person comes to the group meeting having prepared the material for which he or she is responsible. They not only work toward a goal, but they also do what they can to make sure each member of the group is successful. Trust naturally develops among the members of this kind of group.

Activity 12.3

Whom Do You Trust—and Why?

Take a moment and reflect on the people in your life whom you trust. Your initial thoughts might be of a family member, a church leader, a close friend, or a sports teammate. For this activity, however, please picture someone you have met *since you have been on campus.* It might be a classmate, a professor, a counselor, an office worker—or anyone else.

1. Write the first name of this trusted individual.

2. Why do you trust this person?

3. Review your answer. Can you point to a shared experience that led to the formation of this trusted relationship? If so, briefly explain the experience.

When you meet and must work with new classmates or professors during the remainder of your school career—and beyond into the world of work—remind yourself that while it takes time to develop trust, the results are energizing.

CIVILITY AND CONFLICT

> *Conflict is inevitable, but combat is optional.*
>
> —Max Lucado, author and minister

Conflict describes a state of disharmony in which one set of ideas or values contradicts another. A conflict can be fairly minor—a roommate who rises for morning jogs and disturbs your sleep. Or it can be quite serious—two group members

© Shutterstock

getting into a shouting and shoving match about the group's work. At times, you will have to confront conflicts of various degrees of severity.

ARE YOU HAVING A DISAGREEMENT OR A CONFLICT?

A conflict is not necessarily the same as a disagreement. For our purposes, an argument about which college football team should be the national champion does not constitute a conflict. It is a difference of opinion, to be sure, but this type of disagreement does not pit one person's core system of values and beliefs against that of another.

Conflict, on the other hand, occurs when deeply held ideas, values, or perspectives are contradictory (McNamara, 1997–2008). The conflict can be between two or more people—or it can be an internal conflict between your own values and actions.

Suppose a young man has been reared with the deeply held value that having sexual relations before marriage constitutes a violation of personal integrity. If he finds himself in a situation that challenges his deeply held beliefs, he will experience a period of conflict as he tries to reconcile the contradictory signals.

CONFLICT IS NOT ALWAYS A BAD THING

Earlier in this chapter, you read about the dynamics of group formation. Storming is a real and necessary stage that groups and teams will encounter. Conflict about the exact purpose for the team, who has the best talents to be the leader, and what tasks should be assigned to whom can expose contradictory values and perspectives.

One of the dysfunctions of teams occurs when passionate debate does not take place (Lencioni, 2002). So while an absence of conflict may seem heavenly, it is an unrealistic goal in most human relationships—and it may even be unhealthy. The required ingredient is a mechanism to discuss why the conflict exists and how it can be managed and resolved without loss of trust.

When two or more people come together for any length of time, the risk for conflict presents itself. You do not need to enter every relationship with the dread of impending conflict. But it may be healthy to understand that when conflict does occur, it can produce a positive outcome for you and the other person or people involved.

WAYS PEOPLE DEAL WITH CONFLICT

There are many ways to deal with conflict. If five people are involved in a conflict, there will be probably *at least* five solutions presented. If ten people are present, there is a good chance you will find at least ten ideas.

Given this, any list of strategies to manage conflict will be necessarily incomplete. As you read the following strategies and examples, think about how you might handle each situation (McNamara, 1997–2008):

■ **Ignore the issue.** Some people will do anything to avoid a confrontation. They believe that peace at all costs is better than arguing and raising their voices. But this avoidance could lead to a lose-lose situation, in which the initial flame of conflict gets worse because it has not been controlled. Eventually, the conflict will consume all parties in an inferno of controversy. That may result in ill feelings and resentment.

- ☐ **Example**: One member of your group always complains about the project at hand. He drags down your energy each time you are around him. Rather than say anything to him or her, your group quietly goes about its work, many times taking on tasks that the "complainer" was to do. You all hope this person will change his or her ways or leave the group, but none of you says or does anything.

- **Refusing to see another side.** In this scenario, everyone knows a problem exists, but no one willingly changes position. In fact, as the conflict increases, people may become more entrenched in their views. Depending on the severity of the disagreement, this lose-lose situation can bring a relationship or team to a grinding halt.

  - ☐ **Example**: There are four members in your group. Each person believes his or her direction for the group is the best, and no one is willing to concede on anything. No work gets done, and the deadline for the group product gets closer.

- **Give in to the "demands."** In the interest of peace, once again, one person decides to do whatever the other person wants. This is a win-lose situation: Someone gets his or her way, and someone does not. It may leave the underlying issue of the conflict unresolved.

  - ☐ **Example**: Your roommate likes to party late into the night. Unfortunately, his or her late hours have been interfering with your sleep patterns. Each day, you awaken tired. When you talk to your roommate about this, he or she begins to whine about how you do not appreciate what he or she does around the apartment. In fact, you are told, your early morning routines have bothered him or her. Your roommate threatens to move out and leave you to pay the entire monthly rent. You give in—and buy some earplugs.

- **Compromise.** You give a little, the other person gives a little, and the conflict is minimized if not totally resolved. This creates a modified win-win situation, as each person has not been able to achieve all that he or she had hoped for. But for the sake of harmony, a middle course has been agreed on. Because all situations do not reach the synergy level (see the next strategy), compromise sometimes represents a very positive resolution.

  - ☐ **Example**: Your late-night roommate has agreed to enter the apartment quietly and not turn the television on when he or she returns after midnight. You agree to be quieter when you arise early for your 8:00 a.m. class.

- **Synergy.** When two or more people hit on a solution that is actually better than any of the previous ideas, synergy has been achieved. A win-win situation results. Although highly desirable, this outcome requires considerable effort to achieve.

  - ☐ **Example**: You and your late-night roommate have discovered that two of your good friends are having the same problem: One is an early riser, and one is a "night owl." The four of you decide to switch roommates. The two early risers will live together, and the two night owls will live together. All friendships have been maintained, all four individuals are happier than they were prior to the new arrangement, and you are now able to get a great night's sleep.

AGGRESSIVENESS, ASSERTIVENESS, AND PASSIVENESS

Being able to communicate a message of confidence, competence, and civility will have an impact on how people perceive you. Not only does what you say influence people, but so does *how* you say it (tone of voice) and how you *look* (body language) while saying it. Whether you are speaking to 1 person or 100, your communication is the sum of many interrelated parts.

One key to successful communication is to speak with an air of confidence. A self-assured person captures attention better than someone stammering for the correct words. Self-confidence underlies an assertive communication style. People who communicate with **assertiveness** can stand up for themselves. They can face demands and can make requests in a nonaggressive manner (Marano, 2004).

Aggressive behavior, on the other hand, represents a harsher attitude. It can border on hostility or a bullylike approach to dealing with other people. Bullies take advantage of **passive** individuals: people who submit to verbal and, in some cases, nonverbal attacks without resistance. Although every situation presents unique circumstances, generally speaking, assertive behavior is seen as the favored road to travel.

DEALING WITH BULLIES

Mention the word *bully*, and people tend to think of the elementary school playground. A larger boy seeks out and finds a smaller fellow, whom he proceeds to verbally and/or physically assault. However, school-age children do not have a monopoly on bullying behavior. It exists in the workplace, and it exists on college campuses (Saillant, 2005).

Bullies repeatedly seek to control other people by means of physical or verbal aggression. The bully sees the victim as "easy pickings." Bullying can arise in any situation where one person holds power over another. Supervisors and coworkers can bully people, for instance. A student can be bullied because of his or her sexual orientation. A boyfriend can bully his girlfriend, and a girlfriend can bully her boyfriend. Domestic violence is bullying taken to a more extreme level. Faculty can bully students, and students can bully faculty. No one is immune.

If you suspect a friend is being bullied—or if you are the victim of a bully—seek assistance as quickly as possible. Find someone—a friend, a faculty member, a counselor, or a family member—you trust and get help.

WHO ARE THE "ENERGY VAMPIRES" OF YOUR LIFE?

"Toxic" people "poison" our lives. They can affect us on various levels. A toxic person can be a bully who perpetuates a physically abusive or psychologically demeaning relationship. In whatever manner they come to us, these toxic people seem to take the life right out of us. Like a balloon losing air, we can almost hear our energy leaving our bodies.

In the book *Positive Energy*, Judith Orloff (2004) writes of **"energy vampires"**—people in our lives who continually drain us of energy (pp. 288–320). They whine about their lives, berate us for our actions, and monopolize our conversations. Energy vampires do not typically engage in conversations, because that would involve a two-way exchange. Rather, energy vampires usually deliver monologues about their ailments, opinions, or prejudices. When they finish with us, *they* feel more energized—but *we* feel exhausted, having had our energy zapped.

The metaphor of an energy vampire is powerful (Goldberg, n.d.). The same concept is sometimes referred to as "psychic parasitism." After draining us and leaving us tired and wasted, these people move on. Perhaps you have experienced this with a roommate, a classmate, an instructor, a friend, a co-worker, or even a family member. The experience may be subtle. You are not really sure what happened. But after talking with this person, you feel more tired than you did before. And in some cases, you can feel the energy draining from your body as the person moves closer to you and begins to speak.

In short, these people spread "toxins" into your life that affect you as severely as if you immersed yourself in a polluted river.

Two cautionary notes must be added to this discussion of energy vampires:

1. As with many things in life, there are shades of gray. Not every situation is black or white. Obviously, a friend who comes to you in distress about a traumatic event that just occurred is not the same as the person who continually seeks you out to complain or criticize and drains energy from your relationship.
2. Every relationship is a two-way street. If you continually find yourself in draining relationships, you should evaluate your actions. Do you do something that draws these types of people to you and encourages their behavior?

© Shutterstock

Activity 12.4

Identifying the Energy Vampires of Your Life

This activity is particularly personal. The intent is not to ridicule or denigrate another person. Rather, it will help you to identify those people in your life who are tiring *on a regular basis*. Only after that has been accomplished can you work to take ownership and remedy the situation. Seek assistance (say, from a counselor or mentor) as needed.

Think of people in your life who drain you of your energy on a regular basis. How do you know these people drain your energy? Specifically, what do they do, and what emotional or physical reactions do you experience after having encountered them?

1. What do they do?

   ....

   ....

2. Emotional consequences for you:

   ....

   ....

3. Physical consequences for you:

   ....

   ....

Table 12.2   Protecting your energy

What the Person Does to Drain Energy from You	What You Can Do to Minimize or Avoid a Loss of Energy
The person constantly whines and rehashes past events.	Attempt to redirect the conversation.
No solution is really sought. The problems seem to give a purpose to this person's life.	Ask the person to stop rehashing the same scenarios over and over.
Everything constitutes a major crisis.	Set limits on the conversation. Take a deep breath.
The person is angry and negative.	When you can, limit your time with this person.
The person blames others for his or her misfortunes.	When you can't walk away from the person, set boundaries of appropriate conversation.
The person dumps problems on you and wants you to fix them.	You are responsible for your life, and the other person is responsible for his or her life.

Source: Based on Orloff (2004), pp. 288–320.

HOW TO GUARD AGAINST ENERGY VAMPIRES

After you identify the source of your energy loss, what can you do to plug the hole? Orloff provides a number of prescriptions—"antidotes" to the toxin, in effect—including redirecting the conversation, setting limits, and simply spending less time with the person. A few of her suggestions are summarized in Table 12.2. For further information, refer to Orloff's book *Positive Energy*—especially Chapter 9, which is called "The Ninth Prescription: Protect Yourself from Energy Vampires." (In this chapter, Orloff clearly describes nine types of energy vampires and offers specific suggestions for dealing with each one.)

Activity 12.5

Are You an Energy Vampire?

Pause for a moment and reflect on how you interact with other people. Then answer the questions that follow. Ask someone who really knows you well to share his or her perception of your interaction with others.

Remember: If you ask someone for honest feedback, be prepared to accept what he or she says. Do not request information and then argue with the person because you disagree. Consider feedback a wonderful gift.

1. When talking with people, do you continually "replay" your same stories over and over?

    ❏ Yes   ❏ No

2. Do you hold a conversation with people, or do you engage in a self-centered monologue about your life?

    ❏ Yes   ❏ No

3. When someone speaks with you, do you avoid asking meaningful and substantive questions? Do you lack interest in the other person's "stories"?

    ❏ Yes   ❏ No

4. When describing events that have occurred, do you typically describe things as being devastating and particular only to you? That is, do you believe no one could ever experience the hardships that you have experienced?

    ❏ Yes   ❏ No

5. Do you start most of your conversations with "You are never going to believe what happened to me!" or something similar?*

    ❏ Yes   ❏ No

6. When in a group, do you always have to be the focus of attention?

    ❏ Yes   ❏ No

7. Do you find your conversations peppered with insults, anger, and attempts to make others look bad?

    ❏ Yes   ❏ No

8. Any "Yes" answers may indicate that you have a tendency to drain energy from others. Think of the list you made of people who drained your energy. Do you think your name will appear on anyone else's list of energy vampires?

    ❏ Yes   ❏ No

9. Based on your answers, what do you plan to do to make sure you do not drain energy from those around you? What will you do to be a "nutritious person"?

    ....

    ....

    ....

    Dealing with energy vampires may be tiring and counterproductive to group results. If you feel ill equipped or not up to the task, draw on support and advice from trusted friends and mentors. And remember never to place yourself in a dangerous or compromising position. Your emotional well-being is important, as is your physical safety.

    *Orloff (2004, p. 299) refers to these people as "drama queens." And of course, there are "drama kings," too.

BOUNDARIES AND LIMITS

Another strategy is to be proactive. Let people know just how far you will go—and how far you will let them go. Setting boundaries and understanding limits allows for having a more satisfying life (Lee, 2009, pp. 125–142.).

Boundaries show where we begin and end. They let others know what is acceptable and unacceptable. They tell people how far they can go with us. When our boundaries are clearly established, there is no question. People know where they can and cannot go as it relates to you.

Limits, on the other hand, let people know how far *you* will go. Your limits clearly tell people what you will or will not do. If you establish your limits correctly, people will not be left guessing about what to expect from you. People without clearly established limits end up giving more—physically, emotionally, occupationally—than they want to give. This can result in resentment, hurt feelings, and even rage. But these people do it to themselves!

Boundaries and limits can be adjusted along the way, as additional information is learned. But for boundaries and limits to be effective and healthy, they have to be clear to both you and those you live and work with. You should not get upset when someone breeches a boundary if you have not been clear on what your boundaries are. The same goes for limits. If you do not set—and respect—your own limits, you may find yourself overstretched and ready to snap (see Piscitelli, 2010).

Activity 12.6

How Can You Regain Your Energy?

Review your answers from Activity 12.4, and then answer the following questions:

1. In the past, when you have been confronted with an energy-depleting individual, what have you done? Did you do nothing and let the situation escalate? Did you argue and still feel depleted? Did you walk away? Did you feel you were in danger? Did you do something else?

....

....

....

2. How effective or ineffective were your actions?

....

....

....

3. What new strategies can you apply the next time you are confronted by an energy vampire?

....

....

....

FINDING "NUTRITIOUS PEOPLE" FOR YOUR LIFE

One way to protect your energy and sanity is to associate with **"nutritious people"** (see Leider, 1997, p. 64; Leider & Shapiro, 1995, Chapter 7). These people help to ward off the poison spewed by the energy vampires.

A nutritious person has three main characteristics:

© Shutterstock

1. When this person sees you, he or she is genuinely glad to see you. His or her face brightens with a smile.
2. When you speak, this person *listens* to you. He or she asks questions about what you say and about what matters to you. He or she exhibits a genuine interest in what you have to say.
3. The nutritious person accepts you as you are. This individual does not try to make you into someone he or she would like you to be.

The more nutritious people we have in our lives, the better. It is almost as though we can feel our energy level rising when we see their faces.

Identify the nutritious people in your life. Thank them for being there for you. Finally, on this topic, ask yourself, "Am I nutritious for other people?"

Chapter SUMMARY

Before leaving this chapter, keep the following points in mind:

- While groups present opportunities for people to share talents and develop better products than one person could produce alone, they can be unpredictable and create challenges.

- Beware of people who constantly drain energy from you—the energy vampires.

- Seek out nutritious people, who will help energize you.

- If you want to be considered a nutritious person, listen to and acknowledge what others have to offer.

- Effective communication is an art form that has no room for collective monologues.

- Conflict can be positive, when appropriately managed.

CRITICALLY THINKING
What Have You Learned in This Chapter?

Let's apply what you learned in this chapter to help Hakeem's group from the chapter-opening scenario. However, before you address the group's situation and propose your solution, take a moment to think about the main points of the chapter.

Review your notes from this chapter and also the key terms, chapter learning outcomes, boldface chapter headings, and figures and tables. For instance, consider how the chapter learning outcomes may be used to help Hakeem and his group:

- Identify the stage of group development that you have found most difficult—and practice a strategy to cope with that challenge.

- Explain at least two considerations for forming your own group.

- Identify at least one healthy way to minimize how negative people affect you.

© Shutterstock

- Use at least three active-listening techniques to improve your communication skills.

- Use at least one conflict management strategy.

TEST YOUR LEARNING

Now that you have reviewed the main points of this chapter and reread the group's story, what advice do you have for Hakeem and his group. Using the R.E.D. Model of critical thinking, help Hakeem critically review any concerns he might have:

Recognize Assumptions:

Facts: What are the facts in the group's situation? List them.

....

....

Opinions: What opinions do you find in this situation? List them here.

....

....

Assumptions: Are Hakeem's assumptions accurate?

....

....

Evaluate Information:

Help Hakeem compile a list of questions that will help him and the group make the most appropriate decision.

....

....

What emotions seem to be motivating Hakeem?

....

....

What, if anything, is missing from Hakeem's thought process?

....

....

Do you see any confirmation bias?

....

....

Draw Conclusions:

Based on the facts and the questions you have presented, what conclusions can you draw?

....

....

What advice do you have for Hakeem? What solutions do you propose?

....

....

Based on your suggestions, do you see any assumptions?

....

....

Finally, based on what you learned about using critical thinking and interpersonal skills, what plan of action do you suggest for this group?

....

....

The Choices

13

YOU MAKE

Everybody, sooner or later, sits down to a banquet of consequences.

—*Robert Louis Stevenson, author*

CHAPTER LEARNING OUTCOMES

By the time you finish reading this chapter and completing its activities, you will be able to do the following:

■ Evaluate the progress you have made this term toward minimizing or eliminating your study skill challenges.

■ Explain at least three strategies that have had the biggest impacts on your academic success this term.

■ Identify one study skill challenge that you still have to improve, and write a goal that addresses that challenge.

INTRODUCTION
Chapter

You have covered a lot of ground since you first opened this book. You have read about strategies and completed activities to apply your knowledge. Only you (and perhaps your instructor) know how well you have internalized this material.

End-of-the-book chapters, like this one, run the risk of being cliché. Phrases such as "Preparing for the End," "A New Beginning," "Taking the

© Shutterstock

Next Step," and "Where Do You Go from Here?" often appear as the titles of these chapters. In reality, all of them reflect excellent sentiments and accurate thoughts. They let students know that while the work for this term is nearly done, more work and decisions are still to come.

This chapter will discuss these issues within the context of choices. In particular, you will be asked to do the following:

MyStudentSuccessLab

MyStudentSuccessLab (www.mystudentsuccesslab.com) is an online solution designed to help you 'Start strong, Finish stronger' by building skills for ongoing personal and professional development.

- Reflect on the choices—specifically, study skill choices—you have made since the beginning of this school term.
  - Consider the consequences those choices have had for you.
    - Think about the academic choices that lie ahead of you.

Before you close this book one final time, take a last accounting of what you have accomplished—and what you still would like to work on in the future. As you complete the final activities, keep two questions in mind:

- Are you satisfied with the choices you have made this term?
- Did your results match your expectations?

This chapter is short, but it will require you to look back at the previous chapters and activities in this book. In so doing, you will be able to draw important conclusions.

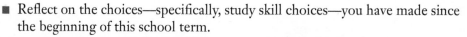

© Shutterstock

THE CHOICES YOU HAVE MADE

> *Success seems to be connected with action. Successful people keep moving. They make mistakes, but they don't quit.*
> —Conrad Hilton, founder of Hilton Hotels

You probably have heard someone say that "He has so much potential." Or perhaps someone made the observation that "She will definitely go far. She has so much ambition."

While **ambition** (a desire to reach a goal) and **potential** (the possibility of becoming something greater than you are) are important characteristics, they are useless without **initiative**. Responsible decision making and follow-through are needed to put potential and ambition into action. Ambition is the desire, potential is the ability, and initiative is the doing.

Throughout this school term, you have had to make **choices** every day to put your ambition and potential into action. Your choices reflect what you consider important in your world. They reflect your priorities—the paths you have decided to take.

RETURNING TO THE BEGINNING

So, let's reflect on what you have done, how far you have progressed since the first day of the term, and what you plan for the future.

First, Activity 13.1 will allow you to once again review your strengths and challenges as they exist now after an entire term of study. Then, the final activity of this chapter will give you the opportunity to apply your critical-thinking skills and evaluate the choices you have made and will need to make for continued success.

Activity 13.1

Assessment of Strengths and Challenges

In completing this activity, focus on what you have *done* (steps you have taken) to become a more capable student in your classes. First, check your strengths when it comes to academic success. What do you do well? Check as many or as few of the following as apply. Take your time, and think about each choice carefully.

- ☐ Setting goals
- ☐ Supporting an opinion with facts
- ☐ Completing goals
- ☐ Organizing an essay
- ☐ Establishing priorities
- ☐ Writing and completing a strong essay
- ☐ Completing work on time
- ☐ Establishing relationships and connections with class notes
- ☐ Eliminating distractions
- ☐ Taking notes from class lectures
- ☐ Remembering important information for exams
- ☐ Controlling test anxiety
- ☐ Taking notes from the textbook
- ☐ Allowing plenty of time to prepare for exams
- ☐ Taking organized notes
- ☐ Completing exams in the time allotted
- ☐ Getting to class on time
- ☐ Learning from previous exam mistakes
- ☐ Participating in class
- ☐ Taking study breaks
- ☐ Keeping an organized notebook
- ☐ Studying alone
- ☐ Regularly reviewing and organizing class notes
- ☐ Studying with friends
- ☐ Coming to class prepared
- ☐ Locating information for research projects
- ☐ Understanding and using my learning style
- ☐ Evaluating information for research projects
- ☐ Using critical-thinking skills to solve problems
- ☐ Using social media for academic and career purposes
- ☐ Getting the main point from a reading assignment
- ☐ Developing respectful relationships with faculty and classmates
- ☐ Other: _____
- ☐ Other: _____

Now, check your challenges when it comes to academic success. What do you still need to improve? Check as many or as few as apply. Take your time, and think about each choice carefully.

- ☐ Setting goals
- ☐ Supporting an opinion with facts
- ☐ Completing goals
- ☐ Organizing an essay
- ☐ Establishing priorities
- ☐ Writing and completing a strong essay
- ☐ Completing work on time
- ☐ Establishing relationships and connections with class notes
- ☐ Eliminating distractions
- ☐ Taking notes from class lectures
- ☐ Remembering important information for exams
- ☐ Controlling test anxiety
- ☐ Taking notes from the textbook
- ☐ Allowing plenty of time to prepare for exams
- ☐ Taking organized notes
- ☐ Completing exams in the time allotted
- ☐ Getting to class on time
- ☐ Learning from previous exam mistakes
- ☐ Participating in class
- ☐ Taking study breaks
- ☐ Keeping an organized notebook
- ☐ Studying alone
- ☐ Regularly reviewing and organizing class notes
- ☐ Studying with friends
- ☐ Coming to class prepared
- ☐ Locating information for research projects
- ☐ Understanding and using my learning style
- ☐ Evaluating information for research projects
- ☐ Using critical-thinking skills to solve problems
- ☐ Using social media for academic and career purposes
- ☐ Getting the main point from a reading assignment
- ☐ Developing respectful relationships with faculty and classmates
- ☐ Other: _____
- ☐ Other: _____

Review your checked boxes in each section above. List below the five strengths you consider your biggest assets, ranking them from 1 to 5 (high to low). Do the same for your challenges.

Strengths

1. ....
2. ....
3. ....
4. ....
5. ....

Challenges

1. ....
2. ....
3. ....
4. ....
5. ....

Look at the strengths you listed. How might you be able to use those strengths to help you minimize or eliminate your challenges? For instance, if one of your challenges is "Getting the main point from a reading assignment" and one of your strengths is "Taking organized notes," how can you use that strength to help with that challenge? That is, how can your strength be used to minimize one of your challenges? Write your response here:

....

....

....

....

....

....

....

....

....

....

....

....

Chapter SUMMARY

If you have completed the activities of this book respectfully, responsibly, and with honesty—congratulations! You have taken the initiative to bring your academic dreams into reality.

You may wish to keep this book on your bookshelf as a ready reference tool. Toward that end, the following list provides you with major "takeaway" points for study skills. Consider this a quick reference guide for each study skill you have learned and will continue to use in the future.

Best wishes for a proud and satisfying future!

Thirteen Strategic Choices for Developing Better Study Habits

1. *Do I REALLY Need This Stuff?* Regardless of your academic abilities, knowing your study skill strengths and challenges will help you become a more successful student. Study skills are for everyone.

2. *Critical Thinking.* A critical thinker logically, precisely, and systematically examines an issue from many sides—even if the conclusions of such thinking may differ with his or her deeply held beliefs. Question your assumptions and gather information before you draw conclusions.

3. *Priority Management.* Being well organized will not only improve your study habits and grades, but it will also allow you to feel in control of your life. Know your priorities, and make time each day to address them.

4. *Information Literacy.* Being an information-literate person will allow you to efficiently and effectively locate, evaluate, and use information. You should also learn how to use social media for your personal, academic, and career benefit.

5. *Motivation and Goal Setting.* When you establish a goal, you actually put together a strategy to obtain what you desire. Whether or not you achieve the goal depends in great part on how effectively you plan and carry out your strategy.

6. *Learning Styles.* You are an individual with your own experiences, skills, and challenges. Your style of receiving and using information will not necessarily be like that of the person sitting next to you in class. If you understand what works best for you and apply that knowledge, your chances of academic success will improve.

7. *Class-Time Listening and Note Taking.* Successful students are actively engaged in classroom activities every day. Remember that active learning is not a one-time event. It requires disciplined practice.

8. *Reviewing and Using Your Notes Outside the Classroom.* Just *taking* and *having* class notes is not enough. You also need to know what to do with them—and when.

9. *Reading.* Effective and skilled readers know that reading is a process. To improve your reading, use the SQ4R method: survey, read, recite, record, and review. It is the most commonly used approach to tackling reading assignments.

10. *Memory.* Three steps are involved in remembering information: noticing, storing, and reclaiming. You must sense something, put it someplace, and then go find it.

11. *Test Preparation and Test Performance.* You have experience with classroom tests. Reflect on your experiences, respect the skills you have, and take responsibility for the changes you need to make. Remember that before you can perform well, you have to prepare effectively.

12. *Civility.* While groups can be unpredictable and create challenges, they also present opportunities for people to share talents and develop a better product than one person could produce alone. Be respectful, responsible, and honest in all your relationships.

13. *The Choices You Make.* While ambition (a desire to reach a goal) and potential (the possibility of becoming something greater than you are) are important characteristics, they are useless without initiative.

CRITICALLY THINKING

What Have You Learned This Term?

The R.E.D. Model (**R**ecognize Assumptions, **E**valuate Information, **D**raw Conclusions) provides a systematic way to approach critical thinking through the use of an easy-to-remember acronym.

To conclude this book, review your notes from this and past chapters. One more time, read the key terms, chapter learning outcomes, boldface chapter headings, and figures and tables.

Using the R.E.D. Model for critical thinking, complete the items that follow:

Sometimes we stare so long at a door that is closing that we see too late the one that is open.

—*Alexander Graham Bell, inventor*

© Shutterstock

288

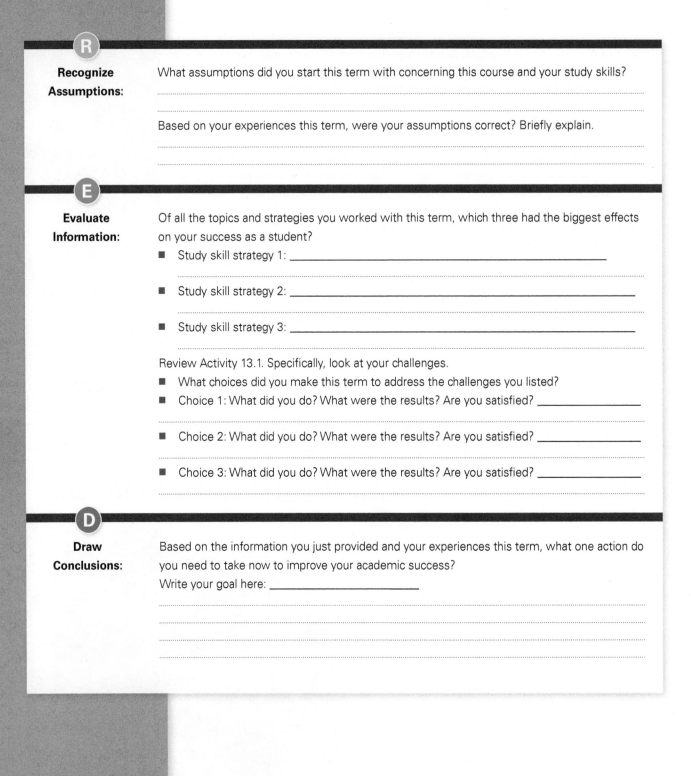

Recognize Assumptions:

What assumptions did you start this term with concerning this course and your study skills?

....

Based on your experiences this term, were your assumptions correct? Briefly explain.

....

....

Evaluate Information:

Of all the topics and strategies you worked with this term, which three had the biggest effects on your success as a student?

■ Study skill strategy 1: _____

....

■ Study skill strategy 2: _____

....

■ Study skill strategy 3: _____

....

Review Activity 13.1. Specifically, look at your challenges.

■ What choices did you make this term to address the challenges you listed?
■ Choice 1: What did you do? What were the results? Are you satisfied? _____

....

■ Choice 2: What did you do? What were the results? Are you satisfied? _____

....

■ Choice 3: What did you do? What were the results? Are you satisfied? _____

....

Draw Conclusions:

Based on the information you just provided and your experiences this term, what one action do you need to take now to improve your academic success?

Write your goal here: _____

....

....

....

About.com/Urban legends. (1998, December 2). Retrieved from http://urbanlegends.about.com/library/weekly/aa120298.htm

Academic integrity policy. (2006, April 6). The University Senate of Michigan Technological University. Retrieved from http://www.sas.it.mtu.edu/usenate/propose/06/8-06.htm

Achor, S. (2010). *The Happiness Advantage: The Seven Principles of Positive Psychology That Fuel Success and Performance at Work*. New York: Crown Business.

Adler, M., & Van Doren, C. (1972). *How to Read a Book*. New York: Simon & Schuster.

American Test Anxiety Association. (n.d.). Retrieved from http://amtaa.org/index.html

Armbruster, B. B., in Flippo, R. F., & Caverly, D. (2000). *Handbook of College Reading and Study Strategy Research*. Mahwah, NJ: Lawrence Erlbaum Associates.

Armstrong, T. (1994). *Multiple Intelligences in the Classroom*. Alexandria, VA: Association for Supervision and Curriculum Development.

Association of College and Research Libraries (a division of the American Library Association). (2006). Information Literacy Competency Standards for Higher Education. Retrieved from http://www.ala.org/ala/mgrps/divs/acrl/standards/informationliteracycompetency.cfm#ildef

Beck, M. (2001). *Finding Your Own North Star: Claiming the Life You Were Meant to Have*. New York: Three Rivers Press.

Budd, J. (n.d.). Facebook. Accessed March 20, 2011.

Carter, C., Bishop, J., & Kravits, S. L. (2006). *Keys to Success* (5th ed.). Upper Saddle River, NJ: Prentice-Hall.

Cherry, K. (2011). Memory retrieval. *About.com Psychology*. New York Times. Retrieved from http://psychology.about.com/od/cognitivepsychology/p/forgetting.htm

Collins, J., & Porras, J. I. (2002). *Built to Last: Successful Habits of Visionary Companies*. New York: Harper Business Essentials.

Computer related repetitive strain injury. (2005). University of Nebraska-Lincoln Electronics Shop RSI Web Page. Retrieved from http://eeshop.unl.edu/rsi.html

Conference Board, Inc., Corporate Voices for Working Families, the Partnership for 21st Century Skills, and the Society for Human Resource Management. (2006). Are they really ready to work? Employers' perspectives on the basic knowledge and applied skills of new entrants to the 21st century U.S. workforce. Retrieved from http://p21.org/documents/FINAL_REPORT_PDF09-29-06.pdf

Critical reading strategies. (2008). Center for Academic Excellence. Saint Joseph's College Connecticut. Retrieved from http://ww2.sjc.edu/archandouts/CriticalReadingStrategies.pdf

Cuseo, J. B. (2004, February). Conference on the First Year Experience, Dallas, Texas.

Dunn, R., & Dunn, K. (1978). *Teaching Students through Their Individual Learning Styles: A Practical Approach*. Reston, VA: Reston.

Elder, L., & Paul, R. (n.d.). Universal intellectual standards. *The Critical Thinking Community*. Retrieved from http://www.criticalthinking.org/page.cfm?PageID=527&CategoryID=68

Energy vampires. (n.d.). Retrieved from www.drbrucegoldberg.com/EnergyVampires.htm

Facebook press room. (n.d.). Retrieved from http://www.facebook.com/press/info.php?statistics

Famous failures. (n.d.). Bluefishtv.com. Retrieved from http://www.youtube.com/watch?v=Y6hz_s2XIAU

Ferguson, C. (2009, June 14). Not every child is a genius. *The Chronicle of Higher Education—The Chronicle Review*. Retrieved from http://chronicle.com/article/Not-Every-Child-Is-Secretly/48001/

Fifty famously successful people who failed at first. (2010, February 16). *Online College.org*. Retrieved from http://www.onlinecollege.org/2010/02/16/50-famously-successful-people-who-failed-at-first/

Fleming, N. (2001–2009a). Read/Write study strategies. *VARK: A Guide to Learning Styles*. Retrieved from http://vark-learn.com/english/page.asp?p=readwrite

Fleming, N. (2001–2009b). Is VARK a learning style? *VARK: A Guide to Learning Styles*. Retrieved from http://vark-learn.com/english/page.asp?p=faq

Florida State College at Jacksonville. (n.d.). Library catalog (LINCC). Retrieved from http://www.fscj.edu/mydegree/library-learning-commons/

Fry, R. (1991). *Improve Your Reading*. Hawthorne, NJ: Career Press.

Gardner, H. (1983). *Frames of Mind: The Theory of Multiple Intelligences*. New York: Basic Books.

Gardner, H., & Moran, S. (2006). The science of multiple intelligence theory: A response to Lynn Waterhouse. *Educational Psychologist, 41*(4), 227–232. Retrieved from http://web.ebscohost.com/ehost/pdfviewer/pdfviewer?sid=b207e2fe-7ac7-49a1-a89f-0a18ffa1db7c%40sessionmgr11&vid=4&hid=11

Gier, V., et al. (2011, Spring). Using an electronic highlighter to eliminate the negative effects of pre-existing, inappropriate highlighting. *Journal of College Reading and Learning, 41*(2), 40.

Glater, J. D. (2006, February 21). To: Professor@University.edu Subject: Why It's All About Me. *New York Times.* Retrieved from http://www.nytimes.com/2006/02/21/education/21professors.html?ex=1298178000&en=361f9efce267b517&ei=5090&partner=rssuserland&emc=rss

Global availability of MSN Messenger and MSN spaces connects people around the world. (2005, April 7). Microsoft PressPass. Retrieved from http://www.microsoft.com/presspass/press/2005/apr05/04-07GlobalMessengerSpacesPR.mspx

Goleman, D. (1997). *Emotional Intelligence.* New York: Bantam Books.

Hallowell, E. M. (2007). *Crazy Busy: Overstretched, Overbooked, and About to Snap!* New York: Ballantine Books.

Healthy weight. (n.d.). Department of Health and Human Services, Centers for Disease Control and Prevention. Retrieved from www.cdc.gov/nccdphp/dnpa/nutrition/nutrition_for_everyone/healthy_weight/index.htm

Hellmich, N. (2002, August 22). USA wallowing in unhealthy ways: Obesity expert points finger at fat-city society. *USA Today.* Retrieved from http://www.usatoday.com/educate/college/firstyear/articles/20020823.htm

Henry, D. J. (2004). *The Effective Reader* (rev. ed.). New York: Pearson/Longman.

Hirsch, J. S. (2004). *Two Souls Indivisible.* Boston: Houghton Mifflin.

Hughes, I. (2011, July). Still winning. *Success Magazine,* pp. 35–37.

Interim academic integrity policy. (2008, September 2). Rutgers University. Retrieved from http://academicintegrity.rutgers.edu/integrity.shtml

Jensen, E. (2000, April). Brain-based learning: A reality check. *Educational Leadership.*

Katzenbach, J. R., & Smith, D. K. (2003). *The Wisdom of Teams: Creating the High-Performance Organization.* New York: Harper Business Essentials.

Keefe, J. (n.d.). *Learning Style Handbook: II. Accommodating Perceptual, Study and Instructional Preferences.* Reston, VA: National Association of Secondary School Principals.

Lee, J. (2009). *The Anger Solution: The Proven Method for Achieving Calm and Developing Healthy, Long-Lasting Relationships.* Philadelphia: Da Capo Press.

Leider, R. (1997). *The Power of Purpose.* New York: MJF Books.

Leider, R., & Shapiro, D. (1995). *Repacking Your Bags: Lighten Your Load for the Rest of Your Life.* San Francisco: Barrett-Koehler.

Lencioni, P. (2002). *The Five Dysfunctions of a Team.* San Francisco: Jossey-Bass.

Lightfoot Matte, N., & Henderson, S. H. (1995). *Success, Your Style: Right- and Left-Brain Techniques for Learning.* Belmont, CA: Wadsworth.

Lin, D. (n.d.). Seize the day. Stumbleupon.com. Retrieved from http://www.stumbleupon.com/su/1JDv8C/www.taoism.net/articles/seizeday.htm

Lyman, P., & Varian, H. R. (2003, October 27). How much information? 2003. School of Information and Management, University of California at Berkeley. Retrieved from http://www2.sims.berkeley.edu/research/projects/how-much-info-2003/execsum.htm#paper

Marano, H. E. (2004, February 1). Assertive, not aggressive. *Psychology Today.* Retrieved from http://www.psychologytoday.com/rss/pto-20040206-000009.html

Marxhausen, P. (2005). Computer related repetitive strain injury. University of Nebraska-Lincoln Electronics Shop RSI Web Page. Retrieved from http://eeshop.unl.edu/rsi.html

Masnjack, T. (2006, February 23). Employers use Facebook in hiring. *Daily Vidette.* Illinois State University. Retrieved from http://www.videtteonline.com/index.php?option=com_content&view=article&id=16275:employers-use-facebook-in-hiring&catid=67:newsarchive&Itemid=53

Matte, N. L., & Henderson, S. H. (1995) *Success, your style: Right- and left-brain techniques for learning.* Belmont, CA: Wadsworth.

McNamara, C. (1997–2008). Basics of conflict management. Retrieved from http://w3.palmer.edu/osd/process/PDF/Basics%20of%20Conflict%20Management.pdf

Mearns, J. (n.d.) The social learning theory of Julian B. Rotter. Department of Psychology, California

State University—Fullerton. Retrieved from http://psych.fullerton.edu/jmearns/rotter.htm

Medina, J. (2008). *Brain Rules: 12 Principles for Surviving and Thriving at Work, Home, and School.* Seattle: Pear Press.

Meyer, P. (2004). Creating S.M.A.R.T. goals. Top Achievement. Retrieved from www.topachievement.com/smart.html

Mihalik, K. (2011, March 19). Phone interview.

Miller, W. (2005, February). Resolutions that work. *Spirituality and Health*, pp. 44–47.

Minninger, J., & Dugan, E. (1994). *Rapid Memory in 7 Days: The Quick-and-Easy Guide to Better Remembering.* New York: Berkeley.

Nadler, R. (n.d.). Text messaging craze. *College Outlook.* Retrieved from http://www.collegeoutlook.net/co_ca_on_campus_c.cfm

NFL prospects: Be careful who you friend. (2009, April 17). *Road to Game Day.* Retrieved from http://roadtogameday.wordpress.com/2009/04/17/nfl-prospects-be-careful-who-you-friend/

Note-taking symbols and abbreviations. (n.d.). *How to be a good student: Study skills from English-Zone.com.* Retrieved from http://english-zone.com/study/symbols.html

Obesity: Fighting one of America's most dangerous conditions. (2011). *One Healthy Life Style.* Retrieved from http://www.onehealthylifestyle.com/physical-health/diseases/obesity.aspx

Orloff, J. (2004). *Positive Energy.* New York: Harmony Books.

Pardini, E. A., et al. (2005, Spring). Parallel note-taking: A strategy for effective use of webnotes. *Journal of College Reading and Learning, 35*(2), 1–18. Retrieved from http://www.eric.ed.gov/PDFS/EJ689655.pdf

Pastor, M. (n.d.). Short-term memory. San Diego State University, College of Education. Retrieved from coe.sdsu.edu/eet/articles/stmemory/start.htm

Patin, M. (n.d.). Correcting Aunt Sally. *Developmental Mathematics: The Order of Operations.* Vernon College. Retrieved from http://www.texascollaborative.org/PatinModule/act1-2.php

Patterson, B. (n.d.). Social media study shows 59 percent of retailers now using Facebook. Reuters. Retrieved from http://www.reuters.com/article/pressRelease/idUS205020+09-Jan-2009+PRN20090109

Pauk, W. (1993). *How to Study in College* (5th ed.). Boston: Houghton Mifflin.

Pew Internet and American Life Project. (n.d.). Pew Research Center. Retrieved from http://pewinternet.org/

Piscitelli, S. (2008). *Rhythms of College Success: A Journey of Discovery, Change, and Mastery.* Upper Saddle River, NJ: Pearson/Prentice-Hall.

Piscitelli, S. (2010, November 14). Know your boundaries—Know your limits. *Steve Piscitelli's Blog.* Retrieved from http://stevepiscitelli.wordpress.com/category/boundaries-and-limits/

Piscitelli, S. (2011). *Choices for College Success* (2nd ed.). Boston: Pearson Education.

Piscitelli, S. (2011, January 16). The student perspective: What do effective teachers do? *Steve Piscitelli's Blog.* Retrieved from http://stevepiscitelli.wordpress.com/2011/01/16/the-student-perspective-what-do-effective-teachers-do/

Posen, D. B. (1995, April). Stress management for patient and physician. *Canadian Journal of Continuing Medical Education.* Retrieved from www.mentalhealth.com/mag1/p51-str.html#Head_1

Procter, M. (n.d.). How not to plagiarize. Writing at the University of Toronto. Retrieved from http://www.writing.utoronto.ca/advice/using-sources/how-not-to-plagiarize

Qualman, E. (2010, May 5). Social media revolution (refreshed): Stats from video. *Socialnomics: Word of Mouth for Social Good.* Retrieved from http://www.socialnomics.net/2010/05/05/social-media-revolution-2-refresh/

Riedling, A. M. (2002). *Learning to Learn: A Guide to Becoming Information Literate.* New York: Neal-Schuman.

Robinson, F. P. (1946). *Effective Study.* New York: Harper and Bros.

Saillant, C. (2005, December). A bulwark against bullies. *LATimes.com.* Retrieved from http://pqasb.pqarchiver.com/latimes/access/936841751.html?dids=936841751:936841751&FMT=ABS&FMTS=ABS:FT&type=current&date=Dec+5%2C+2005&author=Catherine+Saillant&pub=Los+Angeles+Times&edition=&startpage=B.1&desc=A+Bulwark+Against+Bullies

Sapadin, L., with Maguire, J. (1999). *Beat Procrastination and Make the Grade: The Six Styles of Procrastination and How Students Can Overcome Them.* New York: Penguin Books.

Shapiro, E. (2006, May 5). Brain-based learning meets PowerPoint. *Teaching Professor, 20*(5), 5. Retrieved from http://www.vcu.edu/cte/resources/newsletters_archive/TP0605.PDF

Shirky, C. (2010). *Cognitive Surplus: Creativity and Generosity in a Connected Age.* New York: Penguin Press.

Skills and abilities for the 21st Century: A workforce readiness initiative, The. (n.d.). The Career Center and the Community/Mental Health Counseling PRogram. The University of South Florida. Retrieved from http://www.coedu.usf.edu/zalaquett/workforce/sa.htm

Smith, B. D. (2008). *Bridging the Gap: College Reading* (9th ed.). New York: Pearson/Longman.

Smith, M. K. (2005). Bruce W. Tuckman—Forming, storming, norming, and performing in groups. *Infed: The Encyclopaedia of Informal Education.* Retrieved from www.infed.org/thinkers/tuckman.htm

SQ4R: A classic method for studying texts. (2007). University of Guelph (The Learning Commons). Retrieved from http://www.lib.uoguelph.ca/assistance/learning_services/handouts/SQ4R.cfm

SQ4R Reading Method. (n.d.). West Virginia University at Parkersburg. Retrieved from www.wvup.edu/Academics/learning_center/sq4r_reading_method.htm

Sternberg, R. (1997). *Successful Intelligence: How Practical and Creative Intelligence Determine Success in Life.* New York: Plume.

Stevens, J. (2002). *The Power Path: The Shaman's Way to Success in Business and Life.* Novato, CA: New World Library.

Stiles, T. (2009, February 15). Help I'm addicted to Facebook! *The Huffington Post.* Retrieved from http://www.huffingtonpost.com/tara-stiles/help-im-addicted-to-faceb_b_166726.html

Swartz, R. G. (1991). *Accelerated Learning: How You Learn Determines What You Learn.* Durant, OK: EMIS.

Texting etiquette in college. (2009, March 31). Techiediva. Retrieved from http://www.techiediva.com/2009/03/31/texting-ettiquette-in-college/

Tinto, V. (2002, February 28–March 1). Taking student learning seriously. Keynote address to the Southwest Regional Learning Communities Conference, Tempe, AZ. Retrieved from www.mcli.dist.maricopa.edu/events/lcc02/presents/tinto.html

Twitter statistics. (n.d.). *Kiss Metrics.* Retrieved from http://blog.kissmetrics.com/twitter-statistics/

Understanding stress: Signs, symptoms, causes, effects. (n.d.). *HelpGuide.org.* Retrieved from http://helpguide.org/mental/stress_signs.htm

Urban, H. (2003). *Life's Greatest Lessons.* New York: Simon & Shuster.

USA text messaging statistics. (2009, February 19). *Text Message Blog.* Retrieved from http://www.textmessageblog.mobi/2009/02/19/text-message-statistics-usa

VanderStoep, S. W., & Pintrich, P. R. (2003). *Learning to Learn: The Skill and Will of College Success.* Upper Saddle River, NJ: Prentice Hall.

Watson-Glaser Critical Thinking Appraisal, Forms A/B (WGCTA). (2007). NCS Pearson, Inc.

Wilson, S. B. (1994). *Goal Setting.* New York: American Management Association.

Winget, L. (2004). *Shut Up, Stop Whining, and Get a Life.* New Jersey: John Wiley.

Zadina, J. N. (2007, March 22). The mystery of attention. Presentation at the National Association for Developmental Education Annual Conference, Nashville, TN.

Academic integrity. Research, writing, and homework that is performed in a respectful, responsible, and honest fashion. Both students and professors are held to standards of academic integrity.   97; 255

Accuracy. Correctness. Information is factual.   23

Acronym. A word formed from the first letters of a series of words. Can be used as a memory technique; a mnemonic.   228

Action steps. Specific, measurable, and responsible movements toward a goal.   116

Activation energy. The initial movement needed to "kick-start" a positive habit or help block a negative habit. A way to reduce or minimize the obstacles and increase the chances of doing the task. Also a way to minimize procrastination.   54

Active learning. Students must do what they can to be engaged or involved in the lesson; establishing connections during the learning process.   146

Active listening. Being engaged in what you hear by focusing and participating in the discussion.   220; 265

Active reading. Requires you to do something rather than passively see the words on the page; includes note taking, highlighting, scanning, and asking questions.   189

Aggressive. Harsher than assertiveness; can boarder on bullying; violating another person.   272

Ambition. A desire to reach a goal.   282

Analyzing. Comparing, contrasting, examining, and breaking down information into smaller pieces.   24

Anxiety. A general feeling of unease, uncertainty, anticipation, and even fear about an event.   239

Assertiveness. Acting with confidence but not becoming aggressive; standing up for oneself.   272

Assumption. A theory, paradigm, or view of the world. When we assume, we accept something to be correct regardless of whether we have actual proof. We believe the opinion or position to be accurate and truthful.   20

Attention. Concentration. Listening, observing, and sorting through the vast amount of information presented in class or in homework.   131

Auditory learning preference. A preference to learn by taking in and putting out information orally.   133

Benjamin Bloom. An educational pioneer who developed a six-tier model of thinking skills that has become the backbone of the critical-thinking process; he created the language of critical thinking.   23

Blogs. Written pieces posted on websites. They usually include the opinions or observations of the writer (known as the "blogger") about a topic. Often, the blogger will include visuals or links to support his or her thoughts.   84

Boundaries. Show where we "begin and end"; let others know what is acceptable and unacceptable; tell people how far they can go with another person.   275

Brain-based learning. The brain seeks out meaning. It looks for connections as it establishes patterns that will help it make sense of the world. Studies suggest we can take raw facts and make them mean something.   192

Bullies. People who control others using physical or verbal aggression. The bully sees the victim as "easy pickings."   272

Calendar. Organizes time into years, months, weeks, and days. Provides a way to track activities and commitments over time.   47

Challenge. A difficulty, obstacle, or problem that gets in the way of progress.   4

Choices. Reflect what you consider important (your priorities) in your world; your decisions; the paths you have taken.   282

Citation. A credit that's provided when using the words and ideas of another author. Generally consists of the author's name, the title of the publication, the publisher's name, the place and date of publication, and the page numbers from which the material came. If the material was obtained from the Internet, the URL (www) will be needed, as well.   97

Civility. Acting appropriately and with respect; a basic component of a working and respectful relationship; polite and courteous behavior.   156; 262

Clarity. Clearness and directness. Facts and arguments are clearly and unambiguously presented.   23

Classroom success. Achievement that is fostered by attendance, attention, and participation.   152

Collective monologue. Many people are talking but few are listening.   265

Communication. To construct and pass along thoughts, information, and feelings about a particular subject to another person.   264

Comprehension. Understanding what you read. Being able to describe what you have read in your own words.   191

Confirmation bias. Occurs when preconceived ideas interfere with an unbiased decision.   21

Conflict. A state of disharmony in which one set of ideas or values contradicts another.   269

Connections. Relationships between experiences, textbook readings, and classroom lessons. Note taking provides the chance to build these connections.   172

Context. The words surrounding an unknown word that give it meaning.   204

Creative thinking. Thinking that develops (creates) a new or different product; it requires looking at situations in new ways, from different angles or unique perspectives.   30

Critical thinking. Gathering information, weighing it for accuracy and appropriateness, and then making a rational decision based on the facts that have been gathered.   11; 16

Data retrieval chart (D.R.C.). A technique to organize information; allows for easy categorization, comparison, and contrast of information; can be used to show how one thing impacts another; show connections.   221

"Digital tattoo." Your online reputation. Consists of everything you post online about yourself and everything you write in response to someone else. All the photos, videos, music, and poetry that you post (or someone posts concerning you) or link to say something about who you are.   90

Discipline. The development of habits that move you closer to your goals; you focus on what needs to be done, and you do it.   7

Distracters. Incorrect answer choices given on a multiple-choice test; they distract you from the correct answer.   252

Distraction. Anything that hinders concentration; an interruption in thought or action.   152

"Elephant in the corner." Metaphor for a problem that is so big it is impossible to miss, but the problem is being ignored because no one wants to confront it.   268

Emergency studying. Last-minute studying; not a desirable strategy.   250

Emotional intelligence. The ability to soothe oneself, to recognize emotions in others, and to delay gratification. A person needs more than a high score on an IQ test to be successful.   263

"Energy vampires." People who drain us emotionally and/or physically.   272

Environmental factors (affecting learning). Affect how we learn. Include lighting, temperature, types of furniture being used, and so on.   132

Evaluate. A higher-level thinking skill; to judge an assumption as fact or fiction.   21

Excuse. An attempt to explain a particular course of action to remove or lessen responsibility or blame.   111

"Exit slip" strategy. Helps determine a student's level of understanding of the day's notes. The student writes three new things learned in the lesson; two items from the lesson found to be the most interesting; and one thing found the most confusing.   180

Extinction. Incentive to perform is greatly diminished or entirely removed.   226

Forgetting. The failure of a previously learned behavior to reappear.   218

Goal. A desired end point; a place one wants to reach; a result one wishes to attain.   112

Graphics. Pictures, photos, charts, figures, and tables used by an author to illustrate a point.   205

H.O.G.s. Huge Outrageous Goals; they encourage us to stretch and strive for large goals.   113

Habit. Something repeated with such frequency that it becomes involuntary. It seems as though you cannot help yourself from doing it.   54

Higher-order thinking skills. Critical thinking in which the individual is actively and deeply involved in processing information by applying, analyzing, evaluating, and/or creating information and ideas.   23

Highlighting. A strategic reading behavior; marking the major points of a reading; a form of active learning. Can be done with a colored highlighter, pen, or pencil. 201

Information literacy. Competence in finding, evaluating, and using information. Knowing what information to look for, how to find that information, how to judge the information's credibility and quality once it has been found, and how to effectively use the information once it has been found and evaluated. 71

Initiative. Responsible decision making and follow-through. 282

Instructor styles. May include lecture, question-and-answer, group work, lab work, discussion, and seat work. Regardless of the method of presentation, each instructor has a set of expectations for student performance. 149

Intelligence. What we use to reason or solve problems; a set of skills to interact with our environment. 139

Interlibrary loans. Requesting materials from one library and receiving them at another. 75

Interpersonal skills. One's strengths and challenges when interacting with other people. 262

Keyword search. Using a word or phrase to help you find material (in the library or on the Internet) on your topic. 77

Kinesthetic learning preference. A preference to learn by doing; movement is important; active, physical engagement may tend to keep these learners focused and on task. 133

Learning preference. A component of a person's learning style. Refers to the manner in which individuals process (take in *and* put out) information. 132

Learning style. Consists of various factors that influence learning. Includes our learning preference as well as environmental factors. 132

Limits. Let people know how far you will go. They clearly tell people what you will do or will not do. 275

Locus of control. A continuum of behavior that people use to explain what happens to them. People with an internal locus of control accept responsibility for life and make things happen, whereas people with an external locus of control look for reasons (excuses) that things happen to them. The focus of one's power; influences whether you believe life just happens to you or you can influence what happens. 11, 120

Logic. Sense. Information, a position, or an argument that makes sense. 23

Long-term memory. Holds information that has not been lost; retained information. 225

Lower-order thinking skills. Basic thinking that involves memorizing and understanding information. 23

Main idea. The author's primary purpose for writing a paragraph, a section, a chapter, or a book. 200

Memory. Retention and retrieval of information; the ability to grab, hold, and recall information. 214

Memory block. Something that impedes your ability to notice, store, or reclaim information. 224

Motivated learner. Characterized by the appropriate choice, effort, persistence, engagement, and achievement. 107

Motivation (intrinsic and extrinsic). Moves you to act on or toward something. Can come from within (intrinsic) or from an outside source (extrinsic). 106

Motivational barriers. Obstacles and detours on the way to a goal; may slow one down or completely block a goal. 108

Multiple intelligences. Howard Gardner's theory that people have eight different abilities to pick from when solving problems: linguistic, logical-mathematical, spatial, bodily-kinesthetic, musical, interpersonal, intrapersonal, and naturalistic. 140

Note-taking styles. Particular strategies for recording notes. Can be a traditional outline, a flowchart, a spidergram, some combination or variation of these, or some other format. 159

Notice. To pay attention to surroundings or information; to take note. 215

"Nutritious people." People who are glad to see you; listen to you; accept you as you are. 276

Office hours. The times when instructors make themselves available to meet with students. The hours may be posted in a syllabus, on a website, or outside the instructor's office. 182

Online classess. Courses offered from locations beyond the campus grounds and classroom walls. These courses require a great deal of self-discipline and access to a computer and the Internet. 167

Online profile. A short representation of you for others to see; an online identity that is a brief introduction of yourself to all people who view your site. It can include information about your likes, dislikes, education, travels, career, desires, relationships, and residence. You can also post a photo.   90

Passion. What you are committed to and what you love to do with your days.   202

Passive. To submit to verbal and, in some cases, nonverbal attacks without resistance.   272

Persistence. The ability to stick with a task until it has been completed; stick-to-itiveness.   107

Personal storage area. Effective storage for personal papers, books, supplies, and other items. May include desk drawers, bookshelves, file boxes, plastic bins, or a file cabinet.   57

Personal study area. Your private work area.   57

Plagiarism. A dishonest representation of someone else's work as your own. When writing a paper and submitting work, it is your responsibility to provide appropriate citations to your sources.   97

Postexam analysis. Upon completion of an exam, review how well (or not) you have done; to address challenges before the next exam.   245

Potential. The possibility of becoming something greater than you are   282

Priorities. Things, events, and people that are important to you.   40

Problem solving. The use of critical-thinking skills to examine a dilemma, situation, or person that presents a challenge and then propose a solution.   26

Problem-solving trap. Being blinded to new alternatives by becoming stuck in a routine or trapped by assumptions. Perhaps we continue to look at a particular problem from the same point of view.   30

Procrastination. Avoiding and postponing what you should take care of now.   52

Purpose. Various reasons for reading: to answer specific questions, apply information, find details, get a message, evaluate material, and entertain yourself.   192

R.E.D. Model. An acronym for a three-step model of critical thinking: Recognize assumptions, Evaluate information, and Draw conclusions.   20

R.O.I. (return on investment). A business concept that is used as a metaphor for getting the most return (academic and personal success) for the effort you put into your class time and study time.   174

Read-write learning preference. A preference to learn by taking notes and writing essays. As the name implies, people with this preference are generally comfortable reading and writing during the learning process.   133

Reclaiming. Retrieving information you have stored; typically refers to what you have remembered or forgotten.   215

Reference librarian. A library worker who can help you navigate the library's holdings, introduce you to various search strategies, and direct you to the most appropriate databases.   74

Reframe. To look at a situation from a different perspective or point of view.   240

Relevance. Significance. When information relates to the argument or problem at hand.   23

Repetitive strain injuries (RSIs). Also called *repetitive stress injuries*. Commonly happen to people who spend long hours typing at a keyboard and staring at a computer monitor. As the name implies, the injury results from repetitive (continual) motions or actions.   59

Response competition. When new information competes or interferes with previously learned information; can create storing and/or reclaiming difficulties.   226

Review-Relate-Reorganize strategy. An active note-review strategy that helps to translate notes from the instructor's words to the student's words.   177

Scan. In reading, to get a quick overview of what you are to read; understanding the general idea of the passage.   196

Search engines. They assist in gathering pertinent information from the many databases on the World Wide Web. Provide a strategy to move mindless "surfing" to a focused "ride."   75

Short-term memory. Also known as *working memory*; can manipulate, or work with, the information for a short time; may or may not eventually be transferred to long-term memory.   218

Situational variation. When the situation or setting changes; may interfere with memory recall.   227

Social media. Consumer-generated media.   83

SQ4R. A six-step reading model: survey, question, read, recite, record, review.   195

Status updates. Like mini-blogs. People post short messages about things they have just done or are about to do. They can convey a meaningful message, a funny anecdote, or a question. May include a photo, video, or website link.   89

Storing information. The process of mentally filing noticed information for later recall or retrieval.   215

Strategic reading. Reading in a planned and thoughtful way to achieve your desired goal.   200

Strategy. A plan of action.   104

Strength. Something you do well.   4

Stress. The body's response to external and internal pressures; represents a time of extreme arousal in the body; can compromise one's health. There are two types: distress ("bad" stress) and eustress ("good" stress).   60

Study partner. Part of an academic and social support network. Can help organize notes, brainstorm ideas, cope with failures, and celebrate successes.   183

Study skills. Your abilities to learn how to do academic things well and in a disciplined manner.   8

Study time. Time needed for reading, writing, researching, meeting with study groups, completing assignments, and preparing for tests outside class.   42

Surfing the Web. Has come to describe an aimless ride through the Internet, following one link to another without much thought or direction.   75

T.S.D. strategy. Active learning strategy to review notes. Stands for title, summary, and details.   179

Test anxiety. When thoughts of an examination cause a person to be emotionally and/or physically ill with worry.   239

Test-performance skills. Behaviors related to successful test taking.   251

Test-preparation skills. Behaviors related to getting ready for a test.   238

Texting. Sending short messages from cell phone to cell phone.   83

Trigger words. Key words that direct a test taker what to do.   254

Trust. Recognizing that another person (or group) is supportive of your efforts; meaningful relationship built on respect; built over time and shared experiences.   268

Types of exams. Various formats of exams that include multiple choice, matching, true/false, completion, and essay.   252

Values. Reflect what is important to a person.   104

Visual learning preference. A preference to learn by viewing videos, photos, PowerPoint slides, and graphic illustrations. For visual learners, seeing something helps in understanding and explanation.   133

Vocabulary. Your bank of words; allows you to communicate your feelings and views; has an impact on how well you understand the people—and the world—around you.   204

Wikis. Articles that are posted and revised online by multiple people. Allow people to log on and become content contributors and editors.   85

Working memory. Also known as *short-term memory* (*see* Short-term memory).   218

World Wide Web. The Web is the connection or linking of a vast array of digital books, articles, non-print sources, and personal communications. One of the information resources the Internet allows us to access.   75